1995
clarkie

8
AO.

I0765607

Blues, Ideology, and Afro-American Literature

HOUSTON A. BAKER, JR.

Blues, Ideology, and Afro-American Literature

A Vernacular Theory

The University of Chicago Press
Chicago and London

LIBRARY
ARAPAHOE COMMUNITY COLLEGE
5900 SOUTH SANTA FE
LITTLETON, COLORADO 80120

HOUSTON A. BAKER, JR., is the Albert M. Greenfield Professor of Human Relations at the University of Pennsylvania. He is the author of *The Journey Back: Issues in Black Literature and Criticism*, also published by the University of Chicago Press.

THE UNIVERSITY OF CHICAGO PRESS, CHICAGO 60637
THE UNIVERSITY OF CHICAGO PRESS, LTD., LONDON

© 1984 by The University of Chicago
All rights reserved. Published 1984
Printed in the United States of America

93 92 91 90 89 88 87 86 85 84   54321

Library of Congress Cataloging in Publication Data

Baker, Houston A.
  Blues, ideology, and Afro-American literature.

  Includes bibliographical references and index.
  1. American literature—Afro-American authors—History
and criticism. 2. Blues (Songs, etc.)—United States—
History and criticism. I. Title.
PS153.N5B23   1984   810'.9'896073   84-2655
ISBN 0-226-03536-0

3 1717 00016 5367

Yankee

19.95

SEP 2 3 1986

To My Own Blues People,
CHARLOTTE
and
MARK
Who Have Survived More Than
Any One Will Ever Know,
and Who Teach Me the Subtleties
of Music at the Junctures

Contents

Acknowledgments

It does not matter how much steam one generates or how impressively one quills whistles or sets engine bells dancing if one is on the wrong track. Hence, in the world of railroading there exist innumerable yards where proper tracking is the designated function. The most fascinating switch-yards are those called "humpyards." A humpyard contains a mound up one side of which cars are pushed by a switch engine and down the other side of which cars run by gravity onto the proper track. The humpyard provides a fitting image for the world one enters at the beginning of any new scholarly project. There are humps, obstacles, and barriers to be scaled, and one can never get onto the correct track on one's initiative alone. In the formative stages, the best blessing is the service of strong switch engines.

The powers behind my own present work are too extensive to name in toto. But perhaps I can acknowledge those who have aided me over the most formidable obstacles. In any just accounting, my debts begin with the Center for Advanced Study in the Behavioral Sciences, where Alfonzo Ortiz introduced me to symbolic anthropology and where the energetic Gardner Lindzey encouraged me to spend a brief summer residency in 1979. Professor Gordon Ray, and a fellowship from the John Simon Guggenheim Memorial Foundation in 1979–80, enabled me to read extensively in the literatures of symbolic inversion, pollution beliefs, ritual, and the sociology of knowledge. During the summer of 1981, eleven spirited and insightful colleagues joined me at the University of Pennsylvania for a National Endowment for the Humanities Summer Seminar for College Teachers entitled "Afro-American Literature and the Anthropology of Art." I have never worked so hard (or profitably) in my life. The seminar participants helped me to perceive genuinely useful lines of future inquiry.

In 1982–83, I had the good fortune to spend a year at the National Humanities Center in North Carolina. The staff of the Center was quite helpful, and I owe special thanks to Kent Mullikin. My work in 1982–83 was aided also by an award from the Research Fellowship Program for Minority Group Scholars of the Rockefeller Foundation.

The one unfailing engine during past years—indeed, the past decade—has been the University of Pennsylvania. I am tremendously grateful to the University for the research time it has made available to me, and I am deeply appreciative for the continuing insights and advice of my colleagues there.

In addition to those institutions and individuals already named, I must acknowledge my debts to Barbara Herrnstein Smith, Sacvan Bercovitch, Henry Louis Gates, Jr., Kimberly Benston, Barbara Babcock, Mark Taylor, John Sekora, Catharine Stimpson, Chester Fontenot, Jerry Ward, Joe Weixlmann, Sam Girgus, Joan Stewart, Lance Stell, and Sam Allen. All have either discussed with me ideas vital to my project or read and commented upon portions of my manuscript. Professor Smith has been especially generous, and Professor Taylor was essential to my understanding of the deconstructionist project.

My debts to Henry Louis Gates, Jr., should be explicitly acknowledged since his efforts have been an inspiration to the general project of providing adequate theoretical models for the study of Afro-American expressive traditions. Surely Professor Gates's efforts reveal a coming to fullness of the project initiated by the Black Aesthetic. I wish to thank him, not only for providing a detailed and thorough reading of my manuscript in its final form, but also for paying me the supreme compliment of altering his critical vocabulary to accord with mine. His shift from "idiom" to "vernacular" represents a gratifying conflation of erstwhile disparate generational ideals, but more of this development in the second chapter of the present study.

I should also be explicit in acknowledging the superb aid and advice tendered by my National Humanities Center colleague Joan Hinde Stewart. Professor Stewart's direct encouragement first set me to writing (as opposed to disinterestedly meditating) during the Center year. Further, she provided a generously insightful reading of my entire text when I needed to make important organizational decisions concerning the final manuscript.

I must also express gratitude to the University of New Mexico Press, Cambridge University Press, *Black American Literature Forum*, and *PMLA* for permission to reprint portions of the present manuscript that originally appeared under their auspices.

Laura O'Keefe of the Southern Historical Collection, Leroy Bellamy of the Library of Congress, Michael Thomason of the University of South Alabama Photographic Archives, and Carol Netter of the Association of American Railroads were helpful in my efforts to secure appropriate illustrative photographs.

Susan Jeffords, Tim Martin, and Joyce Jonas have all served as my graduate assistants in recent years; they have been extraordinarily helpful to me. The staff of the University of Pennsylvania English Department has been supportive through all stages of my work. And my parents, brothers, in-laws, and a New York uncle have provided more indispensable support than they will ever know.

In the face of such a list, it seems apparent that I could not have remained stranded for long at the base of any steep grade or severe hump. The people I have named have been indefatigable in their support. Yet they carried me only to the crest of the hump. I descended on my own. And if I somehow managed to get onto a wrong track, the fault is entirely mine. I assume full responsibility for errors in the following pages.

H. A. B.

Chapel Hill and Philadelphia, 1983

Vernacular, adj.: *Of a slave*: That is born on his master's estate; home-born
　　　　　Of arts, or features
　　　　　of these: Native or peculiar to a particular country or locality

Other states indicate themselves in their deputies . . . but the genius of the United
　　　　　States is not best or most in its executives or legislatures, nor in its
　　　　　ambassadors or authors or colleges or churches or parlors, nor even in
　　　　　its newspapers or inventors . . . but always most in the common people
　　　　　. . . these . . . are unrhymed poetry. It awaits the gigantic and generous
　　　　　treatment worthy of it.

Walt Whitman

　　　　　If you see me coming, better open up your door,
　　　　　If you see me coming, better open up your door,
　　　　　I ain't no stranger, I been here before.

Traditional Blues

Introduction

Standing at the crossroads, tried to flag a ride,
Standing at the crossroads, tried to flag a ride,
Ain't nobody seem to know me, everybody passed me by.

Crossroad Blues

In every case the result of an untrue mode of knowledge must not be allowed to run away into an empty nothing, but must necessarily be grasped as the nothing *of that from which it results*—a result which contains what was true in the preceding knowledge.

Hegel, Phenomenology of Spirit

So perhaps we shy from confronting our cultural wholeness because it offers no easily recognizable points of rest, no facile certainties as to who, what, or where (culturally or historically) we are. Instead, the whole is always in cacophonic motion.

Ralph Ellison, "The Little Man at the Chehaw Station"

. . . maybe one day, you'll find they actually do understand exactly what you are talking about, all these fantasy people. All these blues people.

Amiri Baraka, Dutchman

From Symbol to Ideology

In my book *The Journey Back: Issues in Black Literature and Criticism* (1980),[1] I envisioned the "speaking subject" creating language (a code) to be deciphered by the present-day commentator. In my current study, I envision language (the code) "speaking" the subject. The subject is "de-centered." My quest during the past decade has been for the distinctive, the culturally specific aspects of Afro-American literature and culture. I was convinced that I had found such specificity in a peculiar subjectivity, but the objectivity of economics and the sound lessons of poststructuralism arose to reorient my thinking. I was also convinced that the symbolic, and quite specifically the symbolically anthropological, offered avenues to the comprehension of Afro-American expressive culture in its plenitude.[2] I discovered that the symbolic's antithesis—practical reason, or the mate-

1

rial—is as necessary for understanding Afro-American discourse as the cultural-in-itself.

My shift from a centered to a decentered subject, from an exclusively symbolic to a more inclusively expressive perspective, was prompted by the curious force of dialectical thought. My access to the study of such thought came from attentive readings of Fredric Jameson, Hayden White, Marshall Sahlins, and others. While profiting from observations by these scholars, I also began to attend meetings of a study group devoted to Hegel's *Phenomenology of Spirit.*

Having journeyed with the aid of symbolic anthropology to what appeared to be the soundest possible observations on Afro-American art, I found myself confronted suddenly by a figure-to-ground reversal. A fitting image for the effect of my reorientation is the gestalt illustration of the Greek hydria (a water vase with curved handles) that transforms itself into two faces in profile. John Keats's "Ode on a Grecian Urn," with its familiar detailing of the economies of "art" and human emotion, can be considered one moment in the shift. Contrasting with Keats's romantic figurations are the emergent faces of a venerable ancestry. The shift from Greek hydrias to ancestral faces is a shift from high art to vernacular expression.

The "vernacular" in relation to human beings signals "a slave born on his master's estate." In expressive terms, vernacular indicates "arts native or peculiar to a particular country or locale." The material conditions of slavery in the United States and the rhythms of Afro-American blues combined and emerged from my revised materialistic perspective as an ancestral matrix that has produced a forceful and indigenous American creativity. The moment of emergence of economic and vernacular concerns left me, as the French say, *entre les deux*: suspended somewhere between symbolic anthropology and analytical strategies that Fredric Jameson calls the "ideology of form."[3]

Ideology, Semiotics, and the Material

In acknowledging a concern for the ideology of form, however, I do not want to imply that my symbolic-anthropological orientation was untrue, in the sense of deluded or deceived.[4] This symbolic orientation was simply one moment in my experiencing of Afro-American culture—a moment superseded now by a prospect that constitutes its determinate negation.[5] What was true in my prior framework remains so in my current concern for the ideology of form. Certainly the mode of ideological investigation proposed by Jameson is an analysis that escapes all hints of "vulgar Marxism" through its studious attention to modern critiques of political economy, and also through its shrewd incorporation of poststructuralist thought.[6]

In chapters that follow, I too attempt to avoid a naive Marxism. I do not believe, for example, that a fruitful correlation exists when one merely claims that certain black folk seculars are determinate results of agricultural gang labor. Such attributions simply privilege the material as a substrate while failing to provide detailed accounts of processes leading from an apparent substrate to a peculiar expressive form. A faith of enormous magnitude is required to accept such crude formulations as adequate explanations. The "material" is shifty ground, and current critiques of political economy suggest that postulates based on this ground can be understood only in "semiotic" terms. Hence, the employment of ideology as an analytical category begins with the awareness that "production" as well as "modes of production" must be grasped in terms of the sign. An example of a persuasive case for "political economy" as a code existing in a relationship of identity with language can be found in Jean Baudrillard's *For a Critique of the Political Economy of the Sign*.[7] To read economics as a semiotic process leads to the realization that ideological analyses may be as decidedly intertextual as, say, analyses of the relationship between Afro-American vernacular expression and more sophisticated forms of verbal art. If what is normally categorized as *material* (e.g., "raw material," "consumer goods") can be interpreted semiotically, then any collection of such entities and their defining interrelationships may be defined as a *text*.[8]

In the chapters in this book, however, I do not write about or interpret the *material* in exclusively semiotic terms. Although I am fully aware of insights to be gained from semiotics, my analyses focus directly on the living and laboring conditions of people designated as "the desperate class" by James Weldon Johnson's narrator in *The Autobiography of an Ex-Colored Man*. Such people constitute the vernacular in the United States. Their lives have always been sharply conditioned by an "economics of slavery" as they worked the agricultural rows, searing furnaces, rolling levees, bustling roundhouses, and piney-woods logging camps of America. A sense of "production" and "modes of production" that foregrounds such Afro-American labor seems an appropriate inscription of the material.

The Matrix as Blues
The guiding presupposition of the chapters that follow is that Afro-American culture is a complex, reflexive enterprise which finds its proper figuration in blues conceived as a matrix. A matrix is a womb, a network, a fossil-bearing rock, a rocky trace of a gemstone's removal, a principal metal in an alloy, a mat or plate for reproducing print or phonograph records. The matrix is a point of ceaseless input and output, a web of intersecting, crisscrossing impulses always in productive transit. Afro-

American blues constitute such a vibrant network. They are what Jacques Derrida might describe as the "always already" of Afro-American culture.[9] They are the multiplex, enabling *script* in which Afro-American cultural discourse is inscribed.

First arranged, scored, and published for commercial distribution early in the twentieth century when Hart Wand, Arthur "Baby" Seals, and W. C. Handy released their first compositions, the blues defy narrow definition. For they exist, not as a function of formal inscription, but as a forceful condition of Afro-American inscription itself. They were for Handy a "found" folk signifier, awakening him from (perhaps) a dream of American form in Tutwiler, Mississippi, in 1903.[10] At a railroad juncture deep in the southern night, Handy dozed restlessly as he awaited the arrival of a much-delayed train. A guitar's bottleneck resonance suddenly jolted him to consciousness, as a lean, loose-jointed, shabbily clad black man sang:

> Goin' where the Southern cross the Dog.
> Goin' where the Southern cross the Dog.
> Goin' where the Southern cross the Dog.

This haunting invocation of railroad crossings in bottleneck tones left Handy stupified and inspired. In 1914, he published his own Yellow Dog Blues.

But the autobiographical account of the man who has been called the "Father of the Blues" offers only a simplistic detailing of *a progress*, describing, as it were, the elevation of a "primitive" folk ditty to the status of "art" in America. Handy's rendering leaves unexamined, therefore, myriad corridors, mainroads, and way-stations of an extraordinary and elusive Afro-American cultural phenomenon.

Defining Blues

The task of adequately describing the blues is equivalent to the labor of describing a world class athlete's awesome gymnastics. Adequate appreciation demands comprehensive attention. An investigator has to *be* there, to follow a course recommended by one of the African writer Wole Soyinka's ironic narrators to a London landlord: "See for yourself."

The elaborations of the blues may begin in an austere self-accusation: "Now this trouble I'm having, I brought it all on myself." But the accusation seamlessly fades into humorous acknowledgment of duplicity's always duplicitous triumph: "You know the woman that I love, I stoled her from my best friend, / But you know that fool done got lucky and stole her back again." Simple provisos for the troubled mind are commonplace, and drear exactions of crushing manual labor are objects of wry, *in situ* commentary. Numinous invocation punctuates a guitar's resonant back beat with: "Lawd, Lawd, Lawd . . . have mercy on me / Please send me someone, to end this misery." Existential declarations of lack combine with lustily macabre prophecies of the subject's demise. If a "matchbox" will hold his clothes, surely the roadside of much-traveled highways will be his memorial plot: "You can bury my body down by the highway side / So my old devil spirit can catch a Greyhound bus and ride." Conative formulations of a brighter future (sun shining in the back door some day, wind rising to blow the blues away) join with a slow-moving *askesis* of present, amorous imprisonment: "You leavin' now, baby, but you hangin' crepe on my door," or "She got a mortgage on my body, and a lien on my soul." Self-deprecating confession and slack-strumming growls of violent solutions combine: "My lead mule's cripple, you know my off mule's blind / You know I can't drive nobody / Bring me a loaded .39 (I'm go'n pop him, pop that mule!)." The wish for a river of whiskey where if a man were a "divin' duck" he would submerge himself and never "come up" is a function of a world in which "when you lose yo' eyesight, yo' best friend's gone / Sometimes yo' own dear people don't want to fool with you long."

Like a streamlined athlete's awesomely dazzling explosions of prowess, the blues song erupts, creating a veritable playful festival of meaning. Rather than a rigidly personalized form, the blues offer a phylogenetic recapitulation—a nonlinear, freely associative, nonsequential meditation—of species experience. What emerges is not a filled subject, but an anonymous (nameless) voice issuing from the black (w)hole.[11] The blues singer's signatory coda is always *atopic*, placeless: "If anybody ask you who sang this song / Tell 'em X done been here and gone." The "signature" is a space already "X"(ed), a trace of the already "gone"—a fissure rejoined. Nevertheless, the "you" (audience) addressed is always free to invoke the X(ed) spot in the body's absence.[12] For the signature comprises a scripted authentication of "your" feelings. Its mark is an invitation to energizing intersubjectivity. Its implied (in)junction reads: Here is my body meant for (a phylogenetically conceived) you.

The blues are a synthesis (albeit one always synthesizing rather than one already hypostatized). Combining work songs, group seculars, field hollers, sacred harmonies, proverbial wisdom, folk philosophy, political commentary, ribald humor, elegiac lament, and much more, they constitute an amalgam that seems always to have been in motion in America—always becoming, shaping, transforming, displacing the peculiar experiences of Africans in the New World.

Blues as Code and Force

One way of describing the blues is to claim their amalgam as a code radically conditioning Afro-America's cultural signifying. Such a description implies a prospect in which any aspect of the blues—a guitar's growling vamp or a stanza's sardonic boast of heroically back-breaking labor—"stands," in Umberto Eco's words, "for something else" in virtue of a systematic set of conventional procedures.[13] The materiality of any blues manifestation, such as a guitar's walking bass or a French harp's "whoop" of motion seen, is, one might say, enciphered in ways that enable the material to escape into a named or coded, blues signification. The material, thus, slips into irreversible difference. And as phenomena named and set in meaningful relation by a blues code, both the harmonica's whoop and the guitar's bass can recapitulate vast dimensions of experience. For such discrete blues instances are always intertextually related by the blues code as a whole. Moreover, they are involved in the code's manifold interconnections with other codes of Afro-American culture.

A further characterization of blues suggests that they are equivalent to Hegelian "force."[14] In the *Phenomenology*, Hegel speaks of a flux in which there is "only *difference* as a *universal* difference, or as a difference into which the many antitheses have been resolved. This difference, as a *universal* difference, is consequently the *simple element in the play of Force itself* and what is true in it. It is the *law of Force*" (p. 90). Force is thus defined as a relational matrix where *difference* is the law. Finally the blues, employed as an image for the investigation of culture, represents a *force* not unlike electricity. Hegel writes:

> Of course, given *positive* electricity, negative too is given *in principle*; for the positive *is*, only as related to a negative, or, the positive is *in its own self* the difference from itself; and similarly with the negative. But that electricity as such should divide itself in this way is not in itself a necessity. Electricity, as *simple Force*, is indifferent to its law—*to be* positive and negative; and if we call the former its *Notion* but the latter its being, then its Notion is indifferent to its being. It merely *has* this property, which just means that this property is not *in itself* necessary to it. . . . It is only with law as law that we are to compare its *Notion* as Notion, or its necessity. But in all these forms, necessity has shown itself to be only an empty word. [P. 93]

Metaphorically extending Hegel's formulation vis-à-vis electricity, one might say that a traditional property of cultural study may well be the kind of dichotomy inscribed in terms like "culture" and "practical reason." But even if such dichotomies are raised to the status of law, they never constitute the necessity or "determinant instances" of cultural study and explanation conceived in terms of *force*—envisioned, that is, in the analytic notion of a blues matrix as force. The blues, therefore, comprise a mediational site where familiar antinomies are resolved (or dissolved) in the office of adequate cultural understanding.

Blues Translation at the Junction

To suggest a trope for the blues as a forceful matrix in cultural understanding is to summon an image of the black blues singer at the railway junction lustily transforming experiences of a durative (unceasingly oppressive) landscape into the energies of rhythmic song. The railway juncture is marked by transience. Its inhabitants are always travelers—a multifarious assembly in transit. The "X" of crossing roadbeds signals the multidirectionality of the juncture and is simply a single instance in a boundless network that redoubles and circles, makes sidings and ladders, forms Y's and branches over the vastness of hundreds of thousands of American miles. Polymorphous and multidirectional, scene of arrivals and departures, place betwixt and between (ever *entre les deux*), the juncture is the way-station of the blues.

The singer and his production are always at this intersection, this crossing, codifying force, providing resonance for experience's multiplicities. Singer and song never arrest transience—fix it in "transcendent form." Instead they provide expressive equivalence for the juncture's ceaseless flux. Hence, they may be conceived as translators.[15]

Like translators of written texts, blues and its sundry performers offer interpretations of the experiencing of experience. To experience the juncture's ever-changing scenes, like successive readings of ever-varying texts by conventional translators, is to produce vibrantly polyvalent interpretations encoded as blues. The singer's product, like the railway juncture itself (or a successful translator's original), constitutes a lively scene, a robust matrix, where endless antinomies are mediated and understanding and explanation find conditions of possibility.

The durative—transliterated as lyrical statements of injustice, despair, loss, absence, denial, and so forth—is complemented in blues performance by an instrumental energy (guitar, harmonica, fiddle, gut-bucket bass, molasses jug, washboard) that employs locomotive rhythms, train bells, and whistles as onomatopoeic references. In *A Theory of Semiotics*, Eco writes:

> Music presents, on the one hand, the problem of a semiotic system without a semantic level (or a content plane): on the other hand, however, there are musical "signs" (or syntagms) with an explicit denotative value (trumpet signals in the army) and there are syntagms or entire "texts" possessing pre-culturalized connotative value ("pastoral" or "thrilling" music, etc.). [P. 111]

The absence of a content plane noted by Eco implies what is commonly referred to as the "abstractness" of instrumental music. The "musical sign," on the other hand, suggests cultural signals that function onomatopoeically by calling to mind "natural" sounds or sounds "naturally" associated with common human situations. Surely, though, it would be a mistake to claim that onomatopoeia is in any sense "natural," for different cultures encode even the "same" natural sounds in varying ways. (A rooster onomatopoeically sounded in Puerto Rican Spanish is phonically unrecognizable in United States English, as a classic Puerto Rican short story makes hilariously clear.)

If onomatopoeia is taken as cultural mimesis, however, it is possible to apply the semiotician's observations to blues by pointing out that the dominant blues syntagm in America is an instrumental imitation of *train-wheels-over-track-junctures*. This sound is the "sign," as it were, of the blues, and it combines an intriguing melange of phonics: rattling gondolas, clattering flatbeds, quilling whistles, clanging bells, rumbling boxcars, and other railroad sounds. A blues text may thus announce itself by the onomatopoeia of the train's whistle sounded on the indrawn breath of a harmonica or a train's bell tinkled on the high keys of an upright piano. The blues stanzas may then roll through an extended meditative repertoire with a steady train-wheels-over-track-junctures guitar back beat as a traditional, syntagmatic complement. If desire and absence are driving conditions of blues performance, the amelioration of such conditions is implied by the onomatopoeic *training* of blues voice and instrument. Only a *trained* voice can sing the blues.[16]

At the junctures, the intersections of experience where roads cross and diverge, the blues singer and his performance serve as codifiers, absorbing and transforming discontinuous experience into formal expressive instances that bear only the trace of origins, refusing to be pinned down to any final, dualistic significance. Even as they speak of paralyzing absence and ineradicable desire, their instrumental rhythms suggest change, movement, action, continuance, unlimited and unending possibility. Like signification itself, blues are always nomadically wandering. Like the freight-hopping hobo, they are ever on the move, ceaselessly summing novel experience.

Antinomies and Blues Mediation

The blues performance is further suggestive if economic conditions of Afro-American existence are brought to mind. Standing at the juncture, or railhead, the singer draws into his repertoire hollers, cries, whoops, and moans of black men and women working in fields without recompense. The performance can be cryptically conceived, therefore, in terms suggested by the bluesman Booker White, who said, "The foundation of the blues is working behind a mule way back in slavery time."[17] As a force, the blues matrix defines itself as a network mediating poverty and abundance in much the same manner that it reconciles durative and kinetic. Many instances of the blues performance contain lyrical inscriptions of both lack and commercial possibility. The performance that sings of abysmal poverty and deprivation may be recompensed by sumptuous food and stimulating beverage at a country picnic, amorous favors from an attentive listener, enhanced Afro-American communality, or Yankee dollars from representatives of record companies traveling the South in search of blues as commodifiable entertainment. The performance, therefore, mediates one of the most prevalent of all antimonies in cultural investigation—creativity and commerce.

As driving force, the blues matrix thus avoids simple dualities. It perpetually achieves its effects as a fluid and multivalent network. It is only when "understanding"—the analytical work of a translator who translates the infinite changes of the blues—converges with such blues "force," however, that adequate explanatory perception (and half-creation) occurs. The matrix effectively functions toward cultural understanding, that is, only when an investigator brings an inventive attention to bear.

The Investigator, Relativity, and Blues Effect

The blues matrix is a "cultural invention": a "negative symbol" that generates (or obliges one to invent) its own referents.[18] As an inventive trope, this matrix provides for my following chapters the type of image or model that is always present in accounts of culture and cultural products. If the analyses that I provide are successful, the blues matrix will have *taken effect* (and *affect*) through me.

To "take effect," of course, is not identical with to "come into existence" or to "demonstrate serviceability for the first time." Because what I have defined as a blues matrix is so demonstrably anterior to any single instance of its cultural-explanatory employment, my predecessors as effectors are obviously legion. "Take effect," therefore, does not signify discovery in the traditional sense of that word. Rather, it signals the tropological nature of my uses of an already extant matrix.

Ordinarily, accounts of art, literature, and culture fail to acknowledge their governing theories; further, they invariably conceal the *inventive* character of such theories. Nevertheless, all accounts of art, expressive culture, or culture in general are indisputably functions of their creators' tropological energies. When such creators talk of "art," for example, they are never dealing with existential givens. Rather, they are summoning objects, processes, or events defined by a model that they have created (by and for themselves) as a picture of art. Such models, or tropes, are continually invoked to constitute and explain phenomena inaccessible to the senses. Any single model, or any complementary set of inventive tropes, therefore, will offer only a selective account of experience—a

partial reading, as it were, of the world. While the single account temporarily reduces chaos to ordered plan, all such accounts are eternally
troubled by "remainders."

Where literary art is concerned, for example, a single, ordering, investigative model or trope will necessarily exclude phenomena that an
alternative model or trope privileges as a definitive artistic instance. Recognizing the determinacy of "invention" in cultural explanation entails
the acknowledgment of what might be called a *normative relativity*. To
acknowledge relativity in our post-Heisenbergian universe is, of course,
far from original. Neither, however, is it an occasion for the skeptics or the
conservatives to heroically assume the critical stage.

The assumption of normative relativity, far from being a call to abandonment or retrenchment in the critical arena, constitutes an invitation to
speculative explorations that are aware both of their own partiality and
their heuristic transitions from suggestive (sometimes dramatic) images to
inscribed concepts. The openness implied by relativity enables, say, the
literary critic to *re-cognize* his endeavors, presupposing from the outset
that such labors are not directed toward independent, observable, empirical phenomena but rather toward processes, objects, and events that he or
she half-creates (and privileges as "art") through his or her own speculative, inventive energies and interests.

One axiological extrapolation from these observations on invention
and relativity is that no object, process, or single element possesses *intrinsic aesthetic value*. The "art object" as well as its value are selective
constructions of the critic's tropes and models. A radicalizing uncertainty
may thus be said to mark cultural explanation. This uncertainty is similar
in kind to the always selective endeavors of, say, the particle physicist.[19]

The physicist is always compelled to choose between velocity and
position.[20] Similarly, an investigator of Afro-American expressive culture
is ceaselessly compelled to forgo manifold variables in order to apply
intensive energy to a selected array.

Continuing the metaphor, one might say that if the investigator's efforts
are sufficiently charged with blues energy,[21] he is almost certain to remodel
elements and events appearing in traditional, Anglo-American space-time
in ways that make them "jump" several rings toward blackness and the
vernacular. The blues-oriented observer (the *trained* critic) necessarily
"heats up" the observational space by his or her very presence.[22]

An inventive, tropological, investigative model such as that proposed by
Blues, Ideology, and Afro-American Literature entails not only awareness
of the metaphorical nature of the blues matrix, but also a willingness on
my own part to do more than merely hear, read, or see the blues. I must
also play (with and on) them. Since the explanatory possibilities of a blues
matrix—like analytical possibilities of a delimited set of forces in unified

field theory—are hypothetically unbounded, the blues challenge investigative *understanding* to an unlimited play.

Blues and Vernacular Expression in America

The blues should be privileged in the study of American culture to precisely the extent that inventive understanding successfully converges with blues force to yield accounts that persuasively and playfully refigure expressive geographies in the United States. My own ludic uses of the blues are various, and each figuration implies the valorization of vernacular facets of American culture. The Afro-American writer James Alan McPherson is, I think, the commentator who most brilliantly and encouragingly coalesces blues, vernacular, and cultural geographies of the United States in his introduction to *Railroad: Trains and Train People in American Culture.*[23]

Having described a fiduciary reaction to the steam locomotive by nineteenth-century financiers and an adverse artistic response by such traditional American writers as Melville, Hawthorne, and Thoreau, McPherson details the reaction of another sector of the United States population to the railroad:

> To a third group of people, those not bound by the assumptions of either business or classical traditions in art, the shrill whistle might have spoken of new possibilities. These were the backwoodsmen and Africans and recent immigrants—the people who comprised the vernacular level of American society. To them the machine might have been loud and frightening, but its whistle and its wheels promised movement. And since a commitment to both freedom and movement was the basic promise of democracy, it was probable that such people would view the locomotive as a challenge to the integrative powers of their imaginations. [P. 6]

Afro-Americans—at the bottom even of the vernacular ladder in America—responded to the railroad as a "meaningful symbol offering both economic progress and the possibility of aesthetic expression" (p.9). This possibility came from the locomotive's drive and thrust, its promise of unrestrained mobility and unlimited freedom. The blues musician at the crossing, as I have already suggested, became an expert at reproducing or translating these locomotive energies. With the birth of the blues, the vernacular realm of American culture acquired a music that had "wide appeal because it expressed a toughness of spirit and resilience, a willingness to transcend difficulties which was strikingly familiar to those whites who remembered their own history" (p.16). The signal expressive achievement of blues, then, lay in their translation of technological innovativeness, unsettling demographic fluidity, and boundless frontier energy into expression which attracted avid interest from the American masses. By the

1920s, American financiers had become aware of commercial possibilities not only of railroads but also of black music deriving from them.

A "race record" market flourished during the twenties. Major companies issued blues releases under labels such as Columbia, Vocalion, Okeh, Gennett, and Victor. Sometimes as many as ten blues releases appeared in a single week; their sales (aided by radio's dissemination of the music) climbed to hundreds of thousands. The onset of the Great Depression ended this phenomenal boom. During their heyday, however, the blues unequivocally signified a ludic predominance of the vernacular with that sassy, growling, moaning, whooping confidence that marks their finest performances.

McPherson's assessment seems fully justified. It serves, in fact, as a suggestive play in the overall project of refiguring American expressive geographies. Resonantly complementing the insights of such astute commentators as Albert Murray, Paul Oliver, Samuel Charters, Amiri Baraka, and others,[24] McPherson's judgments highlight the value of a blues matrix for cultural analysis in the United States.

In harmony with other brilliant commentators on the blues already noted, Ralph Ellison selects the railroad way-station (the "Chehaw Station") as his topos for the American "little man."[25] In "The Little Man at the Chehaw Station,"[26] he autobiographically details his own confirmation of his Tuskegee music teacher's observation that in the United States

> You must *always* play your best, even if it's only in the waiting room at Chehaw Station, because in this country there'll always be a little man hidden behind the stove . . . and he'll know the *music*, and the *tradition*, and the standards of *musicianship* required for whatever you set out to perform [P. 25].

When Hazel Harrison made this statement to the young Ellison, he felt that she was joking. But as he matured and moved through a diversity of American scenes, Ellison realized that the inhabitants of the "drab, utilitarian structure" of the American vernacular do far more than respond in expressive ways to "blues-echoing, train-whistle rhapsodies blared by fast express trains as they thundered past" the junction. At the vernacular level, according to Ellison, people possess a "cultivated taste" that asserts its "authority out of obscurity" (p. 26). The "little man" finally comes to represent, therefore, "that unknown quality which renders the American audience far more than a receptive instrument that may be dominated through a skillful exercise of the sheerly 'rhetorical' elements—the flash and filigree—of the artist's craft" (p. 26).

From Ellison's opening gambit and wonderfully illustrative succeeding examples, I infer that the vernacular (in its expressive adequacy and adept critical facility) always *absorbs* "classical" elements of American life and

Negroes sitting on the steps of the T&P Railway station, New Roads, Louisiana, 1938. (One train per day passes.) Photo by Russell Lee, Farm Security Administration. Reproduced from the collections of the Library of Congress, Washington, D.C.

art. Indeed, Ellison seems to imply that expressive performers in America who ignore the judgments of the vernacular are destined to failure.

Although his injunctions are intended principally to advocate a traditional "melting pot" ideal in American "high art," Ellison's observations ultimately valorize a comprehensive, vernacular expressiveness in America. Though he seldom loses sight of the possibilities of a classically "transcendent" American high art, he derives his most forceful examples from the vernacular: Blues seem implicitly to comprise the *All* of American culture.

Blues Moments in Afro-American Expression

In the chapters that follow, I attempt to provide suggestive accounts of moments in Afro-American discourse when personae, protagonists, autobiographical narrators, or literary critics successfully negotiate an obdurate "economics of slavery" and achieve a resonant, improvisational, expressive dignity. Such moments and successful analyses of them provide cogent examples of the blues matrix at work.

The expressive instances that I have in mind occur in passages such as the conclusion of the *Narrative of the Life of Frederick Douglass*. Standing at a Nantucket convention, riffing (in the "break" suddenly confronting him) on the *personal* troubles he has seen and successfully negotiated in a "prisonhouse of American bondage," Douglass achieves a profoundly dignified blues voice. Zora Neale Hurston's protagonist Janie in the novel *Their Eyes Were Watching God*—as she lyrically and idiomatically relates a tale of personal suffering and triumph that begins in the sexual exploitations of slavery—is a blues artist par excellence. Her wisdom might well be joined to that of Amiri Baraka's Walker Vessels (a "locomotive container" of blues?), whose chameleon code-switching from academic philosophy to blues insight makes him a veritable incarnation of the absorptively vernacular. The narrator of Richard Wright's *Black Boy* inscribes a black blues life's lean desire (as I shall demonstrate in chapter 3) and suggests yet a further instance of the blues matrix's expressive energies. Ellison's invisible man and Baraka's narrator in *The System of Dante's Hell* (whose blues book produces dance) provide additional examples. Finally, Toni Morrison's Milkman Dead in *Song of Solomon* discovers through "Sugarman's" song that an awesomely expressive blues response may well consist of improvisational and serendipitous surrender to the air: "As fleet and bright as a lodestar he wheeled toward Guitar and it did not matter which one of them would give up his ghost in the killing arms of his brother. For now he knew what Shalimar knew: If you surrendered to the air, you could *ride* it."[27]

Such blues moments are but random instances of the blues matrix at work in Afro-American cultural expression. In my study as a whole, I attempt persuasively to demonstrate that a blues matrix (as a vernacular trope for American cultural explanation in general) possesses enormous force for the study of literature, criticism, and culture. I know that I have appropriated the vastness of the vernacular in the United States to a single matrix. But I trust that my necessary selectivity will be interpreted, not as a sign of myopic exclusiveness, but as an invitation to inventive play. The success of my efforts would be effectively signaled in the following chapters, I think, by the transformation of my "I" into a juncture where readers could freely improvise their own distinctive tropes for cultural explanation. A closing that in fact opened on such inventive possibilities (like the close of these introductory remarks) would be appropriately marked by the crossing sign's inviting "X."

One   Figurations for a New American
Literary History: Archaeology,
Ideology, and Afro-American
Discourse

The old formulas had failed, and a new one had to be made, but,
after all, the object was not extravagant or eccentric. One sought
no absolute truth. One sought only a spool on which to wind the
thread of history without breaking it.

Henry Adams, *The Education*

Relics of by-gone instruments of labour possess the same importance for the investigation of extinct economic forms of society as
do fossil bones for the determination of extinct species of animals.

Karl Marx, *Capital*

(The bluesman Big Bill Broonzy sings:
> *I worked on a levee camp and the extra gangs too*
> *Black man is a boy, I don't care what he can do.*
> *I wonder when—I wonder when—I wonder when will*
> > *I get to be called a man.*

*Big Bill's stanza signifies American meaning embedded in rocky
places. Archaeology employs tropological energy to decode such
meaning. It foregrounds voices raised at the margin of civilization,
at the very edge of the New World wilderness:*
> *The first time I met the blues, mama, they came walking*
> > *through the woods,*
> *The first time I met the blues, baby, they came walking*
> > *through the woods,*
> *They stopped at my house first, mama, and done me all*
> > *the harm they could.*

*Little Brother Montgomery's stanza implies harm's unequivocal
conquest by a blues voice rising. From piney woods, sagging
cabins, and settling levees vernacular tones rise, singing a different
America. Archaeology foregrounds and deciphers this song, and
when its work is finished what remains is not history as such, but
a refigured knowledge. Louis Althusser makes explicit the distinction between* history as such *and* historical knowledge:

> *We should have no illusions as to the incredible force of
> that prejudice, which still dominates us all, which is the very
> essence of contemporary historicity, and which attempts to*

15

> *make us confuse the object of knowledge with the real ob-*
> *ject, by affecting the object of knowledge with the very*
> *"qualities" of the real object of which it is knowledge. The*
> *knowledge of history is no more historical than the knowl-*
> *edge of sugar is sweet.*
>
> *The result of archaeology's endeavors is: "A mood blared by*
> *trumpets, trombones, saxophones and drums, a song with turgid,*
> *inadequate words." The song is a sign of an Afro-American dis-*
> *course that strikingly refigures life on American shores.)*

I

In 1822, Gideon Mantell, an English physician with a consuming interest in geology and paleontology, made a routine house call in Sussex.[1] On the visit, he discovered a fossilized tooth that seemed to be a vestige of a giant, herbivorous reptile. Since he had nothing in his own collection comparable to his find, he traveled to the Hunterian Collection of the Royal College of Surgeons in London and spent hours searching drawers of fossil teeth attempting to find a comparable specimen. When he had nearly exhausted the possibilities, a young man who was also working at the Hunterian, and who had heard of the Sussex physician's quest, presented him with the tooth of an iguana. The match was nearly perfect. On the basis of the similarity between the tooth of the extant iguana and his own fossil discovery, Mantell named the bearer of the older tooth *Iguanodon* ("iguana tooth"). In 1825, his paper "Notice on the *Iguanodon*, a Newly-Discovered Fossil Reptile from the Sandstone of Tilgate Forest, in Sussex" appeared in the *Philosophical Transactions* of the Royal Society in London.

As the nineteenth century progressed and the fossil record expanded, it became apparent that Iguanodon was but one member of a family of reptiles that, in 1841, received the name "dinosaur" from Sir Richard Owen. By mid-century, it was possible to construct a feasible model of Iguanodon. Available evidence (including assumed homologies with living animals) indicated that the prehistoric creature was a giant, quadripedal reptile with a small triangular spike on his nose. The concrete and plaster model that was built on this plan in 1854 can be seen in England today.

The story of Iguanodon does not conclude at mid-century, however. The fossil record was substantially augmented later in the century by a splendid find of Iguanodon fossils at Bernissart, Belgium. Louis Dollo, the French paleontologist who oversaw the Bernissart site, was able to revise all existing models. Through cross-skeletal comparison and ethological inference, he concluded that Iguanodon was, in fact, bipedal. Moreover, he persuasively demonstrated that the triangular bone that had been taken for a nose spike was actually a horny thumb spike peculiar to dinosaurs.

The mode of thought implied by the Iguanodon example is similar to the mode of descriptive analysis which Michel Foucault has designated the "archaeology of knowledge."[2] Foucault writes of his project: The archaeology of knowledge "does not imply the search for a beginning; it does not relate analysis to geological excavation. It designates the general theme of a description that questions the already-said [i.e., a family of concepts] at the level of its existence" (p. 131). He defines a family of concepts as a *discourse* (p. 56). To analyze the mode of existence of a discourse (e.g., medicine, natural history, economics) is to engage in archaeological description.

The aim of Foucault's analysis is to accomplish in relationship to *families of concepts* what Dollo and others accomplished in relationship to Iguanodon. Beginning with limited fossil evidence, nineteenth-century investigators eventually arrived at an informed model of Iguanodon that contextualized the prehistoric reptile and rendered a descriptively adequate image of his living presence. The process through which this model was achieved is known to anthropologists as "descriptive integration."[3] It stands in contrast to archaeological excavation designed to unearth the remains of ancient life.

A more explicit definition of Foucault's project enables one to grasp its usefulness and effects in the study of American literary history. As a method of analysis, the archaeology of knowledge assumes that knowledge exists in discursive formations whose lineage can be traced and whose regularities are discoverable. Hence, the mystery and sacrosanctness that often surround "bodies of knowledge" or "disciplines" are replaced, under the prospect of the archaeology of knowledge, by an acknowledgment of such bodies as linguistic constructs.

Rather than attempting to determine the nature of the human subject's access to, or generation of, knowledge, analyses conducted under the prospect of Foucault's project are designed to plot the line of a family of concepts from its origin in the statement to its full-blown manifestation within a constellation of families. In the analysis that follows in the present chapter, for example, the movement is from American historical statements such as "religious man," "errand," and "wilderness" to a consideration of *American History* as a discourse situated among kindred families such as *Natural History* and *Economics*. The goal of the archaeology of knowledge as project is to advance the human sciences beyond a traditional humanism, focusing scholarly attention on the discursive constitution and arbitrary figurations of bodies of knowledge rather than on the constitution and situation of human subjects (traditional concerns of humanism). The analytical work begins with the minimal, meaningful unit of discourse: i.e., the statement.

II

For Foucault, the "statement" is the fundamental unit of discourse. He defines the statement as a materially repeatable (i.e., recorded) linguistic function. A chart, graph, exclamation, table, sentence, or logical proposition may serve as a statement (pp. 79–87). Statement thus seems to occupy the status of those linguistic gestures (even ones so minimal as letters or sounds of the alphabet) to which we refer when we say, "that makes a statement." Moreover, statement seems to imply a variety of enunciative positions rather than a unique utterance by a determinate speaker. The distribution and combination of statements in a discourse are regulated, according to Foucault, by discoverable principles or laws (p. 56). These laws of formation are referred to as a "discursive formation" (p. 38). They make possible the emergence of the notions and themes of a discourse.

Foucault's concern to set his archaeology in nonsubjective terms leads him to talk of statements and laws rather than of, say, speakers and intentions. His method is thus opposed to explanatory accounts that regard human knowlege as the "majestically unfolding manifestation of a thinking, knowing, speaking subject" (p. 55). He insists, instead, that the locations and authorities for discourse are more productive analytical considerations than the motives, intentions, or transcendent subjectivity of individual speakers. In medicine, for example, doctors, researchers, and clinicians are authorities. But they must speak from institutional sites such as hospitals, laboratories, medical schools, and clinics if their statements are to count as official. Moreover, they are confined to a particular succession of statements and a particular group of objects if their statements are to count as *official* medical discourse. Hence, discourse—its sites, objects, and enunciative positions—conditions the speaking subject rather than vice versa. Foucault's archaeology is statement centered: "We must grasp the statement in the exact specificity of its occurrence; determine its conditions of existence, fix at least its limits, establish its correlations with other statements that may be connected with it, and show what other forms of statement it excludes" (p. 28).

In his attempt to address such matters, Foucault insists that an explanatory model for any family of concepts must be based on a penetrating analysis of the primary conceptual structures of a discourse and the "discursive constellation" (i.e., the group of contemporary or related discourses) of which it forms a part (p. 66). He writes: "Archaeology, may ... constitute the tree of derivation of a discourse. It will place at the root, as *governing statements*, those that concern the definition of observable structures and the field of possible objects, those that prescribe the forms of description and the perceptual codes that it can use, those that reveal the most general possibilities of characterization, and thus open up a whole domain of concepts to be constructed, and, lastly, those that, while constituting a strategic choice, leave room for the greatest number of subsequent options" (p. 147).

To survey the discursive family of "American history" from the perspective of the archaeology of knowledge is to discover certain primary linguistic functions that serve as governing statements. "Religious man," "wilderness," "migratory errand," "increase in store," and "New Jerusalem" are, in my estimation, essential governing structures of a traditional American history.[4] The first—"religious man"—signals a devout believer in God for whom matters of economics and wealth are minimal considerations. "Wilderness" refers to a savage territory devoid of human beings and institutions. "Migratory errand" connotes a singular mission bestowed by God on religious man, prompting him to sail the Atlantic and settle the wilderness. The "New Jerusalem" is the promised end of the errand; it is the prospective city of God on earth. It represents the transformation of the wilderness into a community of believers who interpret an "increase in store" as secular evidence of an abiding spiritual faithfulness.

The graphics of most school history texts—with their portrayals of bleak and barren Pilgrims' landings on New World shores and a subsequent "increase in store" and Thanksgiving—offer ample representations of these primary conceptual structures. The mode of dress, physiognomy, and bearing of the foregrounded figures in such graphics normally suggest seventeenth-century European man as the epitome of religious man. Generally in such pictures non-Europeans are savagely clad, merging with the wilderness. In their proximity to the wilderness, non-Europeans are justifiably interpreted as less than human. The written accounts from which such graphics derive establish quite explicit boundaries of what might be called ethnic exclusion. Describing the Pilgrims' arrival in the wilderness, William Bradford writes: "It is recorded in Scripture as a mercy to the Apostle and his shipwrecked company, that the barbarians showed them no small kindness in refreshing them, but these savage barbarians [Native Americans], when they met them . . . were readier to fill their sides full of arrows than otherwise."[5]

Traditional American literary history is a branch of American history. As a kindred body of concepts, it reflects its parentage with rigorously derivative logic, reading the key statements of the larger discourse onto the ancestry of literary works of art. The literary texts included in Robert Spiller's influential model of American literary history,[6] for example, are arranged and explained in terms of an immigration-and-development pattern of events. And in a recent essay,[7] Spiller clearly implies that his literary-historical model, like the discursive family of which it forms a branch, is characterized by boundaries of ethnic exclusion:

> We can . . . distinguish three kinds of ethnic groups which were not parts of the main frontier movement. These are the immigrant groups which came to this country comparatively late; the blacks who were brought to this country under special circumstances; and the Jews who in all their history have mingled with, but rarely become totally absorbed into, any alien culture. All three are of great importance to the American identity today as expressed in its ever-changing literature, but only immigrations from European countries other than Great Britain followed a course close enough to our model to suggest inclusion here, even though the the remarkable achievements of the Jews and the blacks in contemporary American literature suggest that—given a slightly different model—their contributions to our culture would lend themselves to similar analyses. [p.15]

If one were to produce graphics for the history implied by Spiller, they would consist of a foregrounded European author (or a succession of such authors) turning out ever more sophisticated literary works of art. Spiller's notion of a "basic evolutionary development" of American literature (p.15) is equivalent to the larger historical discourse's notion of European, or Euro-American, progress toward the "New Jerusalem." Within the larger discourse, God's divine plan is assumed to reveal (and, ultimately, to fulfill) itself only through the endeavors of religious, European men.[8] And just as such men are considered sole builders of the New Jerusalem, so, too, they are considered exclusive chroniclers of their achievements in the evolutionary phases of an American national literature.

A secularized Hegelian version of the framework implied by traditional American history would claim that the American *Volkgeist* represents the final form of absolute Spirit on its path through history. The millennium, the self-awareness of Spirit, the prophetically augured "fullness of time" are all embodied, in other words, in that primary conceptual structure of American historical discourse—the New Jerusalem. Similarly, the world triumph of an absolute literary creativity finds its ground properly prepared in the evolutionary labors of American writers.[9] In his brilliant study *American Jeremiad*,[10] Sacvan Bercovitch demonstrates that American authors repeatedly conflated New World literary and spiritual missions by adopting the prototypical, scriptural form of rhetoric known as the jeremiad. According to Bercovitch, such authors not only spoke of a divine destiny in America but also employed a divine form modified specifically for American ears.

Given the Providential framework of American history and literary history, it is not surprising that the authorities for the enunciation of historical statements have been ministers and college professors. The institutional sites guaranteeing the official status of such statements have been pulpits and academic classrooms.[11] From the seventeenth century to the twentieth, ministerial and lay professors of the white American academy have been official spokespersons, working as teachers, scholars, critics, editors, and so on. Their ranks have been confined, for the most part, to European or Euro-American males. The early Providential aura of their instruction has been secularized through time, but one still receives the impression on reading their works that lay ministers are at work, taking account of and perpetuating literary workers and works of art that manifest adherence to the original errand—securing a New Jerusalem.

The exclusionist tendencies of Spiller, for example, are amply reinforced by the work of Cleanth Brooks, R.W.B. Lewis, and Robert Penn Warren in their giant anthology *American Literature: The Makers and the Making*.[12] In an introductory "Letter to the Reader," the editors write:

> Since this book is, among other things, a history, it is only natural that its organization should be, in the main, chronological. But it is not strictly so; other considerations inevitably cross-hatch pure chronology. We have mentioned the two sections on southern writing, which overlap periods treated elsewhere. Similarly, the two sections on black literature together span many decades, for like Faulkner and other white southern writers, black writers in America, whether of the North or the South, have worked in terms of a special condition and cultural context. [P. xix]

Although the prose is slightly less penetrable than Spiller's, it is reasonably easy to see that Brooks, Lewis, and Warren are postulating that verbal creativity which lies outside traditional, orthodox patterns of a spiritually evolving American literature is merely a shadow ("cross hatch") on national history and literary history conceived as rigidly determinate chronologies. The telos of such chronologies is, presumably, the New Jerusalem—a recaptured Eden in America.

The "special condition and cultural context" of the editors' introductory "Letter" are identical to Spiller's "special circumstances." And like Spiller, Brooks, Lewis, and Warren begin with the Puritans and trace an evolutionary progression. Unlike their predecessor, however, they find it necessary—presumably for axiological reasons—to ensure that shadows on an exalted past are not mistaken for acts of authentic literary creativity. "Literature of the Nonliterary World" is the title they provide for the concluding section of the first volume of their anthology. The section includes David Walker, Frederick Douglass, Frederick Law Olmstead, "Folk Songs of the White People," Indian Oratory, "Folk Songs of the Black People," non-Puritan historians, Southwest humorists, Abraham Lincoln, Davy Crockett, and so on. On the basis of definitions supplied by the editors, one must suppose that inclusions in this *category of the excluded* exist somewhere between secondary and *non*-literature (p. xii). The editors' definitions obviously conserve a Spillerian orthodoxy.

III

The archaeology of knowledge serves not only to isolate the governing statements of American history and literary history but also to focus attention on such formations as discourse. An emphasis on history and literary history as discourse compels one to think in symbolic, linguistic terms. In his essay "Historical Discourse,"[13] the French semiotician Roland Barthes writes that "the only feature which distinguishes historical discourse from other kinds is a paradox: the 'fact' can only exist linguistically, as a term in a discourse, yet we behave as if it were a simple reproduction of something on another plane of existence altogether, some extra-structural 'reality'" (p. 153).

Barthes's formulation enables us to conceive of the governing statements of American history and the evolutionary stages of American literary history as materially repeatable entities that assume the status of facts only because they are inscribed in historical discourse. On first view, this formulation seems to imply the presence of a human recorder, or noter, and thus to run counter to Foucault's decentering of the subject. But a further consideration indicates that the semiotician, like the archaeologist, is more concerned with the constraints of discourse than with a constraining subjectivity. Barthes says of historical facts, for example, that they "can only be defined tautologically: we take note of what is notable; but the notable . . . is nothing more than the noteworthy [i.e., that which has been 'already-said'] " (p. 153).

This tautology is clarified by an analogy between the fact linguistically conceived and the photograph of a scene. We say that a fact, like a scene, represents a bedrock reality. But since our sole access to the fact is through language we are ever aware of an intervening presence—that of the noted, the recorded, the already said. Similarly, our access to a scene by means of a photograph makes us aware of an intervening process, with its "arranged" objects, croppings, burning, enlargements, and so on. Reality becomes an elusive matter.

Where historical facts are concerned, the implications of the analogy lead one to concur with Barthes that historical discourse "does not follow reality, it only signifies it" (p. 154). What one derives from linguistic, historical facts, therefore, is not reality, but *meaning*. And meaning is always contingent upon the figurative, semantic resources available to us as readers, viewers, or auditors.

If we recur for a moment to the paleontological example with which the present essay began, we might equate Mantell's fossilized tooth with a potential signifier, dependent for its meanings on a host of factors. After the initial model of Iguanodon had been constructed, it was soon apparent that meanings quite different from those conceived by early modelers could be derived from Mantell's discovery. (And the Sussex physician would doubtless have accepted such meanings. American literary historians, by contrast, constrained by a quasi-religious orthodoxy, stand always opposed to new evidentiary considerations.) While the fossil signified dentition homologous to the iguana's, it did not signify quadripedalism. What occurred in the case of the tooth was a further accumulation of evidence that made it possible to provide an enlarged context of meaning. A substantially expanded perspective resulted in a descriptively integrated set of meanings.

Just as an enlarged context altered the conception of Iguanodon, so a consideration of the discursive constellation can alter our view of historical discourse. When the discourses and practices contemporary with American history are brought to bear, its religious orientation, site, and authorities are subject to radical reinterpretation. The savage barbarians of William Bradford's account manifest themselves, in the light of a contemporary seventeenth-century natural history, not as scriptural reprobates, but as negative functions of a philosophico-scientific practice that classified European man as the acme of being.

Both religious man and increase in store are subject to similar revisions if one considers them from the perspective of economics. Euro-Americans who engaged in the trans-Atlantic slave trade maintained a favorable

Inspection and sale of slaves, by Miguel Covarrubias. From Theodore Canot, *Adventures of an African Slaver*, ed. Malcolm Cowley (New York: Albert & Charles Boni, 1928).

balance of trade (both economic and spiritual) by defining Africans whom they loaded into ships' holds not only as heathens to be transported to occidental salvation, but also as property, bullion, or real wealth. In an act of bizarre Western logic, Africans forcefully deported from their home-land to the New World became spiritual revenue.[14] The Afro-American poet Robert Hayden succinctly captures this spiritually aberrant mercan-tilism in the following lines from "Middle Passage":

> Deep in the festering hold thy father lies,
> of his bones New England pews are made,
> those are altar lights that were his eyes.[15]

If we consider historical discourse a family of concepts, we might say that the secular-economic perspective implied by a larger interpretive context signals the possibility of new governing statements from which a new genealogical line may be derived. (We might say, indeed, that the prospect of "standing Hegel on his feet" becomes imminent.) In the novel *Season of Adventure*[16] by the West Indian author, George Lamming, the protagonist reflects:

> The Americans took pleasure in their past because they were de-scended from men whose migration was a freely chosen act. They were descended from a history that was recorded, a history which was wholly contained in their own way of looking at the world . . . [but the history of African-descended black people] was a commercial de-portation. [P. 93]

As a new governing structure, "commercial deportation" dramatically alters the construction of traditional American historical discourse. The statement first signifies an involuntary transport of *human beings* as opposed to the export or import of will-less merchandise. And instead of bleak and barren beginnings on New World shores yet to be civilized, the history signified by commercial deportation implies European man as slavetrader, divider of established civilizations, dealer in "hides of Fella-tah/Mandingo, Ibo, Kru."[17] The transportable stock on American vessels is no longer figured as a body of courageous Pilgrims but as "black gold." And a providential American history reveals itself as a spiritual discourse coextensive with the nondiscursive, economic practices of men who turned the middle passage to profit.

The graphics accompanying a historical formation derived from com-mercial deportation are strikingly different from those accompanying the accounts of a traditional American history. They evoke Armageddon rather than the New Jerusalem.[18] And the shift effected in the larger historical perspective by the governing structure "commercial deporta-tion" opens the way for a corollary shift in perspective on "American literary history." What comes starkly to the foreground are the conditions of a uniquely Afro-American historical and literary historical discourse.

The emergence of conditions for Afro-American literary history is a function not only of an enlarged perspective but also of the "method" of history itself. Moving beyond the explicit levels of discourse, the archaeology of knowledge seeks to discover organizing or formative principles of discourses that it evaluates. Such principles seem aptly conveyed for history by the observation that "history is tied neither to man nor to any particular object. It consists wholly in its method, which experience proves to be indispensable for cataloguing the elements of any structure whatever, human or non-human, in their entirety."[19]

If historical method consists in cataloging elements, then all histories are, at least theoretically, open-ended—the possible inclusions, limitless. In practice, histories are always limited by ideology. Catalogs are not merely constituted. They are instituted on the basis of principles of selection—on the basis of ideologies. In the essay cited earlier, Barthes writes: "historical discourse is essentially a product of ideology, or rather imagination if we accept the view that it is via the language of imagination that responsibility for an utterance passes from a purely linguistic entity to a psychological or ideological one" (p. 253). A history may be conceptualized as an ideologically or imaginatively governed catalog of figurative elements. The catalog is inconceivable in the absence of ideology, and a shift, or rupture, in ideological premises promotes strikingly new figurations.

The ideological orientation foregrounded for "Afro-American literary history" under the prospect of the archaeology of knowledge is not a vulgar Marxism, or an idealistically polemical black nationalism. The most appropriate ideological principles of formation, that is, do not suggest an outlook Fredric Jameson ascribes to a "familiar Western critique of *ideology*":

> the concept of ideology [in a "familiar" critique] already implies mystification, and conveys the notion of a kind of floating and psychological world view, a kind of subjective picture of things already by definition unrelated to the external world itself. The consequence is that even a proletarian world view is relativized, and felt to be ideological, while the ultimate standard of truth becomes the positivistic one of some "end of ideology" which would leave us in the presence of the facts themselves, without any subjective distortions.[20]

Rather than an ideological model yielding a new "positivism," what interests me is a form of thought that grounds Afro-American discourse in concrete, material situations. Where Afro-American narratives are concerned, the most suitable analytical model is not only an economic one, but also one based on a literary-critical frame of reference. The type of ideological model I have in mind is suggested by the scholarly reflections both of Jameson and of Hayden White, another well-known critic of dialectical thought.

Hayden White insists that a literary work of art can be evaluated as a discretely "social" action only if its commodity status in a society's exchange system is acknowledged. In "Literature and Social Action: Reflections on the Reflection Theory of Literary Art,"[21] White tells us that "the solution to the problem of the social status of 'literature' in the modern age, insofar as such a solution can be hoped for in the application of the Marxist method to its study, must consist of the explication of the different statuses that 'literature' has enjoyed or suffered in the hierarchy of value which assesses the worth of everything in terms of its exchange value for money or gold" (p. 377). Jameson argues, in turn, that the relationship between a literary text and its social ground is the relationship that is "reinvented" by ideological analysis. In "The Symbolic Inference: or, Kenneth Burke and Ideological Analysis,"[22] Jameson writes: "The term 'ideology' stands as the sign for a problem yet to be solved, a mental operation which remains to be executed. It does not presuppose cut-and-dried sociological stereotypes like the notion of the 'bourgeois' or the 'petty bourgeois' but is rather a mediatory concept: that is, it is an imperative to re-invent a relationship between the linguistic or aesthetic or conceptual fact in question and its social ground" (p. 510). The "social ground" can be identified as the *economics* or the *modes of production* characterizing the milieu in which an expressive work emerges.

To bring White and Jameson together in an analysis of Afro-American narratives—an analysis designed to provide a fit ideological perspective on "Afro-American literary history"—is to gain a view of subtextual dimensions of Afro-American discourse that have never been effectively evaluated. The efficacious results for practical criticism that derive from what might be called the ideology of form should be apparent in critical analyses that follow.

IV

In Afro-American literary study, a shift from a "traditional" to an economic perspective, from a humanistic to an ideologically oriented frame of reference, evokes what might be called the "economics of slavery." The phrase, like "commercial deportation," stands as a governing statement in Afro-American discourse. In specifically Afro-American terms, the "economics of slavery" signifies the social system of the Old South that determined what, how, and for whom goods were produced to satisfy human wants. As a function of the European slave trade, the economy of the Old South was an exploitative mode of production embodied in the plantation system and spirited by a myth of aristocratic patriarchalism. The formative relationship of the plantation system, as Eugene Genovese argues in *The Political Economy of Slavery* and *The World the Slaveholders Made*, was that between master and slave, lord and bondsman.[23]

At the level of economic production, the slave's labor was brutally exploited to maximize the master's profit. He existed exclusively for the master's greater gain. Genovese argues, however, that the more profoundly grotesque features of "Mr. Moneybags" (Marx's prototypical entrepreneur in *Capital*) are inappropriate for a representation of the planters of the American South. While the "economics of slavery" promoted the dehumanizing plunder of African labor, it also produced a corollary southern mythology of the ruling class. The primary features of this mythology were "patriarchy" and "economic paternalism."[24]

The southern planter, unlike his absentee counterpart in the Caribbean, was a full-fledged, resident member of his own plantation. He conceived of himself as a beneficent patriarch responsible to the full population of his estate. This populace, in fact, was deemed an "extended family" toward which he was obligated to display courtesy and concern. The second feature of Old South mythology, however, cast a bizarre shadow on the face of this assumed patriarchy.

"Economic paternalism" signified the master as the owner of all stock in his "children-as-slaves." Contrary to the free-market economics of an expanding European capitalism, the southern master was not forced to negotiate with a laborer who was, in Marx's words, "the untrammelled owner of his capacity for labour, i.e., of his person."[25] The southern master, therefore, was always a functionary of an economics predicated on the cash nexus. Yet he always, paradoxically, posed as a stern adversary to capitalism.

No sharply qualifying mythology such as that of the Old South— Genovese and others have argued—stood in the way of the West Indian absentee planter's quest for profit. Indeed, the quest for profit proceeded in its own right, far from the (absentee) master's day-to-day concern.[26] Slavery in the Caribbean was a purely capitalistic matter, an investment expected to yield return. As a form of commercial gain, it could conveniently be replaced by alternative economic forms. Genovese writes: "The planters of the British Caribbean argued their case in London for years and finally, faced with defeat, roared their protests, accepted monetary compensation, transferred investments, and made the best of it. For a capitalist an investment in black bodies could be transformed into an investment in cotton textile machinery anytime, for the transformation was a matter of business."[27]

The consequences of the differing views of slavery in the West Indies and in the Old South are reflected in the possible degrees of freedom available to the enterprising West Indian and Afro-American slave. As I shall make clear in my subsequent discussions, the necessity to negotiate an "economics of slavery" was always present for the slave, whether in the Old South or in the Caribbean. But the degree of the masters' intransigence and resistance varied. West Indian slavery was more inclined than that of the Old South to permit the substitution of one form of capital for another. Southerners fought a civil war to avoid abolition. British planters accepted government compensation and altered their investment portfolios.

Both West Indian and Afro-American slavery resulted in the creation of an excluded group of black men and women subjugated by violence and deprived of the fruits of their labor. The condition of existence of this caste (and its descendants) is sometimes extrapolated by historians from birthrate data. Southern patriarchalism, for example, is assumed to have been less harsh than slave treatment in, say, the Caribbean because the United States slave population grew by reproducing itself rather than by fresh deportations from Africa. But as anyone familiar with the spiraling rates of teenaged pregnancies in today's bleak inner cities can appreciate, an increase in population is not necessarily a reliable index of a tolerable life. It is not birthrates, one might suggest, but buildings that best signify the existence of Africans in America.

A *metaphorical* extension of the economics of slavery seems to verify W. E. B. Du Bois's claim that the size and arrangements of a people's homes are no unfair index of their condition.[28] While monographic histories of slavery describe important dimensions of the economics of slavery, it is possible to telescope many dimensions of such economics by means of a vertical, associative, metaphorical decoding. The diachrony of traditional historiography can be productively complemented, I think, by a nonsuccessive, synchronic prospect. The employment of such a prospect amounts to the introduction of what Hayden White defines as "tropological" thought.[29]

Tropological thought is a discursive mode that employs unfamiliar (or exotic) figures to qualify what is deemed "traditional" in a given discourse. To extrapolate from White, one might assert that attempts to signify the force of meaning of the economics of slavery by invoking buildings *and blues* (as I shall do forthwith) constitute an analytical move designed to incorporate into reality phenomena to which traditional historiography generally denies the status "real." The end of a tropological enterprise is the alteration of reality itself.

In White's account, a tropological approach constitutes a metalogical operation which turns logic against itself. Its conscious employment of metaphor releases us from what Hegel conceived as a tyranny of conceptual overdeterminations (p. 10). The process of tropological understanding is coextensive with dialectical thought. It, too, is designed to achieve an enlarged, altered, more adequate discursive rendering of the object of knowledge. A survey of images of Afro-American dwellings demonstrates the effect of tropological thought in defining the economics of slavery.

In *The Slave Community*, the historian John Blassingame writes: "The slaves often complained bitterly about what their masters describe as 'adequate' housing. Most of the [slave] autobiographers reported that they lived in crudely built one-room log cabins with dirt floors and too many cracks in them to permit much comfort during the winter months."[30] After his own observation on the "size and arrangements" of a people's dwellings in *The Souls of Black Folk*, Du Bois goes on to describe Negro homes in the black belt of Georgia at the turn of the century: "All over the face of the land is the one-room cabin,—now standing in the shadow of the Big House, now staring at the dusty road, now rising dark and sombre amid the green of the cotton-fields. It is nearly always old and bare, built of rough boards and neither plastered nor ceiled" (p. 159). In a report on

Africans aboard a slaver. From *Harper's Weekly*, 2 June 1860.

American working conditions in the late-1920's prepared for the Labor Research Organization, Charlotte Todes wrote of a logging camp owned by the Great Southern Railroad and worked by blacks as follows: "Across the railroad track from the depot and company store were about one-hundred shacks for Negro workers. These are one room with a window at one end—not always glass but with a wood flap to let down."[31]

The scant diachronic modification in "size and arrangements" of black dwellings allows them, I suggest, to stand as *signs* for the continuing impoverishment of blacks in the United States. The places where Africans in America have lived (and continue to live) signify the economics of slavery. An "army-style barracks"formed the home of Horace Taft of Philadephia, for example, while he was in North Carolina engaged in an experience that he describes as follows:

> It was real slavery-time work I did down there. My first week's salary was $3. That was a week's pay. They kept all the rest. It was just horrible, the things I seen at those camps. I seen men beat with rubber hoses. I seen a woman beat. There was always someone guarding and watching you. You couldn't get away because they were sitting out there with guns.

Taft was kidnapped into slave labor in 1979. His story appeared as "Slavery in a 'Migrant Stream' " in *The Philadelphia Inquirer* for 17 January 1982.

Yet, if the profile of the masters cannot be confined to capitalist grotes-querie, neither can the dwellings of Africans in America be confined exclusively to an economic signification. The nonmonetary, "mythical" dimensions that arise from the size and arrangements of black homes are supplied by an Afro-American expressiveness that can be succinctly de-noted as "blues." Samuel Charters offers the following bleak description of a dwelling on the outskirts of Brownsville, Tennessee:

> About a mile and a half from the turnoff into Brownsville there is a sagging red cabin, the bare patch of ground in front is littered with bits of clothing, dirty dishes, a broken chair. . . . The cabin has two rooms; one of them empty except for a few rags that lie in the filth of the floor. . . . In the other room is a chair, a rusted wood stove, and two dirty, unmade beds. In the heat of a summer afternoon it looks like the other empty buildings scattered along Winfield Lane.[32]

But while the sagging cabin is like all such Afro-American dwellings in its dilapidation and overcrowding (a man, his wife, and five children inhabit it), it presents identity with a difference. For the sagging red cabin outside Brownsville is the home of Sleepy John Estes, one of the greatest traditional blues singers to take guitar in hand. His brilliant expressiveness modifies, ameliorates, orders, and sharply qualifies the bleakness of a sagging cabin's size and arrangements. His song rises from a "slave community" and is fittingly designated by the single word "blues."

The expressiveness represented by Sleepy John is as much a feature of the economics of slavery as deprivations of material resources that have characterized African life in the New World. It is not, however, the field, country, or classic blues that provide a *first* occasion for examining the operation of "economics of slavery" and "commercial deportation" as governing statements in Afro-American discourse. A first view is provided, instead, by African slave narratives. When such narratives are analyzed in ideological terms, they reveal subtextual contours rich in "blues resources"—abundantly characterized, that is, by aspects of meaning which reveal profoundly brilliant economic expressive strategies designed by Africans in the New World and the Old to negotiate the dwarfing spaces and paternally aberrant arrangements of western slavery.

V

The locus classicus of Afro-American literary discourse is the slave narrative. Appearing in England and America during the eighteenth and nineteenth centuries, the thousands of narratives produced by Africans in England and by fugitive slaves and freed black men and women in America constitute the first, literate manifestations of a tragic disruption in African cultural homogeneity. When the author of *The Life of Olaudah Equiano, or Gustavus Vassa, the African. Written by Himself* (1789) arrived at the African coast in the hands of his kidnappers, he had left behind the communal, familial way of life of his native village of Essaka in the province of Benin.[33] The family member whom he has a final opportunity to embrace is a sister kidnapped in the same slave-trading raid. His sibling serves as sign and source of familial, female love. And the nature of the final meeting is emblematic of the separations that a "commercial deportation" effected in the lives of Africans: "When these people [Africans carrying Vassa and his sister to the coast] knew we were brother and sister, they indulged us to be together; and the man, to whom I supposed we belonged, lay with us, he in the middle, while she and I held one another by the hands across his breast all night; and thus for a while we forgot our misfortunes, in the joy of being together" (p. 24). The phrase, "The man, to whom I supposed we belonged," signals a loss of self-possession. The man's position "in the middle" signals a corollary loss of familial (and, by implication, conjugal) relations. The narrator introduces a sentimental apostrophe to represent his emotional response to loss:

> Yes, thou dear partner of all my childish sport! thou sharer of my joys and sorrows! happy should I have ever esteemed myself to encounter every misery for you and to procure your freedom by the sacrifice of

my own. Though you were early forced from my arms, your image has been always riveted in my heart, from which neither time nor fortune have been able to remove it. [P. 24]

But the full import of loss is felt less in sentiment than in terror. Having arrived at the coast, Equiano encounters the full, objective, reality of his commercially deportable status:

The first object which saluted my eyes when I arrived on the coast, was the sea, and a *slave* ship, which was then riding at anchor, and waiting for its *cargo*. These filled me with astonishment, which was soon converted into terror, when I was carried on board. I was immediately handled, and tossed up to see if I were sound, by some of the crew; and I was now persuaded that I had gotten into a world of bad spirits, and that they were going to kill me . . . When I looked round the ship too, and saw a large furnace of copper *boiling*, and a multitude of *black people* of every description *chained* together, every one of their countenances expressing dejection and sorrow, I no longer doubted of my fate; and, quite overpowered with horror and anguish, I fell motionless on the deck and fainted. [P. 27, my emphasis]

The quotation captures, in graphic detail, the peremptory consignment of the African—body and soul—to a chained and boiling economic hell. He will be forced to extract relief and release through whatever instruments present themselves.

At one interpretive level, the remainder of *The Life of Olaudah Equiano* is the story of a Christian convert who finds solace from bondage in the ministerings of a kind Providence. The Christian-missionary and civilizing effects of the slave trade that were so much vaunted by Europeans find an exemplary instance in the narrator's portrait of himself after a short sojourn in England: "I could now speak English tolerably well, and I perfectly understood everything that was said. . . . I no longer looked upon . . . [Englishmen] as spirits, but as men superior to us [Africans]; and therefore I had the stronger desire to resemble them, to imbibe their spirit, and imitate their manners" (p. 48). Through the kindly instructions of "the Miss Guerins," Englishwomen who are friends of his master, the young Vassa learns to read and write. He is also baptized and received into St. Margaret's church, Westminster, in February 1759 (p. 49). As a civilized, Christian subject, he is able to survive with equanimity the vagaries of servitude, the whims of fortune, and the cruelties of fate. After his manumission, he searches earnestly for the true, guiding light of salvation and achieves (in chapter 10) confirmation of his personal salvation in a vision of the crucified Christ:

On the morning of the 6th October . . . [1774], all that day, I thought I should either see or hear something supernatural. I had a secret impulse on my mind of something that was to take place. . . . In the evening of the same day . . . the Lord was pleased to break in upon my soul with his bright beams of heavenly light; and in that instant, as it were, removing the veil, and letting light into a dark place, I saw clearly with an eye of faith, the crucified Saviour bleeding on the cross on Mount Calvary; the scriptures became an unsealed book. . . . Now every leading providential circumstance that happened to me, from the day I was taken from my parents to that hour, was then in my view, as if it had just then occurred. I was sensible of the invisible hand of God, which guided and protected me, when in truth I knew it not. [Pp. 149-50]

The foregoing passage from *The Life* represents what might be termed the African's providential awakening and ascent from the motionlessness that accompanied a coerced entrance into the mercantile inferno of slavery. To the extent that the narrative reinforces a providential interpretation, the work seems coextensive with an "old" literary history that claims Africans as spiritual cargo delivered (under "special circumstances") unto God Himself.

If, however, one returns for a moment to the conditions of disruption that begin the narrator's passage into slavery and considers the truly "commercial" aspects of his deportation, a perspective quite different from that of the old history emerges. Further, by summoning an ideological analysis grounded in the genuine economics (as opposed to the European-derived "ethics") of slavery, one perceives quite a different *awakening* on the part of the African.

To bring together perspectives of Jameson and White in a discussion of *The Life of Olaudah Equiano* is scarcely to designate "the African" of the narrative's title an exclusively religious product of a trans-Atlantic trade's providential mission. For Vassa's status as transportable property is finally ameliorated as much by his canny mercantilism as by his pious toiling in the vineyards of Anglicanism. *The Life of Olaudah Equiano* can be ideologically considered as a work whose protagonist masters the rudiments of economics that condition his very life. It can also be interpreted as a narrative whose author creates a text which inscribes these economics as a sign of its "social grounding."

The Life, therefore is less a passive "mirroring" of providential ascent than a summoning "into being [by a narrative of] that situation to which it is also, at one and the same time, a reaction."[34] If there is a new, or different, historical subtext distinguishing Vassa's narrative from traditional, historical, and literary historical discourse, that subtext is, at least in part, a symbolic "invention" of the narrative itself. This subtext becomes discernible only under an analysis that explores a determinate relationship between *The Life* and the economics of slavery.

"Now the Ethiopian," writes Vassa, "was willing to be saved by Jesus Christ, the sinner's only surety, and also to rely on none other person or

thing for salvation" (p. 150). The religious "voice" and conversion narrative form implied by this statement stand in marked contrast to the voice
and formal implications characterizing *The Life's* representations of West
Indian bondage. In the "West India climate," according to Vassa, the most
savage barbarities of the trade manifest themselves, resulting in the catalog
of horrors that appears in chapter 5. The savage tides of the Caribbean are
to the calm harbors of England as the gross deceptions and brutalizations
of Montserrat are to the kind attentions of the Guerins and others in
London. It would surely seem, therefore, that if "the Ethiopian" were
anywhere "willing to be saved by Jesus Christ . . . and to rely *on none other
person or thing*" (my emphasis), a "West India climate" would be the
place for such reliance. Yet when the narrator enters the West Indies in
chapter five, the voice dominating the narrative is hardly one of pious
long-suffering.

After a year's labor for Mr. Robert King, his new owner, Vassa writes,
"I became very useful to my master, and saved him, as he used to acknowledge, above a hundred pounds a year" (p. 73). Thus begins a process of
self-conscious, mercantile, self-evaluation—a meditation on the economics of African, or New World, black selfhood—that continues for the
next two chapters of *The Life*. "I have sometimes heard it asserted," Vassa
continues, "that a negro cannot earn his master the first cost; but nothing
can be further from the truth. . . . I have known many slaves whose masters
would not take a thousand pounds current for them. . . . My master was
several times offered, by different gentlemen, one hundred guineas for me,
but he always told them he would not sell me, to my great joy" (p. 73).
These assertions of chapter 5 seem far more appropriate for a trader's
secular diary than a devout acolyte's conversion journal.

Having gained the post of shipboard assistant, or "mate," to Captain
Thomas Farmer, an Englishman who sails a Bermuda sloop for his new
master, Vassa immediately thinks in secular terms that he "might in time
stand some chance by being on board to get a little money, or possibly
make my escape if I should be used ill" (p. 83). This conflation of getting "a
little money" and freedom conditions the narrative experiences leading
from the slave's first trading venture (chapter 6) to his receipt of a certificate of manumission in chapter 7. Describing his initial attempts at mercantilism, the narrator writes in ledger-like detail:

> After I had been sailing for some time with this captain [Mr. Farmer],
> at length I endeavored to try my luck, and commence merchant. I had
> but a very small capital to begin with; for one single half bit, which is
> equal to three pence in England, made up my whole stock. However, I
> trusted to the Lord to be with me; and at one of our trips to St.
> Eustatius, a Dutch island, I bought a glass tumbler with my half bit,
> and when I came to Monserrat, I sold it for a bit, or sixpence. Luckily

we made several successive trips to St. Eustatius (which was a general mart for the West Indies, about twenty leagues from Montserrat), and in our next, finding my tumbler so profitable, with this one bit I bought two tumblers more; and when I came back, I sold them for two bits equal to a shilling sterling. When we went again, I bought with these two bits four more of these glasses, which I sold for four bits on our return to Montserrat. And in our next voyage to St. Eustatius, I bought two glasses with one bit, and with the other three I bought a jug of Geneva, nearly about three pints in measure. When we came to Montserrat, I sold the gin for eight bits, and the tumblers for two, so that my capital now amounted in all to a dollar, well husbanded and acquired in space of a month or six weeks, when I blessed the Lord that I was so rich. [P. 84]

Manifold ironies mark the foregoing account of the slave's transactions. Rather than describing a spiritual multiplication of "talents" in providential terms, shipboard transactions are transcribed as a chronicle of mercantile adventure. The pure product of trade (i.e., transportable "property" or chattel) becomes a trader, turning from spiritual meditations to canny speculations on the increase of a well acquired and husbanded store! The swift completeness of this transformation is apparent when, amidst the lawless savagery visited upon blacks in the West Indies, Vassa calmly resolves to earn his freedom "by honest and honorable [read: mercantile] means" (p. 87). In order to achieve this end he redoubles his commercial efforts.

Eventually *The Life*, in its middle portion, almost entirely brackets the fact that a mercantile self's trans-Caribbean profit-making is a function of an egregious trade in slaves plied between the West Indies and the southeastern coast of the United States. We find, for example, the following statement by the narrator: "About the latter end of the year 1764, my master bought a larger sloop, called the *Prudence*, about seventy or eighty tons, of which my captain had the command. I went with him in this vessel, and we took a load of new slaves for Georgia and Charleston . . . I got ready all the little venture I could; and, when the vessel was ready, we sailed, to my great joy. When we got to our destined places . . . I expected I should have an opportunity of selling my little property to advantage" (p. 91). One explanation for the bracketing of slavery that marks this passage is that the narrator, having been reduced to property by a commercial deportation, decides during his West Indian captivity that neither sentiment nor spiritual sympathies can earn his liberation. He realizes, in effect, that only the acquisition of property will enable him to alter his designated status *as property*. He, thus, formulates a plan of freedom constrained by the mercantile boundaries of a Caribbean situation.

With the blessings of a master who credits him with "half a puncheon of rum and half a hogshead of sugar," Vassa sets out to make "money enough . . . to *purchase my freedom*. . . for forty pounds sterling money, which was only the same price he [Mr. King] gave for me"(pp. 93–94, my emphasis). By chapter 7 the slave's commercial venture is complete. Having entered the "West India trade," he has obtained "about forty-seven pounds." He offers the entire sum to Mr. King, who "said he would not be worse than his promise; and taking the money, told me to go to the Secretary at the Register Office, and get my manumission drawn up" (pp. 101–102). In the act of exchange between lord and bondsman, there appears a clear instance of the West Indian slaveholder's willingness to substitute one form of capital for another. Mr. King's initial reluctance to honor his promise is overcome by a realization that his investment in black bodies can be transformed easily enough into other forms of enterprise.

The most monumental linguistic occurrence in the process that commences with Vassa's shift of voice in chapter 5 is the transcription of his certificate of manumission in chapter 7. The certificate is, in effect, an economic sign which competes with and radically qualifies the ethical piousness of its enfolding text. The inscribed document is a token of mastery, signifying its recipient's successful negotiation of a deplorable system of exchange. The narrator of *The Life* (as distinguished from the author) is aware of both positive and negative implications of his certificate, and he self-consciously prevents his audience from bracketing his achievement of manumission as merely an act of virtuous perseverance in the face of adversity. "As the form of my manumission has something peculiar in it, and expresses the absolute power and dominion one man claims over his fellow, I shall beg leave to present it before my readers at full length" (p. 103).

The document—which gives, grants and releases to "the said Gustavus Vassa, all right, title, dominion, sovereignty, and property" that his "lord and master" Mr. King holds over him—signals the ironic transformation of property by property into humanity. Chattel has transformed itself into freeman through the exchange of forty pounds sterling. The slave equates his elation on receiving freedom to the joys of conquering heroes, or to the contentment of mothers who have regained a "long lost infant," or to the gladness of the lover who once again embraces the mistress "ravished from his arms" or the "weary hungry mariner at the sight of the desired friendly port" (p. 103).

Two frames of mind are implied by the transcription of the manumission certificate and the response of the freeman. First, the narrator recognizes that the journey's end (i.e., the mariner's achievement of port) signaled by manumission provides enabling conditions for the kind of happy relations that seemed irrevocably lost when he departed his sister (i.e., familial relations like those implied by "mother-infant" and conjugal ones suggested by "lover-mistress"). At the same time, he is unequivocally aware that the terribleness of the economics he has "navigated" separated him from such relationships in the first instance. There seems no ambivalence, or split opinion, however, on the part of the *author* of *The Life of Olaudah Equiano*.

The structure of the text of the narrative seems to reflect the author's conviction that it is absolutely necessary for the slave to negotiate the economics of slavery if he would be free. The mercantile endeavors of the autobiographical self in *The Life* occupy the very center of the narrative. Chapters 5, 6, and 7 mark an economic middle passage in a twelve-chapter account.

The work's middle section represents an active, inversive, ironically mercantile ascent by the propertied self from the hell of "commercial deportation." It offers a graphic "re-invention" of the social grounding of the Afro-American symbolic act par excellence. It vividly delineates the true character of Afro-America's historical origins in a slave economics and implicitly acknowledges that such economics *must be mastered* before liberation can be achieved.

Vassa's hardships do not end with the purchase of freedom. Subsequent episodes make it clear that life for a free black in eighteenth-century England was neither simple nor easy. Nonetheless, the dramatic impact of the text following chapter 7 is qualitatively less than that of preceding chapters. This reduction in dramatic effect is at least in part a function of the predictability of the narrator's course once he has undergone economic awakening in the West Indies. The possibility of amorous heterosexual relationships, for example, is introduced immediately after manumission with the narrator's tongue-in-cheek comment on the community's response (especially that of black women) to his liberation:"The fair as well as the black people immediately styled me by a new appellation, to me the most desirable in the world, which was freeman . . . Some of the sable females, who formerly stood aloof, now began to relax and appear less coy . . ." (p. 104). Vassa knows that it is scarcely "coyness" that has distanced him from "sable females" during his servitude. The impediment to union has always been the commercial "man in the middle" first encountered on his departure from his sister.

The economics of slavery not only reduced the African man to laboring chattel, but also reduced African women to sexual objects. After his description of separation from his sister, Vassa concludes the apostrophe cited earlier with the fear that she may have fallen victim to "the lash and lust of a brutal and unrelenting overseer" (p. 24). The probability of such a fate for a young African girl is implicitly heightened in *The Life* by the narrator's own later account of the behavior of his shipmates on a trading sloop:

> It was almost a constant practice with our clerks, and other whites, to commit violent depredations on the chastity of the female slaves; and these I was, though with reluctance, obliged to submit to at all times,

> being unable to help them. When we have had some of these slaves on board my master's vessels, to carry them to other islands, I have known our mates to commit these acts most shamefully, to the disgrace, not of Christians only, but of men. I have even known them to gratify their brutal passion with females not ten years old. [Pp. 73–74]

Not "coyness," then, but a disruptive economics that sanctions rape and precludes African male intervention causes sable females to stand aloof. Yet the successful negotiation of such economics is, paradoxically, the *only* course that provides conditions for a reunification of woman and sable man.

It is, ultimately, Vassa's adept mercantilism that produces the conflation of a "theory" of trade, an abolitionist appeal, and a report of African conjugal union that conclude *The Life of Olaudah Equiano*. After attesting that "the manufactures of this country [England] must and will, in the nature and reason of things, have a full and constant employ, by supplying the African markets" (p. 190), the narrator depicts the commercial utopia that will result when the slave trade is abolished and free commerce is established between Africa and Britain. The abolitionist intent of his utopian commercial theory is obvious. If British manufacturers become fully convinced of the profitability of ending the slave trade, then it must of necessity come to an end for lack of economic and political support. The African who successfully negotiates his way through the dread exchanges of bondage to the type of expressive posture characterizing *The Life*'s conclusion is surely a man who has repossessed himself and, thus, achieved the ability to reunite a severed African humanity.

The conflation of economics and conjugal union is strikingly captured by the last sentence of the penultimate paragraph of Vassa's work. The narrator says: "I remained in London till I heard the debate in the House of Commons on the slave trade, April the 2nd and 3rd. I then went to Soham in Cambridgeshire, and was married on the 7th of April to Miss Cullen, daughter of James and Ann Cullen, late of Ely" (p. 192). A signal image, indeed, is constituted by the free, public African man, aware of and adept at the economics of his era, participating creatively in the liberation of his people and joined, with self-possessed calmness, in marriage. It is an image unique to a discourse that originates in "commercial deportation" and recounts with shrewd adeptness the myriad incumbencies of the "economics of slavery."

The ideological analysis of discursive structure that yields the foregoing interpretation of *The Life of Olaudah Equiano* is invaluable for practical criticism. It discovers the social grounding—the basic subtext, as it were—that necessarily informs any genuinely Afro-American narrative text. What I want explicitly to claim here is that all Afro-American creativity is conditioned by (and constitutes a component of) a historical discourse which privileges certain economic terms. The creative individual (the *black subject*) must, therefore, whether he self-consciously wills it or not, come to terms with "commercial deportation" and the "economics of slavery." The subject's very inclusion in an *Afro-American* traditional discourse is, in fact, contingent on an encounter with such privileged economic signs of Afro-American discourse. The "already-said," so to speak, contains unavoidable preconditions for the practice of Afro-American narrative.

However, a randomly chosen black narrative will not automatically confirm—on the basis of its author's life situation and the "content" of his text—traditional adages about a determinant relationship between means of production and general cultural consciousness (i.e., commerce does not determine consciousness). What seems to hold, instead, is that under ideological analysis certain recurrent, discursive patterns suggest a unified economic grounding for Afro-American narratives. In the nineteenth century, for example, the *Narrative of the Life of Frederick Douglass, An American Slave. Written by Himself* (1845) reads, in ideologically analytical terms, like a palimpsest of Vassa's "traditional" account.[35] To the properly adapted eye, Douglass's work comprises a manuscript where the "already said" is unequivocally visible. And the palimpsestic character of his narrative predicts that its superimposition on Vassa's work will reveal a tracing of the eighteenth-century African's economic topography in all major details. A view of episodes in the *Narrative* foregrounded by the ideological notion of the palimpsest serves to illustrate.

"My mother and I were separated when I was but an infant—before I knew her as my mother," asserts the narrator of *Narrative of the Life of Frederick Douglass* (p. 22). "It is a common custom," he continues, "in the part of Maryland from which I ran away, to part children from their mothers at an early age. . . . I do not recollect of ever seeing my mother by the light of day. She was with me in the night. She would lie down with me, and get me to sleep, but long before I waked she was gone." The disruption of black familial relations signaled by the narrator's separation from his mother is equivalent to Vassa's kidnapping and severance from his sister. Douglass's narrator further announces that "it was rumored that my master [Captain Anthony] was my father," and he goes on to condemn unequivocally the "wicked desires," "lust," and "cunning" of slaveholders, traits which enable them to sustain a "double relation of master and father" to their mulatto children (p. 23).

These assertions of the *Narrative* offer a recapitulation of the "man in the middle" first encountered in Vassa's account. The effect of "owners" destroying Afro-American familial bonds (mother-infant, lover-beloved) is forcefully represented in both the *Narrative* and in *The Life of Olaudah Equiano*. The very possibility of black conjugal or familial bonds (legally sustained) is as anomalous within the slave geography of Douglass's *Narrative* as in the West India climate of *The Life of Olaudah Equiano*. In chapter 6 of Vassa's work, for example, the narrator tells of a "very clever and decent free young mulatto man, who . . . had a free woman for his wife, by whom he had a child" (p. 89). A Bermuda captain boards the vessel on which this free man works, lays "violent hands on him," and carries him into slavery where he is "doomed never more in this world to see [his wife or child]" (p. 89). Similarly, in the *Narrative*, Sandy Jenkins's status as slave prevents his living with his free wife in a sustained, day-to-day relationship. His free wife, in fact, lives "about four miles from Mr. Covey's" and can only be visited on Saturday night (p. 80). In a world where men are property and women victims of the owner's lust, separation and a blunting or eradication of affection are normal. The cruel lengths to which the "man in the middle" will go to reinforce and preserve such norms is indicated not only by Vassa's account of the treatment of African women on trading sloops, but also by Douglass's account of his Aunt Hester's fate:

> Aunt Hester went out one night—where or for what I do not know—and happened to be absent when my master desired her presence. He had ordered her not to go out evenings, and warned her that she must never let him catch her in company with a young man, who was paying attention to her belonging to Colonel Lloyd. The young man's name was Ned Roberts, generally called Lloyd's Ned. Why master was so careful of her, may be safely left to conjecture. [P. 24]

Discovering that Hester has, indeed, been in the company of Ned during her absence, the white owner strips her to the waist, binds her to a hook in the joist of the house, and flogs her until she is bloody. Douglass reports: "I was so terrified and horror-stricken at the sight, that I hid myself in a closet, and dared not venture out" (p. 26). Vassa's words—"I was . . . obliged to submit at all times . . . being unable to help them [African women sexually assaulted by white ship's hands]"—echo through Douglass's report. The only relationship approximating traditional familial or conjugal ones is Douglass's temporary situation with his grandmother. This—like Vassa's brief moments of comfort among those who take him in as youthful servant on his way to the African coast—is a situation that soon ends when Douglass is delivered, as slave property, to the "home plantation of Colonel Edward Lloyd" (p. 27).

The most decisive delivery of the Afro-American slave into a laboring situation takes place, however—like Vassa's own transport—by water. The "commercial deportation" of Douglass occurs when the young boy travels on the trading sloop *Sally Lloyd* to Baltimore to serve in the household of Mr. Hugh Auld. On the day that he is transported, the sloop, which normally transports tobacco, corn, and wheat (p. 27), carries "a large flock of sheep" bound for slaughter at "the slaughterhouse of Mr. Curtis on Louden Slater's Hill" (p. 46). An inland trading vessel and sheep on their way to slaughter are significantly milder features in the representation of deportation than the "slave ship . . . riding at anchor" and the "multitude of black people of every description chained together" encountered in *The Life of Olaudah Equiano*. Nonetheless, the irrevocable break with beginnings, the helplessness of the young boy to determine his own destiny, the cargo status that marks his passage, and his immediately favorable response to the wonders of an alien world of experience are aspects of the voyage from St. Michael's to "the metropole" that cause the *Narrative*'s account to accord with Vassa's work.

A few pages after his account of a terrified response to ships and the sea, Vassa describes the treatment that he and his fellow Africans received on their arrival at Barbados: "We were conducted immediately to the merchant's yard, where we were all pent together, like so many sheep in a fold, without regard to sex or age. As every object was new to me, everything I saw filled me with surprise" (p.32). The conflation of an explicitly powerless situation and an awed and inquisitive response to novelty in *The Life* precedes by more than fifty years Douglass's record of his reaction to Annapolis on his journey to Baltimore: "It was the first large town that I had ever seen, and though it would look small compared with some of our New England factory villages, I thought it a wonderful place for its size—more imposing even than the Great House Farm!" (p. 46). The passage not only signals wonder in the face of chatteldom, but also introduces (through a striking temporal conflation) a contrast between agrarian and industrial modes of existence. The capital of an industrially primitive, southern slave state is less impressive than (in words that could only belong to a traveled narrator) some of "our" New England factory villages. Vassa leaves an agrarian life devoid of "mechanics" (p. 27) only to encounter on shipboard the wonders of the quadrant, a world of "mechanical" invention at the farm of his first Virginia master, and, finally, the captains of industry of his day to whom the concluding remarks of his narrative are directed. Similarly, Douglass moves progressively beyond an agricultural landscape where slavery is omnipotent to the freedom of the "New England factory village." Urban experience mediates the progress of both narrators toward the economic sophistication implied by their privileging of industrial norms.

London, for Vassa, represents the most desirable mode of existence imaginable. The residents of the English metropole and the spiritual and secular possibilities it embodies represent for the African occasions for understanding and self-improvement that he feels are available nowhere else. He even rejects, for example, an opportunity while at Guadaloupe to escape slavery because the fleet in which he would have served as a seaman is bound, not for England, but for "old France" (pp. 90–91). It is in London and among Englishmen that Vassa comes to realize the "superiority" of Europeans to Africans and receives the kindly instructions of the Misses Guerin. Douglass's feelings toward Baltimore are scarcely as warmly affectionate as those of Vassa toward London. Still, the nineteenth-century author writes: "Going to live at Baltimore laid the foundation, and opened the gateway, to all my subsequent prosperity" (p. 46–47). And it is in Baltimore that Douglass (like Vassa in the English city) discovers the "displaced" maternity of a kindly, white womanhood. The familial affections blunted by the "man in the middle" in the feudal regions of slavery find their rejuvenation in the ministrations of white women in the city. Both the Misses Guerin and Mrs. Hugh Auld offer relationships for Vassa and Douglass that satisfy the slaves' needs for emotional affiliation and intellectual advancement.

The women in both the *Narrative* and *The Life of Olaudah Equiano* are represented as examples of the best evangelical-missionary impulses of their day. They are servants and fit disciples of a kind "Providence." Hence, there is a convergence in both Vassa and Douglass of a literacy that accrues from white women's instructions and a Christianity that governs the women's desire to render such instruction. An early result of Vassa's interaction with the Guerins is his baptism. Douglass ascribes his interactions with Sophia Auld to the "interposition of divine Providence in my favor" and also structures his representation of these interactions in implicitly Old Testament terms (p. 47).

Reflecting the slave's literate mastery of Christian instruction and his comprehension of the ironies of his enslaved situation, Douglass's relationship with Sophia Auld is represented in the *Narrative* as a symbolically inverted account of the Fall of Man. On first view, the Edenic calm of the Auld household—a serenity that is emblemized by "a white face beaming with the most kindly emotions"—is seemingly disrupted by the entry of the slave (as serpent?) into the household. The bondsman's presence seems to transform the calm Auld habitat into a domain of "tiger-like fierceness" and calculated deception. Discovering that his wife Sophia has begun to instruct Douglass, Hugh Auld severely reprimands her, prohibits future instructions, and delivers a curt lecture on slaves and education. "She [Mrs. Auld] was an apt woman; and a little experience soon demonstrated, to her satisfaction, that education and slavery were incompatible with each other" (p. 53). She becomes a person of "tiger-like fierceness."

One interpretation of Douglass's first educational encounter suggests that it is scarcely the entry of the bondsman that precipitates Mrs. Auld's transformation to tempestuous ire. If, in fact, Mrs. Auld stands in the role of Eve, it is *the slave* who must be figured as her ironical Adam. For he is the subject of providentially ordained instruction and, finally, a partaker of the Tree of Life. The true serpent in the *Narrative*'s short educational drama is Mr. Auld. He storms about in the rhetorically deceptive guise of a Father (a Patriarch) chastizing the sinful intercourse between his "children." But Hugh Auld is far from a chastizing Providence. He is much more akin to the legendary serpent, playing in fact the "Anti-Christ" by successfully tempting Eve (Sophia) to regard the Tree of Life—the bestowal of a *humanizing* instruction—as an interdicted Tree of Knowledge. He insists that the Tree of Knowledge *must* be denied the slave at all costs.

Douglass listens with fascination. The *Narrative* portrays him in this educational scene "in the garden" as a pristine Adam ignorant of the devious ways of the world the slaveholders made. The words of Auld-as-serpent, however, become for the narrator—in an enfoldingly ironic series of inversions—a "new and special revelation" of the source of slaveholders' power. Auld's words paradoxically take on the character of Providential wisdom.

His master's injunctions to his wife lead the slave to realize that he is not a dweller in an Eden of urban benevolence but a subjugated victim in an inverted paradise of white denial. Primed by this realization, he sets out from a "false Eden" to discover the *true* path to freedom. Like an allegorical pilgrim or knight, he rejects the bower of soul-destroying ignorance and proceeds "with high hope, and a fixed purpose, at whatever cost of trouble, to learn how to read" (p. 49).

The symbolically inversive account of the Fall of Man that the narrator employs to represent his educational encounter signals the slave's mastery as a "reader." He refuses the role of hapless victim of texts (the slavemaster's "false" moral rhetoric) and becomes, instead, an astute interpreter and creator of texts of his own. Hence, though Baltimore, like Vassa's London, bestows a traditional literacy and Christianity, Douglass's acquired skills *as reader* enable him to provide his own interpretations for received texts. His ability ultimately results in a tension between two voices in the *Narrative*. The tones of a Providentially oriented moral suasion eventually compete with the cadences of a secularly oriented economic voice.

This bifurcation of voices parallels the earlier noted duality in *The Life of Olaudah Equiano*. One autobiographical self in the *Narrative* follows a developmental history that leads from Christian enlightenment to the establishment of Sabbath schools for fellow slaves to a career of messianic service on behalf of abolitionism. Of his address to a predominantly white audience at an abolitionist convention in Nantucket, Douglass says: "It was a *severe cross*, and I took it up reluctantly" (p. 119, my emphasis). A self in contrast to this cross-bearing figure in the *Narrative* follows a course dictated by the economics of slavery.

This other self is a function of the slave's ability "to read." It is a self—

or *voice*, if you will—that is *sotto voce*, subtextual, and, in a sense, "after the fact." It provides economic coding for what, on casual first view, appear to be simple descriptions in the service of moral suasion.

Returning for a moment to the first three chapters of the *Narrative*, one of the most striking manifestations of the work's economic voice is the description of the wealthy slaveowner Colonel Lloyd's "finely cultivated garden, which afforded almost constant employment for four men, besides the chief gardener, (Mr. M'Durmond)" (p. 33). This garden, which is found at the outset of chapter 3, prefigures the "false" Eden of the Auld encounter in chapter 6. Its description is coded in a manner that makes it the most significant economic sign in the initial chapters of the *Narrative*. The entire store of the slaveholder's "Job-like" (p. 35) riches is imaged by the garden, which was "probably the greatest attraction of the place [the Lloyd estate]" (p. 33). Abounding in "fruit of every description," the garden is "quite a temptation to the hungry swarms of boys, as well as the older slaves . . . few of whom had the virtue or the vice to resist it" (p. 33). While a garden and its attendant temptations comprise a familiar Christian *topos*, a garden that images *all* the wealth of the "man in the middle" serves Douglass as a very secular sign of "surplus value."

Surplus value is the created exchange value that accrues to the owner after the subsistence costs of the laborer have been deducted from the price of a consumption good. The classical economist David Ricardo floundered when he sought to push through his argument for a rigorous labor theory of value. If the value of the "constant capital," or objective factors of production, and the price or labor are perfectly mirrored in the cost of the resultant commodity, wherein, queried Ricardo, lies the profit for the entrepreneur? Marx resolved this dilemma in *Capital* by making a distinction between *labor power* (i.e., the "capacity for labor") and actual labor. Of the value of labor power, Marx writes, "the minimum value of labour power is determined by the value of the commodities without the daily supply of which the labourer cannot renew his vital energy" (p. 82).

The value of labor power, therefore, is equivalent to a subsistence wage. If such a value can be realized in six hours (i.e., if a commodity can be *produced* in this time yielding the amount paid by the entrepreneur for labor power), then a worker can sustain himself with what, in Marx's day, amounted to a half-day's labor. But then comes the rub:

> The fact that half a day's labour is necessary to keep the labourer alive during 24 hours, does not in any way prevent him from working a whole day. Therefore, the value of labour power, and the value which that labour power creates in the labour process, are two entirely different magnitudes; and this difference of the two values was what the capitalist had in view when he was purchasing the labour power. . . . The owner of the money has paid the value of a day's labour

power; his, therefore, is the use of it for a day; a day's labour belongs to him. The circumstance that on the one hand the daily sustenance of labour power costs only half a day's labour, while on the other hand the very same labour power can work during a whole day, that consequently the value which its use during one day creates is double what he pays for that use, this circumstance is, without a doubt, a piece of good luck for the buyer. [P. 93]

Marx's model of surplus value as one resolution for Ricardo's dilemma and an explanation for the conversion of entrepreneurship into profit begins with free exchange in the marketplace between laborer and entrepeneur. But since the analysis of *Capital* is grounded in the assumption that "the value of each commodity is determined by the quantity of labor expended on and materialized in it" (pp. 89—90), Marx also assumed that the condition of freedom for the laborer was not determinant where surplus value was concerned. "The essential difference between the various economic forms of society, between, for instance, a society based on slave labour and one based on wage labour, lies only in the mode in which . . . surplus labour is in each case extracted from the actual producer, the labourer" (p. 105). Given the very scant rations of southern slaves and their daybreak-to-first-dark regimen, the amount of surplus value resulting from plantation production was substantial.

In the case of Colonel Lloyd's garden the fruits of slave labor are *all* retained by the master. And any attempts by slaves to share such fruits are not only dubbed stealing, but also severely punished. Even so, "the colonel had to resort to all kinds of stratagems [beyond mere flogging] to keep his slaves out of the garden" (p. 33).

The image of vast abundance produced by slaves but denied them through the brutality of the owner of the means of production (i.e., the land) suggests a purely economic transformation of a traditional image of the biblical garden and its temptations. Douglass heightens the import of this economic coding through implicit and ironic detailings of the determination of general cultural consciousness *by commerce*. The folkloric aphorism that a single touch of the "tar brush" defiles the whole is invoked in the *Narrative* as a humorous analogue for Colonel Lloyd's ideological and mystifying designation of those who are denied the fruits of the garden as *unworthy*. The colonel *tars* the fence around his garden, and any slave "caught with tar upon his person . . . was severely whipped by the chief gardener" (p. 33).

The promotion of *tar* (of a *blackness* so sticky and entangling for American conscience that the Tar Baby story of African provenance has been an enduring cultural transplant) to a mark of low status, deprivation, and unworthiness is commented upon by the narrator as follows: "The slaves became as fearful of tar as of the lash. They seemed to realize the impossibility of touching *tar* without being defiled" (p. 33). Blacks, through the *genetic* touch of the tar brush that makes them people of color, are automatically guilty of the paradoxically labeled "crime" of seeking to enjoy the fruits of their own labor.

The "increase in store" of a traditional American history takes on quite other dimensions in light of Douglass's account of the garden in chapter 3. Later in the *Narrative*, he writes of the life of slaves on Thomas Auld's farm: "A great many times have we poor creatures been nearly perishing with hunger, when food in abundance lay mouldering in the safe and smoke-house, and our pious mistress was aware of the fact; and yet mistress and her husband would kneel every morning, and pray that God would bless them in basket and store!" (p. 66). The keenly literate and secular autobiographical self that so capably figures the economics of Lloyd's garden—summing in the process both the nil financial gain of blacks, and their placement in the left-hand, or debit, column of the ledgers of American status—is the same self encountered when the narrator returns as a teenager to southern, agrarian slavery.

At the farm of Mr. Edward Covey, where he has been hired out for "breaking," the *Narrative* pictures four enslaved black men fanning wheat. Douglass comprises one of their number, "carrying wheat to the fan" (p. 77). The sun proves too much for the unacclimatized Douglass, and he collapses, only to be beaten by Mr. Covey for his failure to serve effectively as a mindless ("the work was simple requiring strength rather than intellect") cog in the machine of slave production. Seeking redress from his master (Mr. Thomas Auld) who hired him to Covey, Douglass finds that the profit motive drives all before it: "Master Thomas . . . said . . . that he could not think of taking me from . . . [Mr. Covey]; that should he do so, he would lose the whole year's wages" (p. 79).

The most bizarre profit accruing to the owners in the Covey episode, however, is not slave wages, but slave offspring. If Colonel Lloyd would take the fruit of the slave's labor, Mr. Covey would take the very fruit of the slave's womb. He puts a black man "to stud" with one of his slave women and proclaims the children of this compelled union his property. This is a confiscation of surplus value with a vengeance. It manifests the supreme aberrancy of relationships conditioned by the southern traffic in human "chattel." At Covey's farm, produce, labor, wages, and profit create a crisis that Douglass must negotiate in the best available fashion. He resolves physically to combat Mr. Covey, the "man in the middle."

In contrast to a resolved young Douglass in Chapter 10 of the *Narrative* stands Sandy Jenkins, the slave mentioned earlier in this discussion who has a free wife. Sandy offers Douglass a folk means of negotiating his crisis at Covey's, providing him with "a certain *root*," which, carried "*always on* . . . [the] *right side*, would render it impossible for Mr. Covey or any other white man" to whip the slave (p. 80). What is represented by the introduction of Sandy Jenkins is a displacement of Christian metaphysics by Afro-American "superstition." Ultimately, this displacement reveals the inefficacy of trusting solely to any form of extrasecular aid for relief (or release) from slavery.

The root does not work. The physical confrontation does. Through physical battle, Douglass gains a measure of relief from Covey's harassments. Jenkins's mode of negotiating the economics of slavery, the *Narrative* implies, is not *a man's way*, since the narrator claims that his combat with Covey converted him, ipso facto, into *a man*. In the same chapter in which the inefficacy of Jenkins's way is implied, the text also suggests that Jenkins is the traitor who reveals the planned escape of Douglass and fellow slaves to their master Mr. Freeland. Sandy seems to represent the inescapable limiting conditions of Afro-American slavery in the South; he is the pure, negative product of an economics of slavery. Standing in clear and monumentally *present* (even to the extent of a foregrounding footnote) contrast to the Douglass of chapter 10, Sandy represents the virtual impossibility of an escape from bondage on the terms implied by the attempted escape from Freeland's.

At its most developed, *southern* extension, the literate abolitionist self of the *Narrative* engages in an act of physical revolt, forms a Christian brotherhood of fellow slaves through a Sabbath school, and formulates a plan for a *collective* escape from bondage. But this progress toward liberation in the agrarian South is foiled by one whose mind in so "tarred" by the economics of slavery that he betrays the collective. The possibility of collective freedom is thus foreclosed by treachery within the slave community. A communally dedicated Douglass ("The work of instructing my dear fellow-slaves was the sweetest engagement with which I was ever blessed," p. 90) finds that revolt, religion, and literacy *all* fail. The slave does, indeed, *write* his "own pass" and the passes of his fellows, but the Sabbath school assembled group is no match for the enemy within.

What recourse, then, is available for the black man of talent who would be free? The *Narrative* answers in an economic voice similar to that found in *The Life of Olaudah Equiano*. Returned to Baltimore and the home of Mr. Hugh Auld after a three-year absence, the teenaged slave is hired out to "Mr. William Gardner, an extensive shipbuilder in Fell's Point. I was put there to learn how to calk" (p. 99). In short space, Douglass is able "to command the highest wages given to the most experienced calkers" (p. 103). In lines that echo Vassa with resonant effect, he writes: "I was now of some importance to my master. I was bringing him from six to seven dollars per week. I sometimes brought him nine dollars per week: my wages were a dollar and a half a day" (p. 103). Having entered a world of real *wages*, Douglass is equivalent to the Vassa who realized what a small "venture" could produce. And like Vassa, the nineteenth-century slave recognizes that the surplus value his master receives is but stolen profit: "I was compelled to deliver every cent of that [money contracted for, earned, and paid for calking] to Master Auld. And why? Not because he earned it . . . but solely because he had the power to compel me to give it up" (p. 104).

Like Vassa, Douglass has arrived at a fully commercial view of his situation. He, too, enters an agreement with his master that results in freedom. Having gained the right to hire his own time and to keep a portion of his wages, Douglass eventually converts property, through property, into humanity. Impelled by his commercial endeavors and the opportunities resulting from his free commerce, he takes leave of Mr. Auld. He thus removes (in his own person) the master's property and places it in the ranks of a northern humanity. "According to my resolution, on the third day of September, 1838, I left my chains and succeeded in reaching New York" (p. 111). By "stealing away," Douglass not only steals the fruits of his own labor (not unlike the produce of Colonel Lloyd's garden), but also liberates the laborer— the chattel who works profitlessly in the garden.

The necessity for Douglass to effect his liberation through flight results from the complete intransigence to change of southern patriarchs. Mr. Auld, as the young slave knows all too well, cannot possibly conceive of the child of his "family," of the "nigger" fitted out to work only for his profit, as simply an economic investment. Instead of exchanging capital, therefore, Douglass appropriates his own labor and flees to the camp of those who will ultimately be Auld's adversaries in civil war.

The inscribed document that effectively marks Douglass's liberation in the *Narrative* is, I think, no less an economic sign than Vassa's certificate of manumission:

> This may certify, that I joined together in holy matrimony Frederick Johnson and Anna Murray, as man and wife, in the presence of Mr. David Ruggles and Mrs. Michaels.
>
> > James W. C. Pennington
> > *New York, Sept.* 15, 1838.

What Douglass's certificate of marriage, which is transcribed in full in chapter 11, signifies is that the black man has *repossessed* himself in a manner that enables him to enter the kind of relationship disrupted, or foreclosed, by the economics of slavery.

Unlike Sandy Jenkins—doomed forever to passive acquiescence and weekend visitation—Douglass enters a productive relationship promising a new bonding of Afro-American humanity. As a married man, who understands the necessity for *individual* wage earning (i.e., a mastery of the incumbencies of the economics of slavery), Douglass makes his way in the company of his new bride to a "New England factory village" where he quickly becomes a laborer at "the first work, the reward of which was to be entirely my own" (p. 116).

The representation of New Bedford that the *Narrative* provides—with Douglass as wage-earning laborer—seems closely akin to the economic, utopian vision that closes Vassa's account: "Everything looked clean, new, and beautiful. I saw few or no dilapidated houses, with poverty-stricken inmates, no half-naked children and bare-footed women, such as I had been accustomed to see in . . . [Maryland]" (p. 116). Ships of the best order and finest size, warehouses stowed to their utmost capacity, and ex-slaves "living in finer houses, and evidently enjoying more of the comforts of life, than the average slaveholders in Maryland" complete the splendid panorama. Such a landscape is gained by free, dignified, and individualistic labor—the New England ideal so frequently appearing in Afro-American narratives. (One thinks, for example, of the DuBoisian vision in *The Souls of Black Folk* or of Ralph Ellison's Mr. Norton.) The equivalent vision for Vassa is, of course, comprised by ships of the finest size and best order plying their trans-Atlantic trade between Africa and England. And presiding over the concluding vision in both narratives is the figure of the black, abolitionist spokesman—the man who has arisen, found his "voice," and secured the confidence to address a "general public."

What one experiences in the conclusions of Vassa's and Douglass's narratives, however, is identity with a difference. For the expressive, married, economically astute self at the close of Douglass's work represents a convergence of the voices that mark the various autobiographical postures of the *Narrative* as a whole. The orator whom we see standing at a Nantucket convention at the close of Douglass's work is immediately to become a *salaried* spokesman, combining literacy, Christianity, and revolutionary zeal in an individual and economically profitable job of work. Douglass's authorship, oratory, and economics converge in the history of the *Narrative*'s publication and the course of action its appearance mandated in the life of the author.

Since his identity and place of residence were revealed in the *Narrative*, Douglass, who was still a fugitive when his work appeared, was forced to flee to England. In the United Kingdom, he sold copies of his book for profit, earned lecture fees, and aroused sufficient sympathy and financial support to purchase his freedom with solid currency. While his Garrisonian, abolitionist contemporaries were displeased by Douglass's commercial traffic with slaveholders, the act of purchase was simply the logical (and "traditionally" predictable) end of his negotiation of the economics of slavery.

What is intriguing for a present-day reading of the *Narrative*'s history is the manner in which ideological analysis reveals the black spokesperson's economic conditioning—that is, his necessary encounter with economics signaled by a commercial voice and the implications of this encounter in the domain of narrative transaction. The nineteenth-century slave, in effect, *publicly* sells his voice in order to secure *private* ownership of his voice-person. The ultimate convergence of the *Narrative*'s history is between money and the narrative sign. Exchanging words becomes both a function of commerce and a commercial function. Ideological analysis made available by the archaeology of knowledge, thus, reveals intriguingly commercial dimensions of Afro-American discourse.

VI

The commercial dimensions of male narratives such as Vassa's and Douglass's do not exhaust the subtextual possibilities of Afro-American literary discourse. An analysis of an account by a nineteenth-century black woman demonstrates that gender produces striking modifications in the Afro-American discursive subtext. This gender difference does not eradicate the primacy of such governing statements as "commercial deportation" and the "economics of slavery," but it does alter and expand their scope. A view of Harriet Brent Jacobs's *Incidents in the Life of a Slave Girl: Mrs. Harriet Brent Jacobs, Written by Herself* (1861) serves to illustrate.[36]

On reading the initial chapters of Linda Brent's (the name borne by the narrator of *Incidents*) account, the word that comes to mind is "abandonment." The slave girl's father and mother die when she is young, and she passes only a short time under the tutelage of a "kind" mistress. At twelve years of age, she enters the service of Dr. and Mrs. Flint, whose fictitious surname aptly captures the obdurate character of the sister and brother-in-law of her recently deceased mistress. Though she is actually "bequeathed . . . [to Mrs. Flint's daughter], a child of five years old," the slave girl effectively belongs to the elder Flints. The differences between the works of Vassa and Douglass and Brent's *Incidents in the Life of a Slave Girl* almost immediately manifest themselves in the relatively confined space of movement and absence of adventure characterizing the black woman's account. A world of mistresses and slaves-in-waiting emerges from the first chapters of Brent's narrative as an essentially domestic arena in which the female slave will confront her destiny.

But the domestic world of *Incidents in the Life of a Slave Girl* is far removed from the settled, genteel domesticity found in American sentimental novels. Brent's world is one of sudden transitions and violent disruptions, as chapter 2, "The Slaves' New Year's Day," makes clear. The chapter recounts the effects of "commercial deportation" on the life of the slave community. Noting that "hiring-day" in the South is the first day of January, the narrator asserts: "On the 2nd, . . . slaves are expected to go to their new masters" (p. 25). Slaves, of course, have no voice in deciding their new location; they are transportable property. The plight of the slave mother under such a system is captured as follows:

> To the slave mother New Year's day comes laden with peculiar sorrows. She sits on her cold cabin floor, watching the children who may all be torn from her the next morning; and often does she wish that she and they might die before day dawns. She may be an ignorant creature, degraded by the system that has brutalized her from child-hood; but she has a mother's instincts, and is capable of feeling a mother's agonies. [P. 26]

"Commercial deportation" has its most profound effects in Brent's narrative on the slave woman's issue, disrupting black familial relations at the level of mother-and-infant.

Douglass's and Vassa's recognition of their own worth within the economic system of slavery prompts them to words of condemnation and acts of liberating mercantilism. In *The Life of Olaudah Equiano* and the *Narrative*, the fact that slave skills and labor yield surplus value is a spur to individualistic, economic enterprise. In *Incidents in the Life of a Slave Girl*, by contrast, it is not the value of the female slave's works of hand that is emphasized. Rather, the narrative calls attention time and again to the surplus value deriving from the fruit of the slave woman's womb.

Brent's account explicitly suggests that within the economic system of slavery, the black woman's value is a function of her womb: "Women are considered of no value unless they continually increase their owner's stock. They are put on a par with animals" (p. 76). The narrator does not confine her indictment of this perverse scheme of value to men; she also notes the complicity of southern white women.

> Southern women often marry a man knowing that he is the father of many little slaves. They do not trouble themselves about it. They regard such children as property, as marketable as the pigs on the plantation; and it is seldom that they do not make them aware of this by passing them into the slavetrader's hands as soon as possible, and thus getting them out of sight. [P. 57]

Surely Douglass was aware of the bizarre mores described by Brent; his sketch of life at Edward Covey's demonstrates his awareness. But neither his own life nor his *Narrative* were radically determined by such aberrant mores.

Mulatto children in *Incidents in the Life of a Slave Girl* signify the master's successful, sexual aggression; such offspring both increase his stock and mark his domination. The central relationship in Brent's narrative is, in fact, between an implacable male sexual aggression (Dr. Flint as master) and a strategically effective female resistance and retreat (Linda Brent as slave). The appearance of the indefinite article "a" in the title of the narrative implies that this relationship is defining in the life of *any* slave girl.

At age fourteen, after two years in the Flints's service, Brent becomes the beleaguered object of her master's scathing, verbal sexual abuse. Flint, who has already fathered eleven mulatto children, becomes the clear antagonist. The black slave girl knows that the battle commenced for her is the general lot of black, female adolescents:

> She [the black adolescent girl] will become prematurely knowing in evil things. Soon she will learn to tremble when she hears her master's footfall. She will be compelled to realize that she is no longer a child. If God has bestowed beauty upon her, it will prove her greatest curse. That which commands admiration in the white woman only hastens the degradation of the female slave. [Pp. 45–46]

One of the signal ironies in *Incidents in the Life of a Slave Girl* is that the means adopted by Brent to avoid *conquest* is a willing, sexual liaison with yet another white, southern man.

Mr. Sands, an educated southern male, becomes the father of the slave girl's children. Though she does increase her master's stock through this transaction, the slave girl is quick to point out the psychological advantage the act brings in her war with Flint:

> It seems less degrading to give one's self, than to submit to compulsion. There is something akin to freedom in having a lover who has no control over you, except that which he gains by kindness and attachment. A master may treat you as rudely as he pleases, and you dare not speak; moreover, the wrong does not seem so great with an unmarried man, as with one who has a wife to be made unhappy. There may be sophistry in all this; but the condition of a slave confuses all principles of morality, and, in fact, renders the practice of them impossible. [Pp. 84–85]

What emerges from the "crisis of . . . fate" that leads Brent to a sexual relationship with Sands is a new morality. This new code of ethics emphasizes a woman's prerogative to control her own sexuality—to govern the integrity of her body. Articulating such a code in a violently patriarchal system is a monumental and dangerous accomplishment. For "fatherhood," under the aspect of southern slavery, assumed all the connotations of "rape." The "*patriarchal* institution" (p. 288) appears in the eyes of the black adolescent slave as a vast arena of coerced sexual coupling, a prodigal *fathering* of "stock" by the patriarch-as-rapist. Economics and power conflate in the physical and psychological violations of black victims by white masters.

Linda Brent successfully neutralizes this bizarre equation of dominance and gain. Although she has no power to discount his economic gains ("Dr. Flint did not fail to remind me that my child was an addition to his stock of slaves," p. 94), she does thwart Flint's power of violation by choosing, on her own initiative, the man who will actually father her child.

The economics of the slave girl's situation finally translate in power terms. Submission to the master's will becomes the only act of value the slave woman can perform in a violent patriarchy. Mr. Sands seeks to purchase the freedom of Brent and her children, but his willingness, as the narrator makes clear in chapter 15, is of little consequence: "The money for the freedom of myself and my children could be obtained; but I derived no advantage from that circumstance. Dr. Flint loved money, *but he loved power more*" (my emphasis, p. 122). It would be tedious to enumerate the multiple instances of Flint's violence in *Incidents in the Life of a Slave Girl*—the blows struck and verbal abuse received. It is sufficient, I think, to note that the only stratagem that serves to obviate his power of abuse is the slave girl's total retreat from scenes of daily life, her interiorization and enclosure that are equivalent to burial alive.

At the beginning of chapter 21, the following description of a southern building appears:

> A small shed had been added to my grandmother's house years ago. Some boards were laid across the joists at the top, and between these boards and the roof was a very small garret, never occupied by anything but rats and mice. It was a pent roof, covered with nothing but shingles, according to the southern custom for such buildings. The garret was only nine feet long and seven wide. The highest part was three feet high, and sloped down abruptly to the loose board floor. There was no admission for either light or air. [P. 173]

For seven years, this garret (which is certainly more akin to a grave than a garret) serves as Brent's habitat. She takes refuge in it after fleeing the plantation of Dr. Flint. The chapter in which this habitat is described is entitled "The Loophole of Retreat," a phrase rich in connotation. For although the slave girl chooses "retreat" as a strategy, the new position that she occupies is very much a "loophole"—a hole in the wall from which she wages effective combat. Her battle plan results, finally, in the significant transformation of her children's status.

The implacable Dr. Flint, who on several occasions has taken a razor to her throat in attempts to make her submit, eventually comes to regard possession and domination as all-subsuming ends in themselves. "You are mine," he raves after the birth of her first child, "and you shall be mine for life. There lives no human being that can take you out of slavery" (p. 123). The slave's children become, for Flint, means toward his goal of domination. The power he possesses as master of her children compels the slave girl to bear his furious abuse. Brent eventually realizes, however, that if she puts herself beyond his range, Flint will be forced to alter his conception of her children. He will come to perceive them as commercial ends rather than empowering means. "Dr. Flint, would soon get discouraged, and would be willing to sell my children, when he lost all hopes of making them a means of my discovery" (p. 159).

The slave, therefore, creates commodifying conditions for her children's disposition. In a tactically brilliant act of withdrawal, she converts the fruit of her womb (rather than the skill of her hand or the capital of a husbanded store) to merchandise. Her retreat culminates in the children's sale to Mr. Sands. Thus, she not only chooses her children's father, but also controls, in the final analysis, that second aspect of what Douglass described as the "double relation of master and father." She provides conditions for Mr. Sands to become both father *and* master.

While the commercial, autobiographical selves in Douglass's and Vassa's narratives achieve advantage through derring-do and shrewd financial arrangements with masters, the slave girl in Brent's account secures commercial success by retreat, by nullification of the conditions of the master's implacable force. Fleeing the patriarch-as-rapist, she maintains a physical and psychological integrity that bring the fruits of her labor nearer her own possessing. If in the act of withdrawal she does not achieve immediate conversion of property through property into humanity, she at least provides necessary conditions for such a conversion to occur.

Mr. Sands eventually manumits Brent's children and sends them north. The mother soon follows, making her escape on board a ship to Philadelphia. She moves to New York and enters the service of a white family named Bruce. The second Mrs. Bruce purchases the slave's freedom from Dr. Flint's son-in-law for three hundred dollars. Hence, the garreted withdrawal of chapter 21 commences a commercially successful course of events whose rewards finally include the liberation of Brent and her children.

With the foregoing analysis in mind, it is possible to assert that gender does not alter a fundamentally commercial set of negotiations represented as liberating in the black narrative. The gender of Brent and her narrator does, however, immeasurably broaden the descriptive scope of "commercial deportation" and the "economics of slavery." The implied domain of sexual victimization (so briefly represented in male narratives) becomes the dramatically foregrounded *topos* of the woman's account. And the subtextual dimensions of Afro-American narrative that receive full voice *only* in the work of the black woman include representations of the psychologically perverse motivations of the patriarch-as-rapist, the female slave's manipulation of a sexual and financial partnership outside the boundaries of the master's power, and the strategy of retreat that leads to commercial advantage and physical freedom.

In a sense, the world of the slave woman represented in *Incidents in the Life of a Slave Girl* constitutes "an idea in fiction."[37] Ultimately, Brent is but one figure in what Nina Auerbach calls a "community of women," a sisterhood of slavery that possesses "no majestic titles . . . but must create . . . [its] own, somewhat quirky and grotesque authority" (p. 8). The "grotesqueness" of the authority that accrues to the female slave community (or to any of its individual sisters) is a function of southern patriarchal economics. This system granted such bizarre power to white males that it might well have been designated an "economics of rape."

Linda Brent, her grandmother, mother, fellow slaves including Betty and Fanny, her daughter and countless others implied by the indefinite article of the narrative's title share a collective identity that makes them, in a final phrase from Auerbach's searching study, "a furtive, unofficial . . . underground entity" (p. 11). This entity has its being in seclusion, but achieves its expressive effects in the generic expansions that it entails for Afro-American discourse.

A community of women, as represented by Linda Brent, controls its own sexuality, successfully negotiates (in explicitly commercial terms) its liberation from a crude patriarchy, and achieves expressive fullness through the literate voice of the black, female author. *Incidents in the Life of a Slave Girl* is intended, we are told in the work's "Preface," to make manifest to "the women of the North" the "condition of two million women at the South, still in bondage, suffering what I suffered, and most of them far worse" (p. 6). Unlike the narratives of Vassa and Douglass, Brent's work gives a sense of *collective*, rather than individualistic, black identity. Nurtured and supported by a sisterhood yoked by common oppression, Brent does not seek the relationship of marriage that signals a repossession of self and the possibility of black reunification in male narratives. True to a governing condition of her communal status, Brent's account concludes with a vision that stands in dramatically marked contrast to the image of a black woman miserably awaiting the commercial deportation of her children:

> Reader, my story ends with freedom; not in the usual [read: male] way, with marriage. I and my children are now free! We are as free from the power of slaveholders as are the white people of the north; and though that, according to my ideas, is not saying a great deal, it is a vast improvement in *my* condition. [P. 302]

A new bonding of Afro-American humanity consists, for Brent, in the reunion of mother and child in freedom.

Brent's narrative was edited by Lydia Maria Child, the white abolitionist noted for her *Appeal in Favor of That Class of Americans Called Africans* (1833). And *Incidents* contains an appendix by another nineteenth-century white woman by the name of Amy Post. The laudatory testimony to Brent's character and achievement provided by both white women—in "introduction" and "appendix" respectively—suggests that the author's expressive goal of arousing "women in the North" was admirably accomplished. That we recognize, in a present-day reading, the strong contours of a "community" of black women joined by common economics and capable of stunning negotiations of a mercantile oppression testifies to the nineteenth-century black woman's enduring success.

In *Archetypal Patterns in Women's Fiction*, Annis Pratt decodes the image of Apollo's rape of Daphne as a "displacement."[38] The warlike male, according to Pratt, attempts to rape the nymph-goddess and institute his authority in her dominions by controlling "logos," or the word. Daphne's alternative is biological change: she transforms herself into a laurel. There is a striking difference between Pratt's decoding of a traditional archetype and the explanation one might offer of Linda Brent's figuration of a community of female slaves. In Brent's account, women must indeed *transform* themselves in order to avoid the implacable, warlike aggression of masters. But unlike Daphne, they retain both human form and a quintessentially human power of the word. Transforming herself into a withdrawn celibate, the slave woman issues, even from her gravelike garret, letters to Dr. Flint that foil his schemes of possession and domination. Once in the north, her power of the word is transmuted to public abolitionism and the communally oriented ends of sisterly liberation. By successfully negotiating the economic domain traditionally marked and controlled by a male exteriority, Brent achieves an effective expressive posture. She attains a voice that can both arouse public sympathy and invoke sisterly communion by imaging a quite remarkable community of black women. Under the aegis of ideological analysis, this community reveals itself as a striking expansion of the subtextual dimensions of traditional Afro-American discourse.

VII

The subtext that emerges from ideological analyses of male and female slave narratives reveals the "traditional" dimensions of such narratives. The commercial, subtextual contours of eighteenth- and nineteenth-century black narratives find their twentieth-century instantiations in works that are frequently called "classic" but that are seldom decoded in the ideological terms of a traditional discourse. It is vital, however—if we are to derive full value from the archaeology of knowledge in discovering a uniquely Afro-American discourse—to recognize the subtextual bonding between a novel such as, say, Zora Neale Hurston's *Their Eyes Were Watching God* and its *Afro-American* narrative antecedents.

An ideological analysis of *Their Eyes Were Watching God* reveals the endurance and continuity of a discourse that finds its earliest literate manifestations in slave narratives. By revealing the effects of "commercial deportation" and the "economics of slavery" in Hurston's work, ideological analysis makes available, from the standpoint of practical criticism, new meanings. At a more general level of the archaeology of knowledge, the analysis moves us closer to the realization that a Foucaultian "rupture" exists between traditional American history and literary history and an alternative Afro-American discourse. The relationship between Hurston's subtext and that of narratives discussed so far in this chapter provides adequate grounds for postulating a literary history quite different from a traditional "American literary history." An examination of *Their Eyes Were Watching God* serves to clarify.

The property designation of an "economics of slavery," as Linda Brent's narrative makes abundantly clear, meant that the owner's sexual gratification (forcefully achieved) was also his profit. The children resulting from such a violation followed the enslaved condition of their mother, becoming property. "Succeeding generations," as we have seen in the previous discussion, translated as "added commodities" for a master's store. The Civil War putatively ended such a commercial lineage.

Zora Neale Hurston's *Their Eyes Were Watching God* traces a fictive history that begins with the concubinage of Nanny to her white owner. The relationship results in the birth of the protagonist's mother.[39] Nanny's experiences have endowed her with what she describes as "a great sermon about colored women sittin' on high" (p. 32). There are, however, no observable phenomena—either in her own progress from day to day or in the surrounding world—to lend credibility to her unarticulated text. She feels that the achievement of a "pulpit" from which to deliver such a sermon is coextensive with the would-be preacher's obtaining actual status on high. In a sense, Nanny conflates the securing of property with effective expression. Having been denied a say in her own fate because she was *property*, she assumes that *only* property enables expression. *Their Eyes Were Watching God* implies that she is unequivocally correct in her judgment and possesses a lucid understanding of the economics of slavery.

The pear tree metaphor—the protagonist's organic fantasy of herself as an orgasmic tree fertilized by careless bees—is a deceptively prominent construct in *Their Eyes Were Watching God*; it leads away from the more significant economic dimensions of the novel so resonantly summed up by Nanny. This romantic construct is, in fact, introduced and maintained in the work by a nostalgic, omnipresent narrator. For Janie's true (author-

ial?) grounding is in the parodic economics of black, middle-class respect-
ability marked by Logan Killicks and Joe Starks.

These two black men are hardly "careless" bees. Rather, they possess
the busyness characteristic of the proverbial bee in another of his manifestations—the "industrious bee." Joe Starks is so intent on imitating the
economics of Anglo-American owners that he, paradoxically, manages to
obtain a fair abundance of goods; he becomes wealthy, that is to say, by
Afro-American standards. It is finally Starks's property, gained through
industriousness, that enables Janie's "freedom."

When Starks dies, the protagonist discovers that she is left with both
"her widowhood and property" (p. 139). One might suggest that Vergible
Woods, or "Tea Cake," the young man who appears to fill the bee's slot in
Janie's fantasy, is less a "cause" of freedom than a derivative benefit. Janie
confidently asserts of her relationship with Tea Cake: "Dis ain't no
business proposition, and no race after property and titles." But she is able
to make this claim because she sells Starks's store to finance the relationship (p. 171). The attentions of a young man, after all, do not in
themselves guarantee that a relationship will be a "love game," as the
dreadful example of a deceived and stranded Mrs. Annie Tyler proves (pp.
177–179). It is important to note, however, that the term "Starks's store"
disguises, at least in part, the fact that a share of the store as a commodity is
surely a function of the protagonist's labor. Janie works for years in the
store without receiving more than subsistence provisions. The "surplus
value" that accrues from her labor as equity is rightfully hers to dispose of
as she chooses.

Their Eyes Were Watching God is, ultimately, a novel that inscribes, in
its very form, the mercantile economics that conditioned a "commercial
deportation." If Janie is, in the last analysis, a person who delivers a text
about "colored women sittin' on high," she is one who delivers this text
from a position on high. Her position derives from the petit bourgeois
enterprises she has shared with her deceased husband.

To say this is not to minimize the force of Janie's lyrical, autobiographical recall. She can, indeed, be interpreted as a singer who (ontogenetically)
recapitulates the blues experience of all black women treated as "mules of
the world." She is, indeed, a member of a community of black women.
And the expressiveness that she provides in her bleak situation in a racist
South is equivalent to the song of Sleepy John Estes which qualifies the
bleakness of Winfield Lane.

The descent to the "muck" that provides Janie's artistic apprenticeship
among the "common folk" is, nonetheless, unequivocally a function of
entrepreneurial, capitalistic economic exchange. (Zora Hurston's own
trip to the South to collect her people's lore was financed by a rich white
patron, Mrs. Rufus Osgood Mason.) The duality suggested by Janie's

blues song and its capitalistic enabling conditions is simply one manifestation, finally, of the general dilemma of the Afro-American artist born from an economics of slavery.

The protagonist of *Their Eyes Were Watching God* is known to her childhood cohorts as "Alphabet" because she has been given so many "different names" (p. 21). Likewise, the Afro-American artist has been marginally situated in American culture, without a single, definite name, but embodying within herself the possibility of all names—the alphabet. The only way to shape a *profitable*, expressive identity in such a situation is to play on possibilities—to divide one's self, as Janie does, into "public" and "private" personalities.

In the example of the Afro-American artist, this has meant shaping an expression to fit the marketplace—an act akin to Janie's voluntary silences and seeming complicity in the public, commercial world of her husband's store. Once adequate finances are secured, however, the alphabet can be transformed (as Vassa, Douglass, and Jacobs all demonstrate) into the manifold combinations that make for expressive authenticity. Janie, for example, goes South, gains experience, and returns to the communal landscape of Etonville as a storyteller and blues singer par excellence.

Her striking expressiveness within the confines of Etonville, however, is framed, or bracketed, by the bourgeois economics of Anglo-America. The terrible close of her arcadian sojourn on the "muck" is a return, in the company of a rabidly infected Tea Cake, to a viciously segregated world. A sign of the type of relationships sanctioned by such a world is the mad (male) dog atop the back of a terrified female cow (p. 245). (The patriarchal economics of Brent's work come forcefully to mind.) Given a world implied by such a sign, and by the Jim Crow ethics of the urban environs that Janie and Tea Cake enter, where can the protagonist sing her newly found song of the folk? Having discovered the terrible boundaries on her freedom and its expressive potentialities, she returns to sing to an exclusively black audience.

An ideological reading of *Their Eyes Were Watching God*, thus, claims that the novel inscribes not only the economics signaled by commercial deportation but also the economic contours of the Afro-American artist's dilemma. Nanny, Janie's grandmother, is resoundingly correct in her conclusion that the pulpit (a propertied position on high ground) is a prerequisite for a stirring sermon. From an ideological perspective, Hurston's novel is a commentary on the continuing necessity for Afro-Americans to observe property relationships and to negotiate the restrictions sanctioned by the economics of slavery if they would achieve expressive wholeness.

Janie does not *transcend* the conditions occasioned by commercial deportation; she, like the narrative protagonists of her discursive predecessors, adapts profitably to them. And like many thousands gone before, she sings resonantly about the bleak fate and narrow straits that such an adaptation mandates. Her song is not identical to the unmediated, folk expression of those many thousands gone before. Despite its authentic dialectal transcription, her blues for the townfolk's consumption are made possible—financed, as it were—by a bourgeois economics. They are, in this respect, allied to entertainment. The full contours of the expressive dilemma she so successfully negotiates become even clearer in the analysis of such succeeding examples of Afro-American narrative as Ralph Ellison's *Invisible Man*—a work to which I will turn in a later chapter.

If my judgment of Hurston's work fails to accord with more romantic readings of *Their Eyes Were Watching God*, at least it possesses the virtue of introducing essential, traditional, subtextual dimensions of Afro-American discourse into the universe surrounding the novel. It is difficult to see how economic and expressive-artistic considerations can be ignored in treating a narrative that signals its own origination in a commercial deportation. Surely *economics*, conceived in terms of an ideology of narrative form like that represented in the foregoing analyses, has much to contribute to an understanding of the classic works of an expressive tradition grounded in the economics of slavery.

The value of the archaeology of knowledge and the ideological perspective it occasions does not lie exclusively in an expanded, practical criticism of Afro-American narratives, however. The specific governing statements I have introduced in this chapter could be replaced (and an entirely different discursive structure constituted) by alternative governing statements. "Territorial invasion," for instance, might serve especially well to structure a Chicano or Native American literary history. The archaeology of knowledge vis-à-vis American literary history need not be confined to a single expressive frame of reference.

The greater utility of archaeology consists in the fact that it asks questions about *the nature and method of history and literary history in themselves*, bringing into question the role of ideology in literary history and literary study in general. The mode of thought occasioned by Foucault's project, therefore, might well be employed to substitute other American constructs for "Afro-American history" and "Afro-American literary history." But such displacements could not occur without further raising the kinds of questions and motivating the type of analyses that have characterized the foregoing discussion.

VIII

In recent years there have been dramatic shifts in both the elements and ideological ordering principles deemed essential for American historical and American literary historical discourse. At the level of practical criticism, such shifts have offered conditions for revised readings of traditional texts. At a more global level, however, reconceptualizations of historical discourse have led to the laying bare, the surfacing and re-cognition, of myriad unofficial American histories. I believe that these seismic shifts in the universe of American historical discourse are precisely the type of upheavals that Foucault has in mind when he speaks of "ruptures."

Epistemological cataclysms in historical discourse bring to view dimensions of experience excluded from extant accounts. And in the reordering effected by such ruptures (i.e., their constitution of revised models), one discovers not only new historical terms but also the variant historicity of the statements and terms of a traditional discourse. In *The Archaeology of Knowledge*, Foucault explains that a rupture is not a "great drift that carries with it all discursive formations at once"; instead, it is a "discontinuity specified by a number of distinct transformations, between two particular positivities" (p. 175).

One would not, by any stretch of the archaeological imagination, expect a resolute totality such as "American history" to disappear without a trace in the transformation that marks the emergence of new positivities. Foucault writes, "To say that one discursive formation is substituted for another is not to say that a whole world of absolutely new objects, enunciations, concepts, and theoretical choices emerges fully armed and fully organized in a text that will place that world once and for all; it is to say that a general transformation of relations has occurred, but that it does not necessarily alter all the elements; it is to say that statements are governed by new rules of formation, it is not to say that all objects or concepts, all enunciations or all theoretical choices disappear" (p. 173). The content of ideologically oriented analyses like those above is a sign of the rupture effected when traditional American history and literary history are subjected to epistemological shift. They suggest a different *America*, without totally discounting the terms of a dated prospect.

A less diachronically analytical view of the epistemological rupture is offered by an example drawn from the very Afro-American literary discourse that stems from "commercial deportation." The illustrative, figurative example that I have in mind appears in Ralph Ellison's *Invisible Man* at the point in that narrative where the protagonist wanders into a New York subway station (and, hence, beneath the official surface of things).[40] Underground, the invisible man studies "three boys . . . tall and slender, walking stiffly with swinging shoulders in their well-pressed, too-hot-for-summer suits, their collars high and tight about their necks, their identical hats of black cheap felt set upon the crowns of their heads with severe formality about their hard conked hair" (pp. 429–430). The boys seem to him "outside . . . historical time." Yet they are undeniably *present* in the fastidiousness of their style. The protagonist is thus compelled to alter both his historical catalog and his tacitly held ideology of history. His observations occasion an epistemological shift—an enlargement of perspective that alters his notions of historicity altogether.

Ascending into Harlem, he surveys an urban scene full of black men and women who share the boys' unique style. He reflects in shock and amazement: "They'd been there all along, but somehow I'd missed them. I'd missed them even when my work had been most successful. They were outside the groove [record, phonograph disc] of history, and it was my job to get them in, all of them" (pp. 432–433).

The experience of *Invisible Man*'s protagonist is like that of a number of "minority" (i.e., those who have little *power* in the academy) literary scholars in recent years.[41] As such spokespersons—in the roles of activist, critic, teacher, scholar, and so on—have pursued what has been specified in this chapter as the archaeology of knowledge, they have revealed the limiting boundaries of traditional American historical discourse. They have also discovered, in the process, new elements and governing statements that they have framed according to specific ideological principles. In brief, such scholars have demonstrated through a form of dialectical (and, at times, extraordinarily "tropological") thought that their literary histories have been present all along, but somehow "missed" by the official historians.

One reason that official historians have missed dimensions of experience currently surfacing is that they have refused to grant due attention to what I have referred to as synchronic and metaphoric signs of unofficial histories. The metaphoric dimensions that arise in Afro-American discourse from sagging cabins, felt blues, and fastidious style must be apprehended in their vertical (or synchronic) completeness if one wishes to elaborate exacting accounts of Afro-American history and Afro-American literary history.

Ellison seems patently aware of this stipulation. In the moment of epistemological rupture and historical renewal in *Invisible Man*, his protagonist slowly becomes aware of "the growing sound of a record shop loudspeaker blaring a languid blues. I stopped. Was this all that would be recorded? Was this the only true history of the times, a mood blared by trumpets, trombones, saxophones and drums, a song with turgid, inadequate words" (p. 433). Indeed, the very fact that the protagonist hears a *recorded* blues (one designed for commercial duplication and sale) speaks to the historical and literary historical possibilities of the single, imagistic figure, or trope. For if the blues heard by the invisible man *are* history, they are not constituted as such in any simple sense. The economics that these recorded blues signal in a modern, technological era of multinational corporations, mass markets, and advertised commodities recapitulates, in striking ways, the black artist's dilemma depicted in *Their*

Eyes Were Watching God. What is one's true history? How can its presentation be *financed*? And for whom can one sing of blues and "the man"? In brief, Ellison's blues of historical renewal may well signify (like the expressiveness of those gone before) the scarcity and brutalization of an economics of slavery. But they also reveal an economic complexity that implies black men and women negotiating slavery's tight spaces in movingly expressive ways. The blues, considered as an economically determined and uniquely black "already-said," are both inscribing and formally inscribed in an Afro-American discourse whose very *presence* demands their comprehension.

> *(And so . . . we are left with the song known at the outset. A traditional American history and literary history give way before the blues artist's restless troping mind:*
>> You know I laid down last night,
>> You know I laid down last night, and tried to take
>>> me some rest,
>> But my mind got to ramblin' like wild geese
>>> from the west.
>
> *Skip James*
>
> *The "rambling" is meaning embedded in rocky places. Its discovery creates a vastly enlarged perspective. Indeed, if one were to put forward a model of American literary history to represent present knowledge, it would be far more akin to Louis Dollo's accounts than to the prosaic quadripedalism of Gideon Mantell's English 1850s.)*

Two   Discovering America:
Generational Shifts,
Afro-American Literary Criticism,
and the Study of Expressive Culture

The fault that lies at the root of the entire history of the idea of
the discovery of America consists in assuming that the lump of
cosmic matter which we now know as the American continent has
always been that, when actually it only became that when such a
meaning was given to it, and will cease to be that when, by virtue
of some change in the current world concept, that meaning will
no longer be assigned to it.

           Edmundo O'Gorman, *The Invention of America*

Considering that the newness achieved by Americans has often
been a matter of adapting to function and a matter of naming—of
designation—we are reminded of how greatly the "Americanness"
of American culture has been a matter of Adamic wordplay—of
trying, in the interest of a futuristic dream, to impose unity upon
an experience that changes too rapidly for linguistic or political
exactitude. In this effort we are often less interested in what we
are than in projecting what we will to be.

           Ralph Ellison, "The Little Man at the Chehaw Station"

(See me comin' better open up your door/I ain't no stranger, I
been here before. *The song is no stranger. It is always extant as
scripted and transforming backbeat, as offbeat signifier of America. It is the expressive site where American experience is named—
where a spade is always called: an instrument of forced (sometimes convicted) labor. A shout rises over furrowed fields or gang-
constructed road project at the close of southern day. Bound
musicians play for a masterful ball. A vibrant backbeat "livelies-
up" country picnics until Mississippi dawn. An innovative melody
spins onto a record company's master disc. A growling rumble
escapes doors and windows of South Chicago's summer functions.
Mastered texts and refined rhythms fill downtown dance halls in
New York winter.*See me comin' better heist your windows high/
If I's to leave you, you know you'd break down and cry. *The song
is no stranger, can never be lost. It is the "changing same" matrix
of America, an elusive juncture where thresholds and boundaries*

This chapter is a revised version of my essay "Generational Shifts and the Recent Criticism of
Afro-American Literature," *Black American Literature Forum*, Winter 1981, pp. 3–21.

are helpless. When it sounds, outside is in, and "insiders" are found out. The song sounds on every uneasy body, breaking down resistance, moving through American windows and doors with the ease of a liminal trickster—one foot among the gods, the other planted squarely in the world of men. The song names American land and intrudes, willy-nilly, into the American creative firmament. I ain't no stranger, *sung to the train-whistle-over-track-juncture accompaniment of guitar and harmonica:* I been here before!

It is not the song that is strange, or a stranger. It is the "artistic" or "creative" firmament that is estranging, striving to scandalize the song's name(ing).

Desiring the Greek hydria always in view, "American art" is outraged by the appearance of ancestral faces.

But how can the matrix, the womb, the vernacular mat producing and reproducing American meaning be a stranger?

If you seek your national identity, says the poet, you must "Ask your mamma!" All those purportedly scandalizing strategies: calling the singers the "lady" of the races, prating about quintessential "mammies," swooning over the Negro's "domestic" virtues. All those strategies are uneasy acknowledgments—rendered in a nervous voice that accompanies magic names—of the matrix, the ancestral and reproductive role of the song and its singers. But artful dodges cannot avoid the song. If I's to leave you, you'd break down and cry.

What has been estranging has been AMERICA. *Black and white alike have sustained a literary-critical and literary-theoretical discourse that inscribes (and reinscribes)* AMERICA *as immanent idea of boundless, classless, raceless possibility in America. The great break with a Europe of aristocratic privilege and division has been filled by virtuoso riffs on* AMERICA *as egalitarian promise, trembling imminence in the New World.*

But the players are always founding (white) fathers, or black men who believe there are only a few more chords to be un-not(ted) before Afro-American paternity is secure—before they are, in Alain Locke's phrases, "initiated" into American Democracy as "contributors" to American civilization. Hah! I ain't no stranger, I been here before.

The song is no stranger. No fatherly riffing can write it out of existence. As sign of vernacular dimensions in America, it insistently demands that if AMERICA *is to found(ed), it will be in the bedrock matrix of a blue-black song. Literary-critical and literary-theoretical (indeed, "expressive cultural investigative") discourse must come to fit, blues terms with the* AMERICA *it inscribes. It must discover its own relationship to* AMERICA.

Integrationist discourse privileges AMERICA. *Black aestheticians, riding the blinds of vernacular freights, seek to destroy it as*

a fatherly mystification of Anglo-male power. Reconstructionists
articulately suggest that America should be AMERICA . . . again.
But present-day listeners—blues critics, as it were, whose intent is
always the foregrounding of ancestral faces—hear an AMERICA
singing that has never been heard before.

   Blues critics know the song ain't no stranger. Their translational
task is to demonstrate the song's power at the junctures of Amer-
ican experience—its power to wed quotidian rituals of everyday
American experience to the lusters of a distinctively American ex-
pressive firmament.

   The blues critic seeks to hold the guests at such a signal Amer-
ican merger, not by gray-bearded venerability, but by displaying
the awesome luminescence of the song itself. He hopes that when
the initiated (those "wiser and better" for their attention) see him
coming, they will open up their doors. Through the gloom of a
"fathered" AMERICA, they might perceive faces of a different
ancestry. They might discover AMERICA and National Identity in
the fact that I ain't no stranger, I been here before.)

I

The disappearance of a traditional American literary history leads to
Afro-American literary history. Afro-American literary history, in turn,
supplies enabling conditions for increased insightfulness in Afro-
American practical criticism. The effectiveness of this practical criticism,
however, is contingent on adequate theories of Afro-American expressive
culture. In order to situate past and future directions of such expressive
cultural theory, one must discover the relationship that has existed between its various paradigm instances and AMERICA. To understand the
Afro-American expressive cultural theoretical enterprise, one must discover AMERICA.

   Writing AMERICA in captials enables one to distinguish between an
idea and what Edmundo O'Gorman describes in one of the epigraphs to
this chapter as a "lump of cosmic matter." As an idea, AMERICA represents the kind of "designated" entity to which Ralph Ellison refers in the
chapter's second epigraph. From an Ellisonian perspective, the sign
AMERICA is a willful act which always substitutes for a state description.
The substitution imposes problematical unity and stasis on an ever-
changing American scene.

   The process of discovering AMERICA in its relationship to Afro-
American expressive cultural theory can be viewed, I believe, as a requisite
first step in the deciphering of such theory. For the sign AMERICA is
always implicitly present in any given theoretical instance, carrying, to be
sure, varying metaphysical force from one instance to another. In order to
focus the enterprise of discovering AMERICA and suggesting strategies

for effective expressive cultural theorizing in the United States, I will confine my discussion in the present chapter to an analysis of the past four decades in the development of Afro-American literary criticism and theory.

There exist any number of possible ways to characterize the various manifestations of Afro-American literary criticism and theory during the past four decades. If one assumes a philosophical orientation, one can trace a movement from democratic pluralism ("Integrationist Poetics") through romantic Marxism (the "Black Aesthetic") to a version of Aristotelian metaphysics (the "Reconstruction of Instruction"). From another perspective, one can describe ascendant class interests that have characterized Afro-America since World War II, forcing scholars in one instance to assess Afro-American expressive culture at a mass level and in another to engage a critical "professionalism" contrary to mass interests. On a third level, one can follow a practice in the contemporary philosophy of science and describe conceptual or "paradigm" changes that have marked Afro-American criticism and theory since the Second World War. Any one of the approaches suggested carries its own distinctive inscription of AMERICA, for each philosophical, class, or paradigmatic instance has been uniquely situated vis-à-vis that idea. The various levels of analysis, however, can be combined and their varying inscriptions of AMERICA studied by invoking the notion of the "generational shift."

A "generational shift" is, in my definition, an ideologically motivated movement overseen by young or newly emergent intellectuals dedicated to refuting the work of their intellectual predecessors and to establishing a new framework for intellectual inquiry. The affective component of such shifts is described by Lewis Feuer: "Every birth or revival of an ideology is borne by a new generational wave: in its experience, each such new intellectual generation feels everything is being born anew, that the past is meaningless, or irrelevant, or non-existent."[1] The new generation's break with the past is normally signaled by its adoption of what Thomas S. Kuhn (to whose work I shall return later) designates a new "paradigm": a new set of guiding assumptions that unifies an intellectual community.[2]

The contours of the approach that I am suggesting for the analysis of expressive cultural theory are more sociological than archaeological; they find their object in discrete theoretical "communities" rather than in the larger epistemes of which such communities form a part. If an archaeology of knowledge is required to establish conditions of existence for Afro-American literary history, then a sociology of knowledge is appropriate for determining conditions of existence for paradigms in the practice of Afro-American literary theory.

In the recent criticism and theory of Afro-American literature, there have been two distinct generational shifts. Both have involved ideological reorientations, and both have originated in shifts in literary-critical and literary-theoretical paradigms. The first shift occurred during the mid-1960s. It led to the displacement of what might be termed "Integrationist Poetics" and gave birth to a new object of scholarly investigation.

II

The dominant critical and theoretical perspective in Afro-American literary and expressive cultural study during the late 1950s and early 1960s was "Integrationist Poetics." Richard Wright's essay "The Literature of the Negro in the United States" offers a fit illustration of such poetics.[3] In his essay, Wright optimistically predicts that *Afro-American* literature may soon be indistinguishable from the "mainstream" of American arts and letters. The basis for his optimism was the then recent Supreme Court decision in *Brown v. Topeka Board of Education* (1954) wherein the Court held that the doctrine of "separate but equal" was inherently unequal.

According to Wright, the Supreme Court's decision ensured a future "equality" in the experiences of blacks and whites in America. This equality of *social* experience would translate, according to Wright, into a homogeneity of *represented* experiences (pp. 103–5). And Afro-American writing would soon achieve expressive equality and homogeneity with a white mainstream. In short space, Afro-America would stand at one with the dominant white culture of America—in a relationship that Wright calls "entity" (p. 72).

But these stipulations apply only to what Wright calls the "Narcissistic Level"—the self-consciously literate level of Afro-American expression (pp. 84–85). At the folk, mass, or vernacular level, the relationship between Afro-America and a dominant Anglo-American culture has always been one of "identity," or separateness (p. 72). And though Wright argues that self-consciously literate products of Afro-America which signify a division between cultures such as "protest" poems and novels may disappear relatively quickly under the influence of the *Brown* decision, he is far less optimistic about the vanishing of the "Forms of Things Unknown" (p. 83)—the vernacular expressive products of the Afro-American masses.

Blues, work songs and hollers, and such verbal forms as folktales, boasts, toasts, and dozens are functions of the black masses' relationship of "identity" vis-à-vis mainstream culture. Such forms, in Wright's view, signal *an absence of equality* and represent a "sensualization" of the Afro-American masses' ongoing suffering (p. 83). Black vernacular expression, according to Wright, consists of improvisational forms filled "with a content wrung from a bleak and barren environment, an environment that stung, crushed, all but killed" (p. 84). One will be able to argue that egalitarian ideals have been achieved in America only after the

"Forms of Things Unknown" have disappeared altogether, or after they have been completely elevated to a level of conscious art. The course that leads to such an egalitarian disappearance is marked by momentous social actions like the Supreme Court's ruling in the *Brown* case.

The black spokesman who champions "Integrationist Poetics" is constantly in search of social indicators (such as the *Brown* decision) that signal democratic pluralism in American life. The implicit goal of the paradigm's democratic-pluralistic philosophical orientation is a future raceless, classless society of men and women in America (p. 105). The integrationist critic, therefore, as Wright demonstrates, founds his prediction of such a future, homogeneous body of Americans on such social *evidence* as the Emancipation Proclamation, constitutional amendments, Supreme Court decisions, or any one of many other documented claims that suggest America is moving toward AMERICA.

Under an integrationist prospect, an immanent AMERICA appears in the immaculate robes and cornucopian bounty that mark early paeans to the idea such as those of St. Jean de Crèvecoeur. Integrationist Poetics, that is to say, institutes an optimism that reads documentary statements of ideals as positive signs of a promised land to come. Ideas—Adamically and willfully posited in definition of AMERICA—are ontologically privileged by integrationism as a metaphysical grounding for theoretical presuppositions. For integrationists, an adequate theory of Afro-American expression must be grounded in the belief that blacks and whites in America will soon actualize AMERICA.

The ontology of integrationism validates, in turn, an epistemology with sharply exclusive horizons. Vernacular levels of Afro-American expression such as the blues remain "things unknown." The reason such vernacular manifestations are "unknown" is not far to seek.

As resonantly distinctive products of a way of life in contradiction to the white, educated, wealthy power matrix responsible for the articulation of AMERICA, the blues must be bracketed by Integrationist Poetics. They must be confined to a kind of *terra infirma*, a pre-AMERICA soon to be superseded. They occupy, moreover, "unknown land" insofar as they fit no category extant in the analyst's epistemology. Hence, blues become bracketed contradictions: *forms* of "things unknown." The metaphysical privileging of AMERICA by Integrationist Poetics renders the vernacular, in the governing terms of the poetics themselves, an *aporia*—a self-engendered paradox.

Arthur P. Davis offers another striking example, an earlier one than Richard Wright, of an Afro-American critic who has repeatedly sought to discover evidence to support optimistic arguments that a oneness of all Americans and a harmonious merger of disparate forms of American creative expression are impending American social realities. What seems implicit in Davis's critical formulations is a call for Afro-American writers to speed the emergence of such realities by offering genuine, "artistic" contributions to the kind of classless, raceless literature that he and other integrationists assume will carry the future. An injunction of this type can be inferred, for example, from the 1941 "Introduction" to *The Negro Caravan*, the influential anthology of Afro-American expression that Davis coedited with Sterling Brown and Ulysses Lee:

> The editors . . . do not believe that the expression "Negro literature" is an accurate one, and in spite of its convenient brevity, they have avoided using it. "Negro literature" has no application if it means *structural peculiarity*, or a Negro school of writing. The Negro writes in *the forms evolved* in English and American literature. . . . The editors consider Negro writers to be American writers, and literature by American Negroes to be a segment of American literature. . . . The chief cause for objection to the term is that "Negro literature" is too easily placed by certain critics, white and Negro, in an alcove apart. The next step is a double standard of judgment, which is dangerous for the future of Negro writers. [My emphasis][4]

What must be avoided at all cost, if an AMERICAN unity of black and white is to be achieved, is "structural" or "formative" *peculiarity*. The distinctive *forms* of Afro-American culture must remain *unknown*, or they must be transcended by Negro writers who adopt "evolved" forms of English and American literatures. It is somewhat uncanny that scholars as perspicacious as Davis and Brown inscribe a Darwinian "naturalness" in their critical prescriptions by suggesting American and English literary forms as *evolved* ones. Presumably, integrationism holds that structurally peculiar *Negro* forms are trapped in an evolutionary backwater. To even invoke the term "Negro" in conjunction with "literature," therefore, is a progressivist anathema, suggesting that works of Afro-American writers anthologized by Davis, Brown, and Lee may share some identity with "unfit" forms of expression. There seems no possibility in the editors' statement that a separate, Afro-American line of development exists in the United States.

In the 1950s and 1960s, Davis continued to champion the poetics implicit in such earlier work as *The Negro Caravan*. His essay "Integration and Race Literarure," which was presented to the first conference of Afro-American writers sponsored by the American Society of African Culture in 1959, states:

> The course of Negro American literature has been highlighted by a series of social and political crises over the Negro's position in America. The Abolition Movement; the Civil War, Reconstruction, World War I, and the riot-lynching period of the twenties all radically influenced Negro writing. Each crisis in turn produced a new tradition in our literature; and as each crisis has passed, the Negro writer has dropped the social tradition which the occasion demanded and moved

towards the mainstream of American literature. The integration con-
troversy is another crisis, and from it we hope that the Negro will
move permanently into full participation in American life—social,
economic, political, and literary.[5]

The stirring drama implied here of Afro-American writers finding their
way through various "little" traditions to the glory of the great mainstream is a function of Davis's solid faith in American pluralistic ideals. He
regards history and society from a specific philosophical and ideological
standpoint: Afro-Americans and their expressive traditions, like other
"minority" cultures, have always moved unceasingly toward unity with
Anglo-American culture. He thus predicts—like Wright—the eventual
disappearance of social conditions that produce literary works of art
identifiable (in structurally peculiar terms) as "Negro" or "Afro-American."

Wright and Davis represent a generation whose philosophy, ideology,
and attendant poetics support the vanishing of Afro-American expression
qua *Afro-American* expression. I shall examine this proposition at greater
length in the next section. For the moment, I simply want to suggest that
the consequences of their generational posture for literary-critical axiology can be inferred from the "Introduction" to *The Negro Caravan*. The
editors assert: "They [Afro-American writers] must ask that their books be
judged as books, without sentimental allowances. In their own defense
they must demand a single standard of criticism" (p. 7). The assertion
suggests that black writers must construct expressive products in ways
that make them acceptable in the sight of those who mold a "single
standard of criticism" in America. These standards, for many years, were
molded exclusively by a small community labeled by black spokesmen of
the 1960s the "white literary-critical establishment." Only a poetics but-
tressed by a philosophical viewpoint that augured an eventual unification
of *all* talented creative men and women as judges—that augured, in
short, the emergence of AMERICA—could have prompted such able
spokesmen as Wright, Brown, and Davis to assert that works of Afro-
American expression should be subjected exclusively to the "single standard" of such a narrow community.

III

The generational shift that displaced Integrationist Poetics brought forth a
group of intellectuals most clearly distinguished from its predecessors by a
radically different ideological and philosophical posture vis-à-vis AMER-
ICA. After the beatings, arrests, bombings, and assassinations that comprised the white South's reaction to nonviolent, direct action protests by
hundreds of thousands of civil rights workers from the late fifties to the
mid-sixties, it was difficult for even the most committed optimist to feel

that anything like AMERICA was an impending American social reality.[6] Rather than seeking documentary evidence—that panoply of words arguing for an ideal, *future* egalitarianism in the United States—the emerging generation set itself the task of analyzing the nature, aims, ends, and arts of hundreds of thousands of Afro-Americans who were assaulting present, racist structures of exclusion in America.

The Afro-American masses demonstrated through violent uprisings ("urban riots") in Harlem, Watts, and other communities throughout the United States that they were intent on social and political sovereignty. Their rebellious and vociferous activities signaled the birth of a new ideology, one that received a proper name in 1966,[7] when Stokely Carmichael spoke of "Black Power":

> [Black Power] is a call for black people in this country to unite, to recognize their heritage, to build a sense of community. It is a call for black people to begin to define their own goals, to lead their own organizations and to support those organizations. It is a call to reject the racist institutions and values of this society.[8]

This definition, drawn from Carmichael's and Charles Hamilton's work *Black Power*, expresses a clear imperative for Afro-Americans to focus their social efforts and political vision on their *own* interests. This particularity of Black Power—its sharp emphasis on the immediate concerns of Afro-Americans themselves—was a direct counterthrust by an emergent generation to an Integrationist Poetics' call for a general, raceless, and classless community of men and women in America. The community of interest to the emergent generation was not a future AMERICA, but a present, vibrant group of men and women constituting the heart of Afro-America. The Afro-American masses became, in the late sixties and early seventies, both subject and audience for the utterances of black political spokesmen moved by a new ideology.

The poetics accompanying this new ideological orientation were first suggested by Amiri Baraka (LeRoi Jones) in an address entitled "The Myth of a 'Negro Literature' " which was presented (in what now almost seems an inversive rejoinder to Davis) to the American Society of African Culture in 1962. Baraka begins with a probing question and then moves to a scathing response:

> Where is the Negro-ness of a literature written in imitation of the meanest of social intelligences to be found in American culture, i.e., the white middle class? How can it even begin to express the emotional predicament of black Western man? Such a literature, even if its "characters" *are* black, takes on the emotional barrenness of its model, and the blackness of the characters is like the blackness of Al Jolson, an unconvincing device. It is like using black checkers instead of white. They are still checkers.[9]

Baraka suggests that at the self-consciously literate level of Afro-American expression spokesmen have deserted the genuine emotional referents and authentic experiential categories of Afro-American life. The homogeneity between their representations of experience and those of the white mainstream, contrary to Wright's positive assessment of such a situation, is cause for disgust rather than joy.

Finally, Baraka's remarks imply that the merger of black and white expression at the "Narcissistic Level" (to use Wright's phrase) of Afro-American life is an enervating result of the black writer's acceptance of a "single standard of criticism" dictated by white America. Baraka thus inverts the literary-critical optimism and axiology of an earlier generation, rejecting entirely the notion that "Negro Literature" should not stand apart as a distinctive body of expression. Afro-American writers' desertion of aspects of their culture that foster uniqueness and authenticity is severely condemned.

Where, if not in self-consciously literate works of art, does one discover in Afro-America genuine reflections of the true emotional referents and experiential categories of black life? Like the more avowedly political spokesmen of his day, Baraka turned to the world of the masses in order to secure a vernacular answer to this question. At the mass level, he discovered the "forms of things unknown," specifically, musical inscriptions of such forms:

> Negro music alone, because it drew its strengths and beauties out of the depth of the black man's soul, and because to a large extent its traditions could be carried on by the lowest classes of Negroes, has been able to survive the constant and willful dilutions of the black middle class. Blues and jazz have been the only consistent exhibitors of "Negritude" in informal American culture simply because the bearers of its tradition maintained their essential identities as Negroes; in no other art (and I will persist in calling Negro music Art) has this been possible. [P. 107]

In this statement, Baraka seems to parallel the Richard Wright of an earlier generation. But while Wright felt that the disappearance of the "forms of things unknown" would signal a positive stage in the integration of American life and art, Baraka went on from his discovery of the vernacular to establish the Harlem Black Arts Repertory Theatre/School in 1965 as an enterprise devoted to the continuance, development, and strengthening of the "coon shout," blues, jazz, hollers, and other expressive forms of the "lowest classes of Negroes."[10]

Baraka and other artists who contributed to the establishment of the school felt that the perpetuation of Afro-American vernacular forms would aid the growth of Afro-American social and political autonomy in America. Larry Neal, who worked with Baraka during the mid-sixties, delineated both the complementarity of the Black Arts and Black Power movements and the affective component of a generational shift in his much quoted essay "The Black Arts Movement":

> Black Art is the aesthetic and spiritual sister of the Black Power concept. As such, it envisions an art that speaks directly to the needs and aspirations of Black America. In order to perform this task, the Black Arts Movement proposes a radical reordering of the western cultural aesthetic. It proposes a separate symbolism, mythology, critique, and iconology.[11]

The Black Arts Movement, like its ideological counterpart, the Black Power political front, was concerned with the articulation of experiences (and the satisfaction of audience demands) that found their essential character among the black urban masses. The guiding assumption of the Black Arts Movement was that if a literary-critical investigator looked to characteristic musical and verbal forms of the masses, he could discover unique aspects of Afro-American creative expression—aspects of both *form and performance*—that lay closest to the verifiable emotional referents and experiential categories of Afro-American culture. The result of such critical investigations, according to Neal and other spokesmen such as Baraka and Addison Gayle, Jr. (to name but three prominent advocates of the Black Arts), would be the discovery of a "Black Aesthetic"—a distinctive code for the creation and evaluation of black art.

From an assumed "structural peculiarity" of Afro-American expressive culture, an emergent generation of Afro-American intellectuals proceeded to assert a *sui generis* tradition of Afro-American art and a unique "standard of criticism" suitable for its elucidation. The essay "The Forms of Things Unknown," which is the introduction to Stephen Henderson's anthology *Understanding the New Black Poetry*, offers one of the most suggestive illustrations of the Black Aesthetic discovery process at work.[12] Henderson's formulations mark a high point in the first generational shift in the recent criticism of Afro-American literature. They are the reflections, finally, of the spokesman par excellence for an entirely new object of literary-critical and literary-theoretical investigation. Before turning to the specifics of Henderson's arguments, however, I want to focus for a moment on the work of Thomas Kuhn to clarify what is meant here by a "new object" of investigation.

IV

In *The Structure of Scientific Revolutions*, Kuhn sets out to define the nature of a scientific "revolution" or shift in the fundamental ways in which the scientific community perceives and accounts for phenomena.[13] He first postulates that the guiding construct in the practice of normal science is what he defines as a "paradigm": a constellation of "beliefs, values, techniques and so on shared by the members of a given community" (p. 175). He further defines a paradigm as the "universally recognized scientific achievements that for a time provide model problems and solutions to a community of practitioners [of normal science]" (p. viii). Thus, a paradigm sets the parameters of scholarly investigation, constraining both the boundaries of an investigator's perception and the degree of legitimacy attributed to various problems and methodologies. A forceful example of a scientific revolution and its enabling paradigm shift was the displacement of geocentricism by a Copernican cosmology. Kuhn writes: "The Copernicans who denied its traditional title 'planet' to the sun were not only learning what 'planet' meant or what the sun was. Instead, they were changing the meaning of 'planet' so that it could continue to make useful distinctions in a world where all celestial bodies, not just the sun, were seen differently from the way they had been seen before" (pp. 128–29).

The effects of this kind of paradigmatic shift on the assumptions and higher-order rules of a scholarly community are clarified further when Kuhn writes:

> Led by a new paradigm, scientists adopt new instruments and look in new places. Even more important, during revolutions scientists see new and different things when looking with familiar instruments in places they have looked before. It is rather as if the professional community had been suddenly transported to another planet where *familiar objects are seen in a different light and are joined by unfamiliar ones as well* . . . paradigm changes . . . cause scientists to see the world of their research-engagement differently. In so far as their only recourse to that world is through what they see and do, we may want to say that after a revolution scientists are responding to a different world. [P. 111, my emphasis]

Kuhn cites as an experimental instance of such perceptual changes the classic work of George M. Stratton. Stratton fitted his experimental subjects with goggles that contained inverting lenses. Initially, the subjects saw the world upside down and were extremely disoriented. Eventually, however, their entire visual field flipped over:

> Thereafter, objects . . . [were] again seen as they had been before the goggles were put on. The assimilation of a previously anomalous visual field . . . reacted upon and changed the field itself. Literally as well as metaphorically . . . [the subjects] accustomed to inverting lenses . . . [underwent] *a revolutionary transformation of vision.* [P. 112, my emphasis]

Kuhn, whose influential work appeared in 1962, has been taken to task by a subsequent generation of philosophers, scientists, and historians of science who find his notion of the paradigm shift extremely variable and much too coarse-grained to describe actual events in the practice of science.[14] He has been variously labeled a "relativist" who claims that scientific practices shift from one generation to another in irrational ways and a "sociologist" who unduly emphasizes the determinately communal nature of shifts in scientific practices. (Less polite detractors accuse him of advocating "mob psychology" as the motivation for shifts from one paradigm to another.) Critics who have turned particular attention on Kuhn's specific examples from the history of science suggest that his model of the paradigm shift will not adequately charaterize, say, the Copernican revolution or the ascendancy of Darwinian evolution.

But while critics of Kuhn's model (not the least of whom was Sir Karl Popper) make us aware of limiting cases and possible reservations, we are also aware of how profoundly exciting and energetically disruptive the very notion of the "paradigm" was in the study of science. It seems clear that what Kuhn provided was a tropological vehicle (a "paradigm," as it were) for the study of science that forced an upheaval in familiar conceptual categories.

By insisting that "science" (perhaps a last privileged mode of cognition allowed to *Man* as an autonomous *subject*) was not a cumulative body of knowledge progressively unfolding toward the truth, Kuhn disrupted an array of comforting intellectual assumptions. As an advocate for a kind of perspectival relativism that sees scientific praxis moving from a crisis of faith to revolution to normal science and then, abruptly and indeterminately, repeating the steps again, Kuhn was called an irrationalist. Actually what he instituted with his own paradigm of the paradigm shift was a trope for the study of science that not only focused attention on the normal (quotidian and always communally determined) nature of scientific practice but also denied privileged status to claims that truth arises from coherently progressive, individual acts of scientific rationality. Kuhn's trope became (and remains) a useful tool for the sociology of knowledge. It wrought a basic change in our ways of conceptualizing the nature of any epistemological revolution. And its focus on community determination (i.e., the determination of practice by a specialized and identifiable "disciplinary matrix") and gestalt-like perceptual shifts make his trope of the paradigm quite suggestive for the sociology of Afro-American literary-theoretical practice.

I suggest that Stephen Henderson and other Afro-American intellectuals of a Black Aesthetic generation produced a change in the perceptual field of Afro-American literary study that amounted, finally, to a "revolutionary transformation" of literary-critical and literary-theoretical vision vis-à-vis Afro-American expressive culture. Prior to the mid-1960s, scholars were led by an integrationism that permitted them to apprehend as "literature" or "art" only those Afro-American expressive works that approached or conformed to a "single standard of criticism" like that adjured by the editors of *The Negro Caravan*. Integrationist Poetics bound its perceptual field and constrained its domain of legitimate investigative problems to Afro-American expressive objects and events that most nearly approached such a standard. From an integrationist perspective, therefore, a scholar could not "see" that "Negro music" qua "*Negro* music" or "Negro poetry" qua "*Negro* poetry" constituted *art*. (Hence Baraka's insistence in the previous quotation on calling Negro music "art.") For "Negro-ness" was viewed by the old paradigm as a condition (a set of properties, or, "structural peculiarities") that excluded a phenomenon such as "*Negro* poetry" from the "artworld."[15]

The integrationists assumed as a first principle that art was an American area of achievement in which race and class were not significant variables. To discover or assert that the "Negro-ness" or "Blackness" of an expressive work was *a fundamental condition of its "artistic-ness"* was for a new generation to "flip over" the entire integrationist field of vision. Such a reversed, or inverted, perceptual reorientation is precisely what Henderson and his Black Aesthetic contemporaries achieved. Their efforts made it possible for literary-critical and literary-theoretical investigators to see "familiar objects" in a different light and to include previously "unfamiliar" objects in an expanded (and sharply modified) American artworld. In "The Forms of Things Unknown," Henderson masterfully outlines the hypotheses, boundaries, and legitimate problems of a new paradigmatic framework in Afro-American literary-theoretical practice called the Black Aesthetic.

V

Henderson's principal assumption is that in literature there exists "such a commodity as 'blackness' " (p. 3). He further assumes that this "commodity" should be most easily located in poetry "since poetry is the most concentrated and the most allusive of the verbal arts" (p. 3). Implicit in these statements is the claim that an enabling condition for art (and particularly for "poetry") in Afro-American culture is the possession of *blackness* by an expressive object or event. The ontological status—the very condition of being—of *Afro-American* poetic expression is, therefore, a function of the commodity "blackness." The most legitimate paradigmatic question that a literary-critical investigator or a literary theorist can pose is this, In what place and by what means does "blackness" achieve form and substance?

The title of Henderson's essay suggests his answer. Blackness must be defined, at a *structural* level of expressive objects and events, as an "interior dynamism" that derives force from the "inner life" of the Afro-American folk (pp. 5–6). He is quite explicit that what he means by "inner life" is the constellation of cultural values and beliefs that characterize what Albert Hofstadter calls a "reference public." Hofstadter writes:

> Predication of "good" . . . tends to lose meaningful direction when the public whose valuations are considered in judging the object is not specified. I do not see how we can hope to speak sensibly about the aesthetic goodness of objects unless we think of them in the context of reception and valuation by persons, the so-called "context of consumption." Properties by virtue of which we value objects aesthetically—e.g., beauty, grace, charm, the tragic, the comic, balance, proportion, expressive symbolism, verisimilitude, propriety—always require some reference to the apprehending and valuing person. . . . Any public taken as the public referred to in a normative esthetic judgment I shall call the judgment's *reference public*. The reference public is the group whose appreciations or valuations are used as data on which to base the judgment. It is the group to which universality of appeal may or may not appertain.[16]

Henderson says that the existence of black poetry is a function of a black audience's concurrence that a particular verbal performance (whether written or oral) by some person of "known Black African ancestry" is, in fact, poetry (p. 7). The array of values and beliefs—the cultural codes—that allow a black reference public to make such a normative judgment constitute the *inner life* of the folk. "Inner life," then—assuming the operative codes of a culture are historically conditioned and maintained at a level of interacting cultural systems—is translated as "ethnic roots."

Questions of the ontology and valuation of a black poem, according to Henderson, "can not be resolved without considering the ethnic roots of Black poetry, which I insist are ultimately understood only by Black people themselves" (pp. 7–8). What Henderson seeks to establish or to support with this claim, I think, is a kind of cultural holism—an interconnectedness (temporally determined) of Afro-American cultural discourse—that can only be successfully apprehended through a set of theoretical concepts and critical categories arrived at by in-depth investigation of the fundamental expressive manifestations of a culture.

In order to apprehend the wholeness of a culture, the literary investigator (like the cultural anthropologist) must go to the best available informants—to a "reference public" or, better, to the vernacular "natives" of the culture. "One must not consider the poem in isolation," writes Henderson, "but in relationship to the reader/audience, and the reader to the wider context of the phenomenon which we call, for the sake of convenience, the Black Experience" (p. 62). The tone of "The Forms of Things Unknown" approximates that of cultural anthropology even more closely in the following stipulations on literary-critical axiology:

> ... the recognition of Blackness in poetry is a value judgment which on
> certain levels and in certain instances, notably in matters of meaning
> that go beyond questions of structure and theme, must rest upon one's
> immersion in the totality of the Black Experience. It means that the
> ultimate criteria for critical evaluation must be found in the sources of
> the creation, that is, in the Black Community itself. [Pp. 65–66]

The notion that a conditioning cultural holism is a necessary consideration
in the investigation of a culture's works of verbal art receives yet a further
designation that has anthropological parallels when Henderson talks of a
"Soul Field."

Field theory in anthropology stresses the continuous nature of conceptual structures that make up various areas, or "fields," of a culture, for
example, kinship or color terms and their attendant "connotations" or
"sense." For Henderson, the "Soul Field" of Afro-American culture is "the
complex galaxy of personal, social, institutional, historical, religious, and
mythical meanings that affect everything we say or do as Black people
sharing a common heritage" (p. 41). In this definition, "meanings" is the
operative term, and it situates the author's designation "field" decisively
within the realm of semantics. Henderson's "Soul Field" is, thus, similar to
J. Trier's *Sinnfeld*, or conceptual field: the area of a culture's linguistic
system that contains the encyclopedia or mappings of various "senses" of
lexical items drawn from the same culture's *Wortfeld*, or lexicon.[17]

The theoretical concepts and critical categories for analyzing black
poetry that Henderson sets forth in "The Forms of Things Unknown" are
coextensive with the case he makes for the holism and continuity of
Afro-American culture. His three major categories are *theme, structure,*
and *saturation*. In dividing each category into analytic subsets, he never
loses sight of the "inner life" of the folk—of that interconnected "field" of
uniquely black meanings and values that he postulates as essential determinants of the subsets. He thus seeks to ensure a relationship of identity
between his own critical categories and "real," experiential categories of
Afro-American life. For example, he identifies "theme" with what he
perceives as the *actual* guiding concern of a collective, evolving consciousness of Afro-America. He finds that the most significant concern of this
consciousness has always been "the idea of liberation" (p. 18). He suggests
that the "old word, 'freedom' " might be substituted for this phrase to
denote the overriding theme (i.e., that which is "being spoken of") of
Afro-American expressive culture. Hence, a "real" lexical category ("freedom") and its complex conceptual mappings in Afro-American culture are
identified as one subset of the critical category "theme."

Similarly, the *actual* speech and music of Afro-American culture and
their various forms, techniques, devices, nuances, rules, and so on are

identified as fundamental structural referents in the continuum of black expressive culture:

> Structurally speaking . . . whenever Black poetry is most distinctively and effectively *Black*, it derives its form from two basic sources, Black speech and Black music. . . . By Black speech I mean the speech of the majority of Black people in this country. . . . This includes the techniques and timbres of the sermon and other forms of oratory, the dozens, the rap, the signifying, and the oral folktale. . . . By Black music I mean essentially the vast fluid body of Black song—spirituals, shouts, jubilees, gospel songs, field cries, blues, pop songs by Blacks, and, in addition, jazz (by whatever name one calls it) and non-jazz by Black composers who *consciously or unconsciously* draw upon the Black musical tradition. [Pp. 30–31]

Here, Henderson effectively delineates a continuum of Afro-American verbal and musical expressive behavior that begins with everyday speech and popular music and extends to works of "high art."

Finally, "saturation" is a category in harmony with the assumed distinctiveness of both the Afro-American *Sinnfield* and *Wortfeld*. Henderson insists that "saturation" is a perceptual category that has to do with a distinctive semantics: "Certain words and constructions [e.g., "rock," "jelly," "jook"] seem to carry an inordinate charge of emotional and psychological weight [in Afro-American culture], so that whenever they are used they set all kinds of bells ringing, all kinds of synapses snapping, on all kinds of levels. . . . I call such words 'mascon' words . . . to mean *a massive concentration of Black experiential energy* which powerfully affects the meaning of Black speech, Black song, and Black poetry—if one, indeed, has to make such distinctions" (p. 43).

From an assumed "particularity," wholeness, and continuity of Afro-American culture—characteristics that manifest themselves most clearly among the Afro-American folk or masses—Henderson moves to an articulation of theoretical concepts and critical categories that provide what he calls "a way of speaking about all kinds of Black poetry despite the kinds of questions that can be raised" (p. 10). He proposes, in short, *a theory* to account for the continuity—the unity in theme, structure, and semantics—of black speech, music, and poetry (both oral and written).

From the outset, Henderson refuses to follow a traditional literary-critical path—predicating cultural and expressive continuity on history, or chronology, alone. Instead, he observes the contemporary scene in Afro-American poetry (i.e., the state of the art of black poetry in the 1960s and early 1970s) and realizes that the expressive modes of a black urban vernacular are dominant shaping influences in the work of Afro-American poets. From his observation of this modern instance of reciprocity between expressive vernacular modes and self-conscious, literary expression, he proposes that *all* black poetic expression can be understood in terms of such a pattern. Understanding the new black poetry in its relationship to the black urban vernacular, therefore, provides direction and definition in the larger enterprise of understanding the expressive codes, or the cultural system that is "art," in Afro-American culture as a whole. A comprehension of the "forms of things unknown" and the theoretical assumptions that it presupposes leads to the discovery of a distinctive artistic tradition.

The Black Aesthetic signaled for Henderson and his contemporaries the codes that determine such a distinctive, Afro-American tradition, as well as the theoretical standpoint (one marked by appropriate categories) that enables an investigator to see—to "speak about"—this tradition. And like all new paradigms, the Black Aesthetic had immediate perceptual and semantic ramifications. It changed the meaning of both "black" and "aesthetic" in the universe of American literary-critical discourse so that these terms could continue to make "useful distinctions" in a world where Afro-American expressive products had come to be seen quite differently from the manner in which they were perceived by an older integrationist paradigm.

VI

Earlier, I referred to the philosophical orientation of the Black Aesthetic as romantic Marxism. Having discussed Henderson's work, perhaps I can now clarify this designation. For me, the fact that the aesthetics of the Black Arts movement were idealistically centered in the imagination of the black critical observer makes them "romantic."[18] This critical centrality of the Afro-American mind is illustrated by Henderson's assumption that "Blackness" is not a theoretical reification, but a reality accessible only to those who can "imagine" in uniquely black ways. From this perspective, the word "understanding" in the title of his anthology is a sign for a spiritual journey in which what the *black* imagination seizes upon as *black* must be *black*, whether it existed before or not.

The notion of a "reference public" gives way, therefore, at a lower level of the Black Aesthetic's argument, to a kind of impressionistic chauvinism. For it is, finally, *only* the black imagination that can experience blackness, in poetry, or in life. As a result, the creative and critical framework suggested by Henderson resembles, at times, a closed circle:

> . . . for one who is totally immersed, as it were, or saturated in the Black Experience the slightest formulation of the typical or true-to-life [Black] experience, whether positive or negative, is enough to bring on at least subliminal recognition [of the "formulation" of the experience as "black"]. . . . I have tried to postulate a concept that would be useful in talking about what Black people feel is their distinctiveness, with-

out being presumptuous enough to attempt a description or definition of it. This quality or condition of Black awareness I call *saturation*. I intend it as a sign, like the mathematical symbol infinity, or the term "Soul." It allows us to talk about the thing [a "distinctive" feeling of "blackness"], even to some extent to use it, though we can't, thank God! ultimately abstract and anlyze it: it must be experienced. [Pp. 63, 68]

"Saturation" also gives way, then, at a lower level of the argument to cultural xenophobia. Rather than indicating a *sui generis* semantics, it becomes a mysterious trait of consciousness. In "Saturation: Progress Report on a Theory of Black Poetry," an article that appeared two years after his anthology, Henderson comments on the critical responses that his romantic specifications have evoked:

> Some people—critics, white and Black—have difficulty with this last standard [i.e., the critical standard of "intuition" for judging the successful rendering of "black poetic structure"]. They call it mysterious, mystical, chauvinistic, and even (in a slightly different context) a "curious metaphysical argument" (Saunders Redding). I call it *saturation*. I authenticate it from personal experience. To those critics I say: Remember Keats did the same, proving poetic experience by his pulse and the "holiness of the imagination."[19]

But if Henderson's romanticism led to the chauvinistic positing of an "intuitive sense"—a "saturated" or an "immersed" black imagination—it also led to the suggestive, higher-order arguments that I have discussed in the preceding section. I think the romanticism of Henderson and his contemporaries—like that of romantics gone before who were driven to "create a system or be enslav'd by another Man's"—resided in their metaphysical rebelliousness, their willingness to postulate a positive and distinctive category of existence ("Blackness") and then to read the entire universe under that sign.[20] The predication of such a category was not only a radical political act designed to effect the liberation struggles of Afro-America, but also a bold critical stroke designed to break the interpretive monopoly on Afro-American expressive culture that had been held traditionally by a white minority who set an exclusive and "single" standard of criticism. Henderson writes:

> If the critic is half worth his salt, then he would attempt to describe what occurs in the poem and to *explain*—to the extent that it is possible— how the "action" takes place, i.e., how the elements of the work interact with one another to produce its effect. And if one of those elements is "Blackness"—as value, as theme, or as structure, especially the latter—then he is remiss in his duty if he does not attempt to deal with it in some logical, orderly manner.[21]

Given Henderson's argument for the black person's "intuitive sense" of experience as the only valid guide to the recognition of "Blackness" as an "element," it seems unlikely that any white critic would prove worth his or her "salt" vis-à-vis Afro-American literature and criticism. The implicit exclusion of white judgment from the critical enterprise is complemented by the implicit antinomianism in the following assertion from Henderson's "The Question of Form and Judgment in Contemporary Black American Poetry: 1962–1977":

> Historically, the question of what constitutes a Black poem or how to judge one does not really come to a head until the 1960s and the promulgation of the Black Aesthetic in literature and the other arts. In a special sense . . . "Black" poetry was invented in the 1960s along with the radicalization of the word "Black" and the emergence of the Black Power philosophy.[22]

Here, the faith that postulated "Blackness" as a distinctive category is seen as the generative and exclusively Afro-American source of a new art, politics, and criticism that nullify the interpretive authority of a traditional white, critical orthodoxy.

In a sense, the critical "orthodoxy" repudiated by a Black Aesthetic generation was the customary faith that sustained the idea of AMERICA. The sole basis for privileging the standards of a white, literary-critical establishment was the faith that this establishment's values and practices were instrumental in a dauntless progress toward AMERICA. The Black Aesthetic generation realized that the cost of such a faith was an ironic and unpluralistic relinquishing of one's own particularity ("structural" or otherwise) in the service of a pluralistic immanent idea. Their realization led to a declaration of heterodoxy.

To relinquish "blackness" in the service of a faith established, maintained, and promulgated by (and in the interest of) a minority segment of the American white, male population seemed not an act of democratic rationality but a gesture of rank heresy—or lunacy. Hence, the Black Aesthetic generation, having demystified (having discovered to *uncover*) AMERICA, stated a new immanent idea with its romantic, idealistic, and nationalistic concept of a Black Nation within America. "It's Nation Time!" declared the radical black political front of the 1960s. And nationalism became a radical move by cultural investigators as well. They quickly sought to inscribe and close a black critical circle around Afro-American expressive culture.

The rebelliousness that seemed to close the circle of Afro-American criticism to white participants, however, was not only romantic but also Marxist. Henderson and his contemporaries attempted to base their arguments for an Afro-American intuitive sense of "blackness" on the notion that such a sense was a function of the continuity of Afro-American culture. The distinctive cultural circumstances that comprised the material bases of Afro-American culture—the "economics of slavery"—were always seen by spokesmen for the Black Aesthetic as determinants of a distinctively "black" consciousness. And the most accurate reflection of the economics of slavery (and their subsequent forms) in the American economy was held to take place at a mass or vernacular level. Hence, the expressive forms of black folk consciousness were defined by Black Aestheticians as underdetermined by material circumstances that were held to vary within a narrow range. To take up such forms, therefore, according to Black Aestheticians, is, perforce, to find oneself involved with the *authentic* or *basic* (as in the "material base") categories of Afro-American existence.

"Culture determines consciousness" became a watchword for the Black Aesthetic, and by "culture" its spokesmen meant a complex of material and expressive components that could only be discovered at a vernacular level of Afro-American experience. It was the emphasis on the vernacular—an emphasis motivated by a paradoxical desire to ground idealistic rebelliousness in a materialist reading of history—that led to a deepened scholarly interest during the sixties and early seventies in both Afro-American folklore and other black expressive forms that had long been (in Henderson's words) "under siege . . . [by] . . . white critical condescension and snobbery, and . . . outright pathological ignorance and fear."[23] Through their own investigations of the "forms of things unknown" in recent years, some white critics have been able to enter a black critical circle.[24] They entered, however, not as superordinate authorities, but as scholars working in harmony with fundamental postulates of the Black Aesthetic.

There is a more clichéd sense in which the Black Aesthetic was Marxist, and it finds its best illustration in the insistence by spokesmen for the new paradigm that Afro-American expressive culture has a "social function." Black Aestheticians were too quick to assert that works of verbal art have *direct* effects in the solution of social problems and in the shaping of social consciousness. The prescriptive formulations of a spokesman like Ron Karenga demonstrate this aspect of the Black Aesthetic: "All black art, irregardless of any technical requirements, must have three basic characteristics which make it revolutionary. In brief, it must be functional, collective and committing."[25] Like Mao Ze-dong, whom he is paraphrasing, Karenga and other spokesmen for the Black Arts felt that poems and novels could (and *should*) be designed to move audiences to revolutionary action.

At this point in the discussion, it should be clear that there were blatant weaknesses in the theoretical framework of the Black Aesthetic. Too often in attempts to locate the parameters of Afro-American culture, Black

Aesthetic spokesmen settled instead for romantically conceived boundaries of "race." Moreover, their claims to a scholarly consensus on "culture" sometimes appeared as mere defensive chauvinism. What is en-
couraging, however, in an evaluation of the Afro-American intellectual
milieu that prevailed during the later stages of the Black Arts movement is
that Black Aesthetic spokesmen *themselves* were the first to point out (and
to suggest ways beyond) the critical and theoretical weaknesses of their
new paradigm.

In his essay "The Black Contribution to American Letters: The Writer
as Activist—1960 and After," Larry Neal identifies the Black Aesthetic's
interest in an African past and in African-American folklore as a species of
Herderian nationalism. He goes on to say: "Nationalism, wherever it
occurs in the modern world, must legitimize itself by evoking the muse of
history. This is an especially necessary step where the nation or group feels
that its social oppression is inextricably bound up with the destruction of
its traditional culture and with the suppression of that culture's achievements in the intellectual sphere."[26] A group's reaction in such nationalistic
instances, according to Neal, is understandably (though also regrettably)
one of total introspection—of drawing into itself and labeling the historically oppressive culture as "the enemy" (p. 782). A fear of the destruction
of Afro-American culture by an "aggressive and alien" West, for example,
prompted Black Aesthetic spokesmen to think only in racial terms and to
speak only in "strident" tones as a means of defending their culture against
what they perceived as threats from the West. In Neal's view, such a
strategy represents a confusion of politics and art, an undesirable conflation of the "public" domain of social activism and the "private" field of
language reserved for artistic creation and literary-theoretical investigation.

The nationalistic response represented by the Black Aesthetic is, in
Neal's estimation, finally a form of distorted "Marxist literary theory in
which the concept of race is substituted for the Marxist idea of class"
(p. 783). The attempt to apply the "ideology of race to artistic creation"
(p. 784), says Neal, is simply a contemporary manifestation of Afro-
American literature's (and, by implication, literary criticism and theory's)
historical dilemma:

> The historical problem of black literature is that it has in a sense been
> perpetually hamstrung by its need to address itself to the question of
> racism in America. Unlike black music, it has rarely been allowed to
> exist on its own terms, but rather [has] been utilized as a means of
> public relations in the struggle for human rights. Literature can indeed
> make excellent propaganda, but through propaganda alone the black
> writer can never perform the highest function of his art: that of
> revealing to man his most enduring human possibilities and limita-
> tions. [P. 784]

In order to perform the "highest function" of artistic creation and criticism the black spokesman, in Neal's view, must concentrate on method—on "form, structure, and genre"—rather than on experience or content (pp. 783–84). Neal, therefore, who in the sixties called for a literature and criticism that spoke directly to the needs and aspirations of black people, ends his later essay by invoking a creativity that projects "the accumulated weight of the world's aesthetic, intellectual, and historical experience" as a function of that creativity's mastery of *form*. This revised formalist position leads not only to a condemnation of the critical weaknesses of the intellectual strategies of Neal's former allies in the Black Aesthetic camp but also to a valorization of theoretical formulations of "Western" theoreticians such as Northrop Frye and Kenneth Burke (pp. 783–84).

A new order of literary-critical and literary-theoretical thought—one that sought to situate the higher-order rules of the Black Aesthetic within a contemporary universe of literary-theoretical discourse—was signaled during the mid-seventies not only by Neal's essay but also by symposia and conferences on the Black Arts that occurred throughout the United States.[27] It was at one such symposium that Stephen Henderson presented his essay, "The Question of Form and Judgment," which I have previously cited.[28] Like Neal, Henderson is drawn to a formalist critique. He implicitly rejects an intuitive "saturation" in favor of an empirical approach to literary study: "in criticism, intuition, though vital, is not enough. The canons, the categories, the dynamics must be as clear and reasoned as possible. These must rest on a sound empirical base" (p. 36). This "sound empirical base" is, in the final analysis, a *data base* acquired through the kind of investigation that I suggested when discussing "The Forms of Things Unknown." "Black poetry," Henderson continues, "can and should be judged by the same standards that any other poetry is judged by—by those standards which validly arise out of the culture" (p. 33).

I think it would be incorrect to assert that the mid- and later seventies witnessed a total revisionism on the part of former advocates of the Black Aesthetic. However, by that time some early spokesmen had begun to point out weaknesses of the intellectual structure raised on the ideological foundations of Black Power. The defensive inwardness of the Black Aesthetic—its manifest appeal to a racially conditioned, revolutionary, and intuitive standard of critical judgment—made the new paradigm an ideal instrument for those wishing to usher into the world new and *sui generis* Afro-American objects of investigation. Ultimately, though, such introspection could not answer theoretical questions occasioned by the entry of such black, expressive objects into the world. In a sense, the investigator had been given—through a bold act of the critical imagination—a unique expressive tradition but no distinctive theoretical vocabulary in which to discuss this tradition. He had been brought to perceive linguistic forms of power and beauty, but the language meted out by spokesmen such as Ron Karenga was little more than a curse. A new paradigm, one coextensive with contemporary literary-theoretical practice, was in order.

VII

Discussing the manner of progression of new philosophical postures born of generational shifts, Feuer comments:

> . . . from its point of origin with an insurgent generational group, the new emotional standpoint, the new perspective, the new imagery, the new metaphors and idioms spread to the more conventional sections of their own generation, then to their slightly older opponents and their relative elders. Thus, by the time that conservative Americans spoke of themselves as "pragmatic," and virtually every American politician defined himself as a "pragmatist," the word "pragmatist" had become a cliché, and its span as a movement was done. A new insurgent generation would perforce have to explore novel emotions, images, and idioms in order to define its own independent character, its own "revolutionary" aims against the elders.[29]

One might substitute "Black Aesthetic" and "Black Aesthetician" for the implied "pragmatism" and the explicit "pragmatist" of the foregoing remarks. By the end of the 1970s, the notion of a uniquely Afro-American field of expressive experience marked by unique works of verbal and literary art had become a commonplace in American literary criticism. The philosophical tenets that supported early manifestations of this notion, however, had been discredited by the failure of revolutionary black social and political groups to achieve their stated ends. "Black Power" as a motivating philosophy for the Black Aesthetic was deemed an ideological failure by the mid-seventies; no sovereign Afro-American state within the United States was even vaguely to be hoped for. Hence, those who adopted fundamental postulates of the Black Aesthetic as givens in the late seventies did so without a corresponding acceptance of its initial philosophical buttresses.

The "imagery" of a resplendent NATION of Afro-Americans invested with Black Power—like the emotional standpoint which insisted that this hypothetical NATION could have a collective and "functional" literature and criticism—gave way in the late seventies to a new idiom. In defining its independent character, a new group of intellectuals found it de rigueur to separate a language of expressive cultural theory from the vocabulary of political ideology. The philosophical posture which supported their separation was a dualism predicated on a distinction between literary and extra literary realms of human experience.

The proclaimed mission of the new generation was to "reconstruct"

pedagogy and study of Afro-American literature to reflect the most advanced thinking of contemporary literary-theoretical discourse. This goal
was similar in some respects to the revisionist efforts of Neal and Henderson. Like their immediate predecessors, the "reconstructionists" were
interested in establishing a sound theoretical framework for the future
study of Afro-American expressive culture. In their attempts to achieve
this goal, however, some spokesmen of the new generation (whose work I
shall take up shortly) were hampered by a literary-critical "professionalism" that functioned in the service of newly emergent class interests.

At the outset of the present discussion, I implied that the notion of
"generational shifts" was sufficient to provide an account of "ascendant
class interests that have characterized Afro-America since World War II."
The emergence of the mass, black audience so crucial to the enterprise of
Black Power and the Black Arts was the first instance of such ascendancy.[30]
But the vertical mobility of Afro-Americans that was prompted by black
political activism during the 1960s and early 1970s also resulted in the
emergence of what has been called a "New Black Middle Class."[31]

The opening of the doors, personnel rosters, and coffers of the white
academy to minority groups that was brought about by radical politics
during the past two decades provided conditions for the appearance of
Afro-American critics who have adopted the postures, standards, and
vocabularies of their white compeers. The disappearance of a mass black
audience for literary-critical and revolutionary-political discourse brought
about by billions of dollars and countless man-hours spent to suppress
American radical-leftist activities in recent years has been accompanied
(quite ironically) by the emergence of Afro-American spokesmen whose
class status and privileges are, in fact, contingent on their adherence to the
accepted standards of their various professions. Bernard Anderson's
reflections on the situation of black corporate middle managers who
assumed positions in the late sixties and early seventies also describe the
situation of a new group of Afro-American literary scholars. Anderson
writes:

> As pioneers in a career-development process, these [black] managers
> face challenges and uncertainties unknown to most white managers.
> Many feel an extra responsibility to maintain high performance levels,
> and most recognize an environment of competition that will tolerate
> only slight failure. . . . Some black middle managers feel the need to
> conform to a value system alien to the experience of most black
> Americans but essential for success in professional management.[32]

One result of a class-oriented professionalism among Afro-American
literary scholars has been a sometimes uncritical imposition upon Afro-
American expressive culture of theories and theoretical terminologies

borrowed from prominent white scholars. When such borrowings occurred among the reconstructionist scholars who displaced the Black
Aesthetic movement, the results were sometimes less than favorable for the
course of Afro-American literary study. Instead of furthering the vernacu-
lar-oriented mode of analysis suggested by the higher-order arguments of a
previous generation, the emergent reconstructionist generation chose to
posit Afro-American "literature" as an *autonomous cultural domain* and
to criticize this literature in terms "alien" to the implicitly vernacular
approach of the Black Aesthetic. Rather than attempting to assess the
merits of the Black Aesthetic's methodological assumptions, the reconstructionists adopted the "professional" assumptions (and attendant jargon) of the world of white, academic literary criticism.

If the later stage of the Black Aesthetic paradigm witnessed a situation in
which a vast and intriguing panoply of vernacular concerns existed in the
absence of a suitable theoretical vocabulary, then the early stage of reconstructionism witnessed a situation in which a vast array of borrowed
theoretical terms existed in the absence of any readily discernible Afro-
American expressive cultural referents. Unlike the Integrationist Poetics
workers of earlier years, the reconstructionists did not want to bring an
identifiable corpus of (Afro-American) "literature" under the judgment of
a white, literary-critical establishment. Their goal was not to help actualize
AMERICA by conceding cultural identity. Instead, they assumed that
cultural identity was not at issue, suggesting that an advanced, theoretical
vocabulary for the study of human expression was both transcultural and
constitutive. The reconstructionists seemed to believe that their own position at the right hand of prominent articulators of advanced, theoretical
terminologies indicated that AMERICA had already been actualized.

There appeared to exist, in the early days of reconstructionism, a belief
that only an "inferiority complex" among previous commentators on
Afro-American expressive culture had caused them to reject a hearty
egalitarianism and salutary equality of critical possibilities awaiting them
in an AMERICA of advanced theoretical discourse. The implicit inscription (an extraordinarily naive and perhaps dangerous one in its absence of
political and ideological awareness) of their belief was, "Why insist on
difference when you can now join a white, AMERICAN vanguard simply
by speaking its language?" Hence, early manifestations of reconstructionism reveal a vigorous, if quite often confused and confusing, engagement
with establishment theoretical langauge—an engagement that is meant, I
think, to signal the Afro-American commentator's own personal discovery
of AMERICA. Arthur P. Davis and Sterling Brown wanted an identifiable
Afro-American literature to be judged by an establishment's "single standard of criticism" as a stage in the realization of AMERICA. The recon-

structionists, by contrast, held that AMERICA had been founded and that what remained to be accomplished was the founding of Afro-American literature in theoretical terms.

A positive outcome of an emergent reconstructionist paradigm has been a strong and continuing emphasis on the necessity for an adequate theoretical framework for the study of Afro-American literature. The negative results of reconstructionism include an unfortunate burdening of the universe of discourse surrounding Afro-American expressive culture with meaningless jargon and the articulation of a variety of lamentably confused utterences on language, literature, and culture.

The emergent reconstructionist generation was fundamentally correct, I feel, in its call for serious study of Afro-American literature. But it was hopelessly misguided in its wholesale adoption of terminology and implicit assumptions of white, "professional" critics. A view of essays by principal spokesmen for the new theoretical prospects will serve, I hope, to clarify my judgments. The recontructionist essays that I have in mind appear in *Afro-American Literature: The Reconstruction of Instruction* (1979),[33] which might be called the handbook of the new generation.

Edited by Dexter Fisher and Robert B. Stepto, *Afro-American Literature* "grew out of the lectures and course design workshops of the 1977 Modern Language Association/National Endowment for the Humanities Summer Seminar on Afro-American Literature" (p. 1). The volume sets forth basic tenets of a new paradigm in Afro-American literary theory. The guiding assumption of the reconstructionists—that a literature known as "Afro-American" exists in the world—is stated by Stepto in his "Introduction": Afro-American "literature fills bookstore shelves and, increasingly, the stacks of libraries; symposia and seminars on the literature are regularly held; prominent contemporary black writers give scores of readings; and so the question of the literature's existence, at this juncture in literary studies, is not at issue" (p. 1). The second, fundamental assumption—that literature consists in "written art" (p. 3)—is implied by Stepto later in the same "Introduction" when he describes the unit of *Afro-American Literature* devoted to "Afro-American folklore *and* Afro-American literature as well as Afro-American folklore *in* Afro-American literature" (pp. 3–4). According to the editor, folklore can be transformed into a "written art" that may, in turn, comprise "fiction" (p. 4). Further, he suggests that the "folk" roots of a work like Frederick Douglass's *Narrative of the Life of Frederick Douglass* are to be distinguished from its "literary roots" (p. 5). The conditions signaled by "written," therefore, seem at first glance to be necessary enabling ones for "literary" and "literature" in Stepto's thinking.

There is, however, some indication that Stepto does not wish to confine his definition of the "literary" exclusively to what is "written." At the mid-point of his opening remarks, he asserts that there are "discrete literary texts that are inherently interdisciplinary (e.g., blues) and often multigeneric (dialect voicings in all written art forms)" (p. 3). If "blues" and "dialect voicings" constitute, respectively, a literary text and a genre, then it would appear to follow that any distinctly Afro-American expressive form (not merely written ones) can be encompassed by the "literary" domain. The boundaries of the reconstructionist's theoretical inquiries can apparently be shifted at will to include whatever seems distinctly expressive in Afro-America. Stepto suggests, for example, that "a methodology for an integrated study of *Afro-American folklore* and literature" (p. 4, my emphasis) should form part of the scholar-teacher's tools. He goes on to propose that there are "various ways in which an instructor . . . can present *a collection of art forms* and still respond to the literary qualities of many of those forms in the course of the presentation" (p. 3, my emphasis).

On one hand, then, the reconstructionist project implies a rejection of modes of inquiry that are sociological in character or that seek to explore ranges of experience lying beyond the transactions of an *exclusive* sphere of *written* art: "central . . . to this volume as a whole" is a rejection of "*extraliterary* values, ideas, and pedagogical constructions that have plagued the teaching of . . . [Afro-American] literature" (p. 2, my emphasis). On the other hand, reconstructionism attempts to preserve a concern for the "forms of things unknown" (e.g., blues) by reading them under the aspect of a quite Procrustean category labeled "literary."

Similarly, reconstructionism attempts to maintain certain manifestations of Afro-American "ordinary language" (e.g., dialect voicings) as legitimate areas of study by reading such voicings as *literary* "genre." Finally, the project, as it is tentatively defined by Stepto, implies that the entire realm of Afro-American expressive culture ("arts") can be subsumed by the "literary" since any "collection" of black art forms may be, in his view, explicated in terms of "literary qualities." Such "qualities," under the terms of reconstructionism, take on the character of sacrosanct, cultural universals (a point to which I shall return shortly).

If we return for a moment to Kuhn's work, we note that he claims that a paradigmatic shift in a community's conception of the physical world results in "the whole conceptual web whose strands are space, time, matter, force, and so on," being shifted and "laid down again on nature whole" (p. 149). While the Black Aesthetic was concerned to determine how the commodity "blackness" shaped an Afro-American expressive domain, the emergent reconstructionist paradigm attempted to discover how qualities of a "literary" domain shaped Afro-American life *as a whole*. There is thus a movement with reconstructionism from the whole of culture to the part. What workers under the new paradigm sought to specify was a "literary" conceptual scheme for apprehending Afro-American culture. Such a specification constitutes, in fact, the very motor of their theoretical project. Two of *Afro-American Literature's* most important essays—Stepto's "Teaching Afro-American Literature: Survey or Tradition: The Reconstruction of Instruction" and Henry Louis Gates, Jr.'s "Preface to Blackness: Text and Pretext"—are devoted to making the engine run.

Stepto's basic premise in "Teaching Afro-American Literature" is that the typical (i.e., normative) teacher of Afro-American literature is a harried, irresponsible pedagogue ignorant of the "inner" workings of the Afro-American literary domain. It follows from this proposition that pedagogy surrounding Afro-American literature must be *reconstructed* on a sound basis by a person familiar with the "myriad cultural metaphors," "coded structures," and "poetic rhetoric" of Afro-America (p. 9). Stepto asserts that only a person who has learned *to read* the discrete literary texts of Afro-America in ways that ensure a proximity and "intimacy, with writers and texts outside the normal boundaries of *nonliterary* structures" (p. 16, my emphasis) can achieve this required familiarity. According to Stepto, moreover, it is a specific form of "literacy"—of proficient reading—that leads to the reconstruction of instruction.

Understandably, given Stepto's earlier claims, the achievement of literacy, in his view, is not dependent on the comprehension, or study, of "extraliterary" structures. The epistemological foundations of a requisite literacy lie in a reader's apprehension and comprehension of what Stepto calls the "Afro-American canonical story or pregeneric myth, the particular historicity of the Afro-American literary tradition, and the Afro-American landscape or *genius loci*" (p. 18). This pregeneric myth, according to Stepto, is "the quest for freedom *and* literacy" (p. 18). He further specifies the myth as an "aesthetic and rhetorical principle" that can serve as the basis for constructing a proper course in Afro-American literature (p. 17). Thus Afro-American pregeneric myth is, at one and the same instant, a prelinguistic reality, a quest, and a pedagogical discovery principle.

It is with Stepto's specifications on a pregeneric myth that what I refer to as an "unfortunate burdening" of the universe of discourse surrounding Afro-American expressive culture with jargon becomes apparent. For the author's formulations on a pregeneric myth reflect his metaphysical leanings and orientation toward AMERICA far more clearly than they convey a desirable methodological competence. They signal, in fact, what I called, at the outset of my discussion, a "version of Aristotelian metaphysics." For Stepto's "myth" has the character of prime matter that is capable of assuming an infinite variety of forms. Just as for Aristotle "the elements are the simplest physical things, and within them the distinction of matter and form can only be made by an abstraction of thought,"[34] so for Stepto the pregeneric myth is informed matter serving as the core and essence of that which is "literary" in Afro-America.

The pregeneric myth is for Stepto the substance out of which all black expression molds itself: "The quest for freedom and literacy is found in every major Afro-American text. . . "(p. 18). He further states: "If an Afro-American literary tradition exists, it does so not because there is a sizeable chronology of authors and texts but because those authors and texts seek collectively their own literary forms—their own admixture of genre—bound historically and linguistically to a shared pregeneric myth"(p. 19).

A simplified statement of the conceptual scheme implied by Stepto's notion of cultural evolution would be: The various *structures* of a culture derive from the informed matter of myth. The principal difficulty with this notion is that Stepto fails to make clear the mode of being of a "myth" that is not only pregeneric, but also, it would seem, *prelinguistic*. "Nonliterary structures," he tells us, evolve "almost exclusively from freedom myths devoid of linguistic properties" (p. 18). Such structures, we are further told, "speak rarely to questions of freedom *and* literacy" (p. 18). The question one must pose in light of such assertions is: Are "nonliterary structures" indeed devoid of linguistic properties? If so, then "literacy" and "freedom" can scarcely function as dependent variables in a single, generative myth. Under conditions of a mutual inclusiveness (where the variables are, ab initio, functions of one another) the structures generated from the myth could not logically be devoid of that which is essential to literacy, that is, *linguistic properties*. It is important to note, for example, that the "nonliterary" structure known as the *African Methodist Episcopal Church* preserves in its name, and particularly in the linguistic sign, "African," a marker of the structure's cultural origin and orientation. And it is difficult to imagine the kind of cognition that would be required to summon to consciousness cultural structures devoid of linguistic properties such as a name, a written history, or a controlling interest in the semantic field of a culture's language.

But perhaps what Stepto actually means to suggest by his statement is that "freedom myths" are devoid of linguistic properties. Under this interpretation, however, one would have to adopt a philosophically idealistic conception of myth that seems contrary to the larger enterprise of reconstructionism. For Stepto insists that the "reconstruction" of Afro-American literary instruction is contingent on the discoverability through "literacy" (a process of linguistic transaction) of the Afro-American pregeneric myth. And how could such a goal be achieved if myths existed only as prelinguistic, philosophical ideals? In sum, Stepto seems to have adopted a critical rhetoric that plays him abysmally false. Having assumed intrinsic merit and inherent clarity in the notion "pregeneric myth," he fails to delineate analytically the mode of existence of such a myth or to clarify the manner in which it is capable of generating two distinct kinds of cultural structures.

One sign of the problematical status of this myth in Stepto's formulations is the apparent "agentlessness" of its operations. According to Stepto, the pregeneric myth is simply "set in motion" (p. 20), and one can observe its "motion through both chronological and linguistic time" (p. 19). Yet the efficacy of motion suggested here seems to have no historically based community of agents or agencies for its origination or perpetuation. The myth and its operations, therefore, are finally reduced in Stepto's thinking to an aberrant version of Aristotle's "unmoved mover." Aristotle specifies that the force which moves the "first heaven" has "no contingency; it is not subject even to minimal change (spatial motion in a circle), since that is what originates."[35] Stepto, however, wants both to posit an "unmoved" substance as his pregeneric myth *and* to claim that this myth *moves* as "literary history." In fact, he designates the shape of its literary-historical movement as a circle—a "magic circle," or *temenos*—representing one kind of ideal harmony, or perfection of motion.

At this point in his description, Stepto (not surprisingly) feels compelled to illustrate his formulations with examples drawn from the Afro-American literary tradition. He first asserts that the phrase "the black belt" is one of Afro-America's metaphors for the *genius loci* (a term he borrows from Geoffrey Hartman, signifying "spirit of place") that resides within the interior of the "magic circle" previously mentioned (p. 20). Of the "black belt" metaphor, the late nineteenth-century founder and president of Tuskegee Institute, Booker T. Washington, wrote:

> So far as I can learn the term was first used to designate a part of the country which was distinguished by the colour of the soil. The part of the country possessing this thick, dark soil was, of course, the part of the south where the slaves were most profitable, and consequently they were taken there in the largest numbers. Later, and especially since the war, the term seems to be used wholly in a political sense—that is, to designate the counties where the black people outnumber the white.[36]

Stepto feels this description is disingenuous. When he proceeds to demonstrate that Washington's statement represents a "literary offense" against the metaphor "the black belt," however, he does not summon logical, rhetorical, or linguistic criteria. In condemning Washington for describing only geological and political dimensions of the black belt rather than historical and symbolic ones, Stepto uses "extraliterary" criteria. He insists that the turn-of-the-century black leader's *offense* was committed to ensure his own success in soliciting philanthropic funds for Tuskegee. The author of *Up from Slavery*, in Stepto's view, merely "glossed" the metaphor *the black belt* in order to keep white potential benefactors happy.

We thus find ourselves thrust into the historical dust and heat of turn-of-the-century white philanthropy in America. And what Stepto calls a "geographical metaphor" (i.e., "the black belt") becomes, in his own reading, simply a sign for one American region where such philanthropy had its greatest impact. Contrary to his earlier injunction, therefore, Stepto allows a "nonliterary structure" to become central to his own "reading of art" (p. 20). He assumes, however, that he has reached his interpretation of Washington solely on the basis of his own "literacy" in regard to the black leader's employment of metaphor. He further assumes that when he contrasts W. E. B. Du Bois's use of the phrase "the black belt" with Washington's he is engaged in a purely "literary" act of "reading within tradition" (p. 21). But if the "tradition" that he has in mind requires a comprehension of turn-of-the-century white philanthropy to understand Washington, then surely Stepto does a disservice to his own reader when he fails to reveal that Du Bois's "rhetorical journey into the soul of a race" (p. 21) in fact curtailed white philanthropy to Atlanta University, cost Du Bois his teaching position there, and led the author of *The Souls of Black Folk* to an even deeper engagement with the metaphor "the black belt."

In his attempt to maintain the exclusively "literary" affiliations of a pregeneric myth and its operations, Stepto introduces historical and sociological structures into his reading where they will not appear to conflict dramatically with his claim that *all necessary keys for literacy* in the tradition generated by the pregeneric myth are linguistically situated within the texts of black authors themselves. His reading, however, is at best an exercise in the positing of cultural metaphors followed by attempts to fit such metaphors into a needlessly narrow framework of interpretation. Yet Stepto asserts that "it is reading of this sort that our instructor's new pedagogy should both emulate and promote" (p. 21).

Rather than offering additional examples of such reading, Stepto turns to a consideration of what one early twentieth-century critic called the relationship between "tradition and the individual talent."[37] For Stepto, this relationship is described as the tension between "Genius and *genius loci*" and between *temenos* and *genius loci*. The mediation between these facets of Afro-American culture constitutes what the author calls "modal improvisation." Although his borrowed terminology is almost hopelessly confusing here, what Stepto seems to suggest is that the Afro-American literature instructor must engage in "literate" communion with the inner dynamics of the region of Afro-America comprised of a pregeneric myth and its myriad forms and operations. The instructor's pedagogical "genius" consists in his ability to comprehend the "eternal landscape" (p. 22) that is the pregeneric myth—that is, the sacred domain of the "literary" in Afro-American culture.

An "eternal landscape" (without beginning or end and agentless in its creation and motions) is but another means of denoting for Stepto what he describes earlier in his essay as the "various dimensions of literacy achieved within the *deeper recesses* of the art form" (p. 13, my emphasis). At another point in "Teaching Afro-American Literature," the author speaks of "*immersion* in the multiple images and landscapes of metaphor" (p. 15, my emphasis). This cumulative employment of images of a sacred interiority suggests that Stepto believes there is an inner sanctum of pregeneric, mythic, literary "intimacy" residing in works of Afro-American art. He seems to feel that entrance to this sanctum can be gained only by the initiated. Thus, what is presented by "Teaching Afro-American Literature" is a scheme of Eleusinian literacy that finally comprises what might be called a *theology of literacy*. The "conceptual web" laid on Afro-America by Stepto's essay asserts the primacy and sacredness among cultural activities of the literary-critical and literary-theoretical enterprise. The argument of the essay is, in the end, a religious interpretation *manqué*, complete with an unmoved mover, a priestly class of "literate" initiates, and an eternal landscape of cultural metaphors that can be entered by those free of literary offense. And the "qualities" that derive from such a landscape (since they are coextensive with the generation of cultural structure) operate as "universals."

The articulation of such a literary-critical theology is scarcely a new departure in the history of literary criticism. In his "General Introduction" to *The English Poets* published in 1880, Matthew Arnold wrote: "More and more mankind will discover that we have to turn to poetry to interpret life for us, to console us, to sustain us. Without poetry, our science will appear incomplete; and most of what now passes for religion and philosophy will be replaced by poetry."[38] Like Stepto, Arnold envisions a realm of poetry to which only the worthy have access: "In poetry, which is thought and art in one, it is the glory, the eternal honour, that charlatanism shall have no entrance; that this noble sphere be kept inviolate and inviolable" (p. 3). Stepto's assumption that his "reconstructed" scheme for teaching Afro-American literature may "nurture literacy in the academy" (p. 23) is certainly akin to Arnold's formulations of the exalted mission of poetry. And the reconstructionist's zeal in preserving "inviolate"the sacred domain of the literary surely constitutes a modern instance of an Arnoldian theology of literacy. In his zeal Stepto condemns with fierce self-righteousness any pedagogical contextualization of Afro-American literature that might lead a student to ascribe to, say, a Langston Hughes poem, a use-value, or meaning, in opposition to the kind of linguistic and rhetorical values made available by a reconstructionist approach.

Stepto emerges as a person incapable of acknowledging that the decision to investigate the material bases of the society that provided enabling conditions for Hughes's metaphors is a sound literary-theoretical decision. Semantic and pragmatic considerations of metaphor suggest that the information communicated by metaphor is hardly localized in a given image on a given page (or exclusively within the confines of a magical literary circle). Rather, the communication process is a function of myriad factors interacting: a native speaker's ability to recognize ungrammatical sentences, the vast store of encyclopedic knowledge constituting a speech community's common knowledge, relevant information supplied by the verbal context of a specific metaphoric text, and finally, the relevant knowledge brought to bear by an introjecting listener or reader.[39] Conceived in these terms, metaphoric communication may actually be better comprehended by an investigation of the material bases of society than by an initiate's passage "from metaphor to metaphor and from image to image of the same metaphor in order to locate the Afro-American *genius loci*" (p. 21). For example, Hughes may be more comprehensible within the framework of Afro-American verbal and musical *performance* than within the borrowed framework for the description of *written* inscriptions of cultural metaphor adduced by Stepto. Only a full investigation of Afro-American metaphor—an analysis based on the best theoretical models available—will enable a student to decide.

The myopic zeal that forced Stepto to adopt a narrow, "literary" conception of metaphor should not be totally condemned. For it is correct (and fair) to point out that a kind of sacred crusade did seem in order by the mid-1970s to modify or "reconstruct" the instruction and study of Afro-American literature. While I do not think the type of mediocre instruction and misguided criticism that Stepto describes were, in fact, as prevalent as he assumes, I do feel there were enough villains about in the mid-seventies to justify a renewed vigilance and effort. But though one comes away from "Teaching Afro-American Literature" with a fine sense of the villains, one does not depart the essay (or others in *Afro-American Literature*) with a sense that reconstructionists are broad-minded and well-informed in their preachments. In fact, I think the instructor who seeks to model his course on the formulations of Stepto might find himself as nonplused as the critic who attempts to pattern his investigative strategies on the model implicit in Henry Louis Gates's "Preface to Blackness: Text and Pretext."

Just as Stepto's work begins with the assumption that the pedagogy surrounding Afro-American literature rests on a mistake, so Gates's essay commences with the notion that the criticism of Afro-American literature (prior to 1975) rested on a mistake. This mistake, according to Gates, consisted in the assumption that a "determining formal relation" exists between "literature" and "social institutions."

> The idea of a determining formal relation between literature and social
> institutions does not in itself explain the sense of urgency that has, at
> least since the publication in 1760 of *A Narrative of the Uncommon
> Sufferings and Surprising Deliverance of Briton Hammon, A Negro
> Man*, characterized nearly the whole of Afro-American writing. This
> idea has often encouraged a posture that belabors the social and
> documentary status of black art, and indeed the earliest discrete
> examples of written discourse by slave and ex-slave came under a
> scrutiny not primarily literary. [P. 44]

For Gates, "social institutions" is an omnibus category equivalent to
Stepto's "nonliterary structures." Such institutions include the philosophical musings of the Enlightenment on the "African Mind," eighteenth-century debates concerning the African's place in the great chain of
being, the politics of abolitionism, or (more recently) the economics,
politics, and sociology of the Afro-American liberation struggle in the
twentieth century. Gates contends that Afro-American literature has repeatedly been interpreted and evaluated according to criteria derived from
such "institutions."

As a case in point, he surveys the critical response that marked the
publication of Phillis Wheatley's *Poems on Various Subjects, Religious
and Moral*, discovering that "almost immediately after its publication in
London in 1773," the black Boston poet's collection became "the international antislavery movement's most salient argument for the African's
innate mental equality" (p. 46). Gates goes on to point out that "literally
scores of public figures" provided prefatory signatures, polemical reviews,
or "authenticating" remarks dedicated to proving that Wheatley's verse
was (or was not, as the case may be) truly the product of an African
imagination. Such responses were useless in the office of criticism, however, because "virtually no one," according to Gates, "discussed . . .
[Wheatley's collection] as poetry" (p. 46). Hence, "The documentary
status of black art assumed priority over mere [?] literary judgment;
criticism rehearsed content to justify one notion of origins or another"
(p. 46).

Thomas Jefferson's condemnation (on "extraliterary" grounds) of
Wheatley and of the black eighteenth-century epistler Ignatius Sancho set
an influential model for the discussion of Afro-American literature that, in
Gates's view, "exerted a prescriptive influence over the criticism of the
writings of blacks for the next 150 years" (p. 46). Jefferson's recourse to
philosophical, political, religious, economic, and other cultural systems
for descriptive and evaluative terms in which to discuss black writing was,
in short, a *mistake* that has been replicated through the decades by both
white and Afro-American commentators. William Dean Howells, the
writers of the Harlem Renaissance, and, most recently, according to Gates,
spokesmen for the Black Aesthetic have repeated the critical offense of

Jefferson: They have assumed there is, in fact, a determining formal relation between literature and other cultural institutions and that various dimensions of these other institutions constitute areas of knowledge relevant to literary criticism.

Gates says a thunderous no to such assumptions. As he reviews the "prefaces" affixed to various Afro-American texts through the decades, he finds no useful criteria for the practice of literary criticism. He discovers only introductory remarks that are "pretexts" for discussing African humanity or for displaying "artifacts of the sable mind" (p. 49), or for chronicling the prefacer's own "attitude toward being black in white America" (p. 65).

Like Larry Neal,[40] Gates concludes that such "pretexts" and the lamentable critical situation they imply are functions of the powerful influence of "race" as a variable in all spheres of American intellectual endeavor related to Afro-America. And like Neal, he states that racial considerations have substituted for "class" as a category in the thinking of those who have attempted to criticize Afro-American literature, resulting in what he calls "race and superstructure" criticism: "blacks borrowed whole the Marxist notion of base and superstructure and made of it, if you will, race and superstructure" (p. 56). Gates also believes that Afro-American creative writers have fallen prey to the mode of thought that marks "race and superstructure" criticism. For these writers have shaped their work on polemical, documentary lines designed to prove the equality of Afro-Americans or to argue a case for their humanity. In the process, they have neglected the "literary" engagement that results in true art.

What, then, is the path that leads beyond the critical and creative failings of the past? According to Gates, it lies in a semiotic understanding of literature as a "system" of signs that stand in an "arbitrary" relationship to social reality (pp. 64–68). Having drawn a semiotic circle around literature, however, he moves rapidly to disclaim the notion that literature as a "system" is radically distinct from other domains of culture:

> It is not, of course, that literature is unrelated to culture, to other disciplines, or even to other arts; it is not that words and usage somehow exist in a vacuum or that the literary work of art occupies an ideal or reified, privileged status, the province of some elite cult of culture. It is just that the literary work of art is a system of signs that may be decoded with various methods, all of which assume the fundamental unity of form and content and all of which demand close reading. [P. 64]

The epistemology on which this description rests is stated as follows:

> ... perceptions of reality are in no sense absolute; reality is a function of our senses. Writers present models of reality, rather than a description of it, though obviously the two may be related variously. In fact,

> fiction often contributes to cognition by providing models that high-
> light the nature of things precisely by their failure to coincide with it.
> Such certainly is the case in science fiction. [P. 66]

The semiotic notion of literature and culture implied by Gates seems to combine positivism (reality as a "function of our senses") with an ontology of signs that suggests they are somehow "natural" or "inherent" to human beings. If "reality" is, indeed, a function of our senses (surely an extraordinarily semiotically naive proposition), then observation and study of human physiological capacities should yield some comprehension of a subject's "reality." In truth, it is never brute physiological processes in themselves that interest Gates, but rather the operation of such processes under the conditions of "models" of cognition, which, of course, is a very different matter. If one begins, not with the phenomenal, but with the cognitive, then one is required to ask: How are cognitive "models" conceived, articulated, and transmitted in human cultures? Certainly one of the obvious answers here is *not* that human beings are *endowed* with a "system of signs," but rather that *models of cognition are conceived in, articulated through, and transmitted by language.* And like other systems of culture, language *is* a "social institution." Hence, if cognitive "models" of "fiction" differ from those of other spheres of human behavior, they do so not because fiction is somehow discontinuous with social institutions. In fact, it is the attempt to understand the coextensiveness of language as a social institution and literature as a system within it that constitutes a defining project of literary-theoretical study in our day.

When, therefore, Gates proposes metaphysical and behavioral models that suggest that literature, or even a single text (p. 67), exists as a structured "world" ("a system of signs") that can be comprehended without reference to "social institutions," he is misguided in his claims, appearing only vaguely aware of recent developments in literary study, symbolic anthropology, linguistics, the psychology of perception, and other related areas of intellectual inquiry. He seems, in fact, to have adopted, without qualification, a theory of the literary sign (of the "word" in a literary text) that presupposes a privileged status for the creative writer: "The black writer is the point of consciousness of his language" (p. 67). What this assertion means to Gates is that a writer is more capable than others in society of producing a "complex structure of meanings"—a linguistic structure that (presumably) corresponds more closely than those produced by nonwriters to the organizing principles by which a group's world view operates in consciousness (p. 67).

How can a writer achieve this end unless he is fully aware of language *as a social institution* and of the relationship language bears to other institutions that create, shape, maintain, and transmit a society's "organizing principles"? Surely Gates does not want to suggest that the mind of the writer is an autonomous semantic domain where complex structures are conceived and maintained "nonlinguistically." On the other hand, if such structures of meaning are, in fact, "complex" *because* they are linguistically maintained, then so are similar structures conceived by nonwriters.

That is to say, Gates renders but small service to the office of theoretical distinction when he states that "a poem is above all atemporal and must cohere at a symbolic level, if it coheres at all" (p. 60), or when he posits that "literature approaches its richest development when its 'presentational symbolism' (as opposed by Suzanne Langer to its 'literal discourse') cannot be reduced to the form of a literal proposition" (p. 66). The reason such sober generalities contribute little to an understanding of literature, of course, is that Gates provides no informed notion of the nature of "literal discourse." He fails to admit both its social-institutional status and its fundamental existence as a symbolic system.

On what basis, then, except a somewhat naive belief in the explanatory power of semiotics can Gates suggest a radical disjunction between literature and other modes of linguistic behavior in a culture? The critic who attempted to pattern his work on Gates's model would find himself confronted by a theory of language, literature, and culture that suggests that "literary" meanings are conceived in a nonsocial, noninstitutional manner by the "point of consciousness" of a language and maintained and transmitted, without an agent, within a closed circle of "intertextuality" (p. 68). It does seem, therefore, that despite his disclaimer, Gates feels "literature is unrelated to culture." For culture consists in the interplay of various human symbolic systems, an interplay that is essential to the production and comprehension of meaning. Gates's independent literary domain, which produces meanings from some mysteriously nonsocial, noninstitutional medium, bears no relationship to such a process.

One reason Gates fails to articulate an adequate theory of literary semantics in his essay, I think, is that he allots an inordinate amount of space to the castigation of his critical forebears. And his attacks are often restatements of shortcomings that his predecessors had already recognized and discussed by the later 1970s. Yet Gates provides elaborate detail in, for example, his analysis of the Black Aesthetic.

Among the many charges that he levels against Stephen Henderson, Addison Gayle, Jr., and me is the accusation that spokesmen for the Black Aesthetic assumed they could "achieve an intimate knowledge of a literary text by re-creating it from the inside: Critical thought must become the thought criticized" (p. 66). Though Gates employs borrowed (in this instance from Gérard Genette) terminology here,[41] what he seems to object to in the work of Black Aesthetic spokesmen is their treatment of the text as subject. In short, he charges that these spokesmen postulated a tautological, literary-critical circle, assuming that the thought of an Afro-

American literary text was "black thought" and hence could be "re-thought" only by a black critic. While there is some merit in this charge (as Henderson's and Neal's previously mentioned reconsiderations of their initial critical postures make clear), it is scarcely true, as Gates argues, that Black Aestheticians did nothing but reiterate presuppositions about "black thought" and then interpret Afro-American writings according to the entailments of such presuppositions.

The insular vision that would have resulted from such a strategy would not have enabled Black Aestheticians to discuss and interpret Afro-American verbal behavior in the holistic ways conceived by Henderson, Neal, Gayle, and me. Spokesmen for the Black Aesthetic seldom conceived of the "text" as a *closed* enterprise. At the higher level of their arguments, they thought of the text as an occasion for transactions between writer and reader, between performer and audience. And far from insisting that the written text was, in itself, a repository of inviolable "black thought" to be preserved at all costs, they called for the "destruction of the text"—an open-endedness of performance and response that created conditions of possibility for the emergence of both new meanings and new strategies of verbal transaction.[42] True, such spokesmen never saw the text as discontinuous with its social origins, but then they also never conceived of these "origins" as somehow divorced from the semantics of the metaphorical instances represented in black artistic texts. In short, they never thought of culture under the terms of a semiotic analysis that restricted its formulation to a literary domain alone.

On the other hand, Black Aesthetic spokesmen were certainly never so innocent as Gates might have one believe. Their semantics never permitted them crudely to accept the notion that words of a literary text stand in a one-to-one relationship to "things" in Afro-American culture. In fact, they were so intent on discovering the full dimensions of the artistic word that they attempted to situate its various manifestations within a continuum of verbal behavior in Afro-American culture. Further, they sought to understand the continuum within the complex webs of interacting cultural systems that ultimately give meaning to such words.

Rather than a referential semantics, therefore, what was implicit in the higher-order arguments of the Black Aesthetic (as I have attempted to demonstrate) was an anthropological approach to Afro-American art. I think, in fact, that Gates recognizes this and is, finally, unwilling to accept the kind of critical responsibilities signaled by such an enterprise. Though he expends great energy arguing with Henderson's and my own assumptions on Afro-American culture, he refuses (not without disingenuity) to acknowledge our *actual readings of Afro-American texts*. The reason for this refusal to acknowledge our readings, I think, is that we have always brought together, in what we hope are useful ways, our knowledge of various social institutions, or cultural systems (including language), in attempts to reveal the distinctive character of Afro-American expressive texts. Gates's formulations, however, imply an ideal critic whose readings would summon knowledge only from the *literary system* of Afro-America. The semantics endorsed by his ideal critic would *not* be those of a culture. They would be the specially consecrated meanings of an intertextual world of "written art."

The emphasis on close reading (p. 64) in Gates's formulations, therefore, might justifiably be designated a call for a *closed* reading of selected Afro-American written texts. In fact, Gates implies that the very defining criteria of a culture may be extrapolated from selected written, literary texts rather than vice versa (p. 62). For example, if any Afro-American literary artist has entertained the notion of "frontier," then he feels that "frontier" as a notion must have defining force in Afro-America culture (pp. 63–64). Only by ignoring the mass or vernacular level of Afro-America and holding up the "message" of literary works of art by, say, Ralph Ellison and Ishmael Reed as normative utterances in Afro-American culture can Gates support such a claim. His claim is thus a function of a privileged status granted to the writer and an elite status bestowed on the literary uses of language (p. 62).

But if it is true that scholarly investigations of an Afro-American expressive tradition must begin at a vernacular level—at the level of the "forms of things unknown"—then Gates's claim that "frontier" has defining force in Afro-America would have to be supported by the testimony of, say, the blues, work songs, or early folktales of Afro-America. And emphasis on "frontier," in the sense suggested by Frederick Jackson Turner, is scarcely discernible in such cultural manifestations of Afro-America.

Gates, however, is interested only in what *writers* (as "points of consciousness") have to say, and he seems to feel no obligation to turn to Afro-American folklore. In fact, when he comments on Henderson's formulations on Afro-American folk language, or vernacular, he reveals not only a lack of interest in folk processes but also profound misconceptions about the nature of Afro-American language itself.

Henderson attempts to establish a verbal and musical *continuum of expressive behavior* in Afro-American culture as an analytical category. In this process, he encounters certain terms that seem to claim (through usage) expansive territory in the Afro-American "sign field." Gates mistakenly assumes that Henderson is setting such terms (e.g., "jook," "jelly") apart from a canon of ordinary usage as "poetic discourse." This assumption is a function of Gates's critical methodology, which is predicated on a distinction between ordinary and poetic discourse. It compels him to cast aspersions on the originality of Henderson's work by asserting that practical critics, since the 1920s, have been engaged in actions similar to those of the Black Aesthetic spokesman (p. 61).

The fault with Gates's judgment on Henderson is that he fails to recognize that the Black Aesthetician was *not* seeking to isolate a lexicon of Afro-American poetic usages, nor to demonstrate how such usages superimpose a "grammar" (Gates's term) on nonliterary discourse (p. 61). Instead, Henderson is concerned to demonstrate that Afro-American ordinary discourse is, in fact, *continuous with* Afro-American artistic discourse and that an investigation of the Afro-American oral tradition must finally concern itself, not simply with a lexicon, but also with a grammar (in the fit linguistic sense) adequate to describe the syntax and phonology of *all* Afro-American speech.

Gates cannot grasp Henderson's project because he believes that the artistic domain is unrelated to ordinary social modes of behavior. Hence, he is enamored of the written, literary word, and suggests that a mere dictionary of black poetic words and their "specific signification" would lead to an understanding of how Black English departs from "general usage" (p. 61). This view of language is coextensive with his views of literature and culture. It concentrates solely on words as artistic signs and ignores the complexities of the syntax and phonology that give them resonance. "A literary text," Gates writes, "is a linguistic event; its explication must be an activity of close textual analysis" (p. 68).

It is not, however, the text that constitutes an event (if by this Gates means a process of linguistic transaction). It is, rather, the reading or performance by human beings of a kind of score—or graphemic record, if you will—that constitutes *the event* and, in the process, produces (or reproduces) a meaningful text. And the observer, or critic, who wishes to analyze such a text must have a knowledge of far more than the lexicon of the performers. He should, it seems to me, have at least some theoretically adequate notions of the entire array of cultural forces which shape the performer's cognition, allowing him to actualize a "text" as one instance of a distinct cultural semantics. Gates cannot even conceive of such an investigative posture. And his "Dis and Dat: Dialect and the Descent" reveals the confusion on issues of both language and culture that leaves him theoretically ill-equipped to comprehend Henderson's project.

Briefly, Gates says that "culture is imprisoned in a linguistic contour that no longer matches . . . the changing landscape of fact" (p. 92). At first this appears to be a mild form of Whorfianism.[43] However, if one asks, How do "facts" achieve nonlinguistic existence? the answer is, *They do not achieve such existence*. Placed in proper perspective, Gates's statement simply means that different communities of speakers of the same language have differential access to "modern" ideas. But in his effort to preserve language apart from other social institutions, Gates ignores agents or speakers until he wishes to add further mystery to his own peculiar conceptions of language. When he finally comes to reflect on speakers, he invokes the notion of "privacy," insisting that lying and remaining silent both offer instances of a speaker's employment of a "personal" thesaurus (p. 93). This conception stands in contrast to Gates's earlier Whorfianism.[44] To my knowledge, it possesses little support in the literature of linguistics or semiotics.

The notions that Gates advocates presuppose uniquely "personal" meanings for lexical items that form part of a culture's "public discourse." But what is unique, or personal, about these items is surely their *difference* from public discourse; their very identity is a function of public discourse. Further, the ability to use such lexical items in order to lie, or to misinform, scarcely constitutes an argument for privacy. Umberto Eco, for example, writes:

> A sign is everything which can be taken as significantly substituting for something else. This something else does not necessarily have to exist or to actually be somewhere at the moment in which a sign stands for it. Thus *semiotics is in principle the discipline studying everything which can be used in order to lie*. If something cannot be used to tell a lie, conversely it cannot be used to tell the truth: it cannot in fact be used "to tell" at all.[45]

The *word*, in short, becomes a sign by being able *to tell*, and unless Gates means to propose the idealistic notion that each human mind generates its own system of meaningful, nonpublic signs, it is difficult to understand how he conceives of sign usage in lying as an instance of the "private" use of language. His goal in "Dis and Dat" (an unfortunate choice of lexical items for his title, since the phonological feature *d* for *th* is not unique to Black English Vernacular, but rather can be found in other nonstandard language varieties) is to define Afro-American "dialect" as a kind of "private," subconscious code signifying a "hermetic closed world" (p. 94). The problem with this suggestive notion, however, is that Gates not only misunderstands the issue of privacy in language and philosophy, but also fails to comprehend the nature of Black English Vernacular (BEV).

He bases his understanding of BEV on a nineteenth-century magazine article by a writer named James A. Harrison, who asserted that "the poetic and multiform messages which nature sends him [the Afro-American] through his auditory nerve" are reproduced, in words, by the Afro-American (p. 95). Gates takes Harrison's claims seriously, assuming that there is a fundamental physiological difference between the linguistic behavior of Afro-Americans and that of other human beings: "One did not believe one's eyes, were one black; one believed [presumably on the basis of the Afro-American's direct auditory contact with nature] ... one's ears" (p 109). On the basis of such ludicrously racist linguistic and cultural assumptions, Gates proposes that BEV was essentially musical, poetical, spoken discourse generated by means other than those employed to generate standard English and maintained by Afro-Americans as a code of symbolic inversion.

There are reasons for studying the process of symbolic, linguistic inversion in Afro-American culture, and, indeed, for studying the relationship between the tonal characteristics of African languages (which is, I think, what both Harrison and Gates have in mind when they say "musical") and those of Afro-American speech. Such study, however, should not be grounded on the assertions of Wole Soyinka, Derek Walcott, or James A. Harrison (Gates's sources). It should be a matter of careful, holistic cultural analysis that summons as evidence a large, historical body of comment and scholarship on BEV. Henderson has made a beginning in this direction in "The Question of Form and Judgment," which commences with the assumption that a discussion of Afro-American poetry (whether written in dialect or standard English) must be based on sound historical notions of BEV resulting from detailed research.[46]

Neither Gates nor Stepto, the principal spokesmen for the reconstructionist project in *Afro-American Literature*, has undertaken the detailed research in various domains of Afro-American culture that leads to adequate theoretical formulations. Stepto's stipulations on the ontology of a pregeneric myth from which all Afro-American cultural structures originate are just as problematical as Gate's notions of a generative, artistic point of consciousness whose literary uses of language are independent of social institutions. The narrowness of Stepto's conception of the literary forces him to adopt "nonliterary" criteria in his reading of *Up from Slavery*. And the instability of Gates's views of language and culture forces him to relinquish his advocacy for a synchronic, close reading of literary utterances when he comes to discuss Afro-American dialect poetry. Social institutions, and far more than literary criteria, are implied when he asserts, "When using a word we wake into resonance, as it were, its entire previous history. A text is embedded in specific historical time; it has what linguists call a diachronic structure. To read fully is to restore all that one can of the immediacies of value and intent in which speech actually occurs" (p. 114). Here, contextualization, rethinking the "intent" of the speaker, and "institutional" considerations are all advocated in a way that hardly seems opposed to certain essential strategies of the Black Aesthetic paradigm.

To concentrate exclusively on the shortcomings and contradictions of Stepto's and Gates's work is to minimize their positive achievements. Both writers have suggested, in stimulating ways, that Afro-American literature can be incorporated into a contemporary universe of literary-theoretical discourse. True, the terms on which they propose incorporation amount in one instance to a theology of literacy and in the other to a mysterious semiotics of literary consciousness. Nonetheless, the very act of proposing that a sound, theoretical orientation toward an Afro-American literary tradition is necessary constitutes a logical second step for Stepto, Gates, and other reconstructionists to take after the paradigmatic establishment of that tradition by the Black Aesthetic.

Furthermore, Stepto and Gates are both better critics than theoreticians. They provide interpretations of texts that at times are quite striking (e.g., Gates's reflections on structuralism and his structuralist reading of *Narrative of the Life of Frederick Douglass*). In addition, neither is so imprisoned by his theoretical claims that he refuses to acknowledge the value of radically competing theories. For example, the essay by Sherley Anne Williams, "The Blues Roots of Contemporary Afro-American Poetry" (pp. 72–87), that appears in *Afro-American Literature* is based on Henderson's work and stands in direct contrast in its methodology to the stipulations on written, noninstitutional, literary art adduced by Stepto and Gates. And although Robert Hemenway, in his fine essay on Zora Neale Hurston's relationship to Afro-American folk processes (pp. 122–52), makes a gallant attempt to join the camp of Stepto and Gates, his work finally suggests the type of linguistic, expressive continuum implied by Henderson rather than the segmented model of Gates. Finally, Robert O'Meally's essay on Frederick Douglass's *Narrative* (pp. 192–211) is antithetical at every turn to Stepto's notion that critical literacy is a function of the reader's understanding of written metaphor, or inscribed instances of "poetic rhetoric *in isolatio*" (p. 9). O'Meally's agile contextualizing of Douglass's work within the continuum of Afro-American verbal behavior enables him to provide a reading of the work that suggests intertextual possibilities that are far more engaging than those suggested by Stepto's own reading of the *Narrative* (pp. 178–91).

In his editorial capacity, therefore, Stepto has rendered a service to the scholarly community by refusing to allow his own theory of the "literary" to foreclose inclusion of essays that contradict or sharply qualify his explicit claims. Unfortunately, he and his coeditor did not work as effectively in their choice of course designs—the models of "reconstructed" instruction toward which the whole of *Afro-American Literature* is directed (if we are to believe the volume's title). Briefly, the section entitled "Afro-American Literature Course Designs" reflects all of the theoretical confusions that have been surveyed heretofore. There are models for courses based on: weak distinctions between "literary" and "socio-historical" principles (p. 237); the assumption that literature is an "act" of language (p. 234); the notion that the "oral tradition is . . . a language with a grammar, a syntax, and standards of eloquence of its own" (p. 237); the idea that folk forms are "literary" genres (p. 246); and, finally, the assumption that "interdisciplinary" status can be attained merely by bringing together different forms of art rather than by summoning methods and models from an array of intellectual disciplines (pp. 250–55). The concluding course designs thus capture the novelty and promise, and the shortcomings, of the reconstructionist prospect. The types of distinctions, concerns, and endeavors they suggest are significant for the future study of Afro-American literature and verbal art. What they lack—sound theories of ordinary and literary discourse, an adequate theory of semantics, and a comprehensive theory of reading—will, I hope, be provided in time by scholars of Afro-American literature who are as persuaded as the reconstructionists that the Afro-American literary tradition can both withstand critical scrutiny and survive (as a subject of study) the limitations of early attempts at its literary-theoretical comprehension.

IX

In *Ideology and Utopia*, Karl Mannheim writes:

> To-day we have arrived at the point where we can see clearly that there are differences in modes of thought, not only in different historical periods but also in different cultures. Slowly it dawns upon us that not only does the content of thought change but also its categorical structure. Only very recently has it become possible to investigate the hypothesis that, in the past as well as the present, the dominant modes of thought are supplanted by new categories when the social basis of the group of which these thought-forms are characteristic disintegrates or is transformed under the impact of social change.[47]

The generational shifts analyzed in the foregoing discussion attest the accuracy of Mannheim's observation. The very notion of a "generational shift," as I have defined it, begins with the assumption that changes in the "categorical structure" of thought are coextensive with social change. The literary-theoretical goal of analyses deriving from the concept of generational shifts is a "systematic and total formulation" of problems in the study of Afro-American expressive culture. By investigating the guiding assumptions (the "categories" of thought, as it were) of recent Afro-American literary criticism, one can gain a sense of the virtues and limitations of what have stood during the past four decades as opposing generational paradigms.

What emerges from such an investigation is, first, a realization of the socially and generationally conditioned selectivity, or partiality, of such paradigms. They can be as meetly defined by their exclusions as by their manifest content. A determining feature of the scope of their Afro-American expressive cultural concerns is their relationship to AMERICA. There seems to be an inverse ratio between the weight and importance attached to the idea of AMERICA and the clarity of their theoretical vision of Afro-American vernacular inscriptions. The attempt to "impose unity [signaled by the traditional idea of AMERICA] upon an experience that changes too rapidly for linguistic or political exactitude" has resulted in sometimes egregious faults of omission and commission. Hence, the quasi-political rhetoric of the Black Aesthetic seems to compete (at the paradigm's weakest points) with the quasi-religious and semiotic jargon of reconstructionism for a flawed theoretical ascendancy.

Yet what also emerges from an investigation of generational shifts in recent Afro-American literary criticism is the sense that the study of Afro-American expressive culture has progressed during the past forty years to a point where some "systematic" formulation of theoretical problems is possible. The extremism and shortsightedness of recent generations have been counterbalanced, that is to say, by their dedication to analyses of expressive objects that did not even exist prior to the mid-1960s. The perceptual reorientations of recent generations have served as enabling conditions for a "mode of thought" that takes the theoretical investigation of a unique tradition or *Afro-American* expression as a normative enterprise.

My own preference where such theoretical investigations are concerned is the kind of holistic, cultural-anthropological approach implicit in the work of Henderson and other spokemen for the Black Aesthetic. This does not mean, however, that I would minimize the importance of reconstructionism's necessary and forceful call for serious literary-theoretical endeavors. Still, I am persuaded that the theoretical project that I designated the "anthropology of art" offers one fruitful approach to the study of Afro-American literature and culture.[48] The guiding assumption of the anthropology of art is coextensive with basic tenets of the Black Aesthetic insofar as both assert that works of Afro-American expressive culture cannot be adequately understood unless they are contextualized within the interdependent systems of Afro-American culture. But the anthropology of art *departs from both the Black Aesthetic and reconstructionism in its assumption that art cannot be studied without due attention to the methods and models of many disciplines.*

The contextualization of a work of expressive culture, from the perspective of the anthropology of art, is an "interdisciplinary" enterprise. Rather than ignoring or denigrating the research and insights of scholars in natural, social, and behavioral sciences, the anthropology of art views such efforts as positive attempts to comprehend the multiple dimensions of human behavior. Such efforts serve the investigator of expressive culture as guides and contributions to an understanding of symbolic dimensions of human behavior that comprise a culture's literature and verbal art.

Expressive culture, however, cannot be confined exclusively to a symbolic domain. Perhaps "confined" is not even the appropriate word here.

For what often occurs in the investigation of cultures is an aestheticizing of *all* seemingly anomalous or nonmaterial human products and events. In *The Mirror of Production*, Baudrillard captures the shortcomings of such investigations:[49]

> The limits of the materialist interpretation of earlier societies are the same. Those who have discovered primitive and savage arts have proved their good will and have shown all the luicidity one could ask about the art's originality and complexity. Without bias, they have attempted to "relocate" these "works" into their magical and religious "context." In the kindest yet most radical way the world has ever seen, they have placed these objects in a museum by implanting them in an esthetic category. But these objects are not art at all. And, precisely their non-esthetic character could at last have been the starting point for a *radical perspective* on (and not an *internal critical* perspective leading only to a broadened reproduction of) Western culture. [P. 89]

Though Baudrillard's disparagement is directed specifically at material analyses grounded in a vulgar Marxism, it could be speaking of *any* investigaion of expressive culture that fails to take account of its own conceptual limitations. To displace a bourgeois aesthetic theory that privileges art as a domain apart from normal production and exchange—for example, through a materialist theory that merely brackets "nonfunctional" aspects of culture as "magic," "religion," or "primitive art"—scarcely constitutes a theoretical advance. "Aestheticizing" and naive dualism still remain norms.

Hence, interdisciplinary study, whether it proceeds in symbolic *or* materialist terms, does not automatically guarantee the success of a theory. What is required is an investigator with both an interdisciplinary orientation *and* a tropologically active imagination—an imagination that ceaselessly compels the analyst to introduce tropes that effectively disrupt familiar conceptual determinations. Interdisciplinary study is necessary for the invention of effective tropes, for the investigator must bring to bear as many serviceable models and methods as possible.

Yet the discovery of effective tropes also requires that the investigator have an as yet underdetermined imaginative power. No one can lead an analyst of Afro-American culture, for example, to *discover* the effectiveness of blues, or storytelling, or the signifying monkey for a theory of black expression.[50] "Discovery"—in the tropological view—is not synonymous with learning through rational persuasion. It is akin to an adventurous act of play, or an energetic invention. The effective trope, one might say, is merely the lever long enough for the purpose. One must still risk the leap into space that discovers seemingly unlikely spots from which to move a familiar world.

Here I must add details about a recent and gratifying awareness of secular, folk traditions in Afro-America manifested by the current efforts of Henry Louis Gates, Jr., an erstwhile reconstructionist. Gates's wonderfully suggestive study of the Afro-American cultural practice of signifying—*The Signifying Monkey: Towards a Theory of Afro-American Literary Criticism*—reveals the addition of key imaginative metaphors to his own repertoire of analytical resources. In early sallies onto the folk landscape, Gates assumed that signifying was a form of "idiom," that is a subcomponent of *ordinary* black discourse. After due attention to the corpus of works—in a variety of disciplines—that have emerged from scholarly efforts during the past quarter century to bring Afro-American vernacular concerns into the foreground, Gates has now resituated his formulations in a framework that he pointedly calls the "black vernacular." From a dramatic and somewhat mystifying castigator of black critical thinking about the vernacular, he has become a convert to such thinking. I feel the conversion is salutary for a blues critique of American expressive cultural analysis.

Certainly *The Signifying Monkey* represents a significant move forward in Afro-American literary study. However, its lack of a self-conscious awareness of the politics of its stated myth of origins is troubling. The book's undeniable and enabling derivation from the Black Aesthetic prospect is bracketed by its author with all the cool silence of an Orwellian "re-write"—a quietness produced, I assume, by a strangely "professional" anxiety of influence. Briefly, while the actual explanatory model of Gates's work in the "vernacular" unequivocally reveals his acceptance of the insights of an immediately preceding generation, the curiously apolitical cast of his arguments manifests a continuing allegiance to a politics of professionalism characteristic of the reconstructionists. I believe he would no longer deny his critical parentage; but I believe he would cheerfully select a high cultural (or, high critical) history in describing his *ancestry*. As in all acts of blues criticism, however, we can improvisationally constrain the limitations of his model's politics by signifying on them. This can even be done in supremely self-conscious ways, as when Amiri Baraka playfully proffers his legacy:

> When I die, the consciousness I carry I will to black people. May they pick me apart and take the useful parts, the sweet meat of my feelings. And leave the bitter bullshit rotten white parts alone.

The necessity, in all paradigmatic blues analyses, is to leave the "bitter . . . rotten," and, one might add "overly professional or careerist" parts alone.

From my current space of observation, I want to suggest that a tropological mode—one duly informed by interdisciplinary attention to methods and models of various areas (including the material and economic) of intellectual inquiry—is akin to a blues mode of proceeding. The viability and energy of the blues derive from the bluesman's improvisational skill. When the "break" appears and voices and instruments drop to a quiet decrescendo and someone says "Let me hear you squall, boy, like you never squalled before!" the bluesman must be, in Albert Murray's apt phrase, "Nimble or not at all."[51] His effective performance depends on his knowledge of the tradition of which he is a part and his deft improvisational energies.

Similarly, an investigator of expressive culture gains much from the comprehension of traditional modes of cultural study, but when he is confronted with the "break" constituted by the job of specifying a distinctive tradition in all its resonant fullness, he must know the vernacular or "native" level of the tradition and then be improvisationally nimble enough to advance both the tradition itself and its clearer understanding. The improvisational dynamism of the blues analyst's work is a function of the rapidly changing character of all experience in the New World. There is a constant need for original and suggestive tropes to capture an ever changing American scene.

In today's "break," a blues matrix provides suggestive sound, vision, and space for expressive cultural theory. One can improvisationally posit, in fact, that any future concept of expressive culture in the space constituted by AMERICA in the New World will be informed by vernacular inscriptions that qualitatively alter an *idea* that has prevailed since 1492. The blues matrix—the fluid, mediating vernacular of the New World— enables one to understand that, rather than being a nation of strangers in search of Anglo-male domestication, AMERICA *has no strangers.*

> (There are, as yet, no norms that enough of the land's myriad inhabitants are willing to accept (or to admit, or to inscribe) as a final definition. Moreover, even if a consensus could be arrived at and set down in the propositional terms so familiar to our heritage, the words would always be mismatches. They would always fail to describe or arrest the processes that constitute an ever changing AMERICA—a land without strangers. There would always be a blues critic sitting at, perhaps, a Chehaw Station, tropologically prepared to sing in the break between propositional words and processual actuality, "I ain't no stranger, I been here before!"
>
> Finally, the analytical project that may serve as a paradigm for the future study of Afro-American literature and expressive culture is a vernacular model, one that finds apt figuration in the blues. A Black Aesthetic generation was the first paradigmatic community to demonstrate the efficacy of the vernacular for deciphering—or, far more accurately, enciphering—AMERICA.)

Three A Dream of American Form:
Fictive Discourse, Black (W)holes,
and a Blues Book Most Excellent

We all have had something in mind and we didn't want to talk about it to anybody, but the burden is real heavy until you could make some kinda sound about it, you could express yourself to somebody, sort of lighten the thing up.

> Henry Townsend, blues guitarist

But the real thing, the sequence of motion and fact which made the emotion and which would be as valid in a year or ten years or, with luck and if you stated it purely enough, always, was beyond me and I was working very hard to get it.

> Ernest Hemingway, *Death in the Afternoon*

The possibilities of music. First that it does exist. And that we do, in that scripture of rhythms. The earth, I mean the soil, as melody. The fit you need, the throes. To pick it up and cut away what does not singularly express.

> Amiri Baraka, "Leadbelly Gives an Autograph"

(Fr. verna: a slave born in his master's house; a native of uncertain origin. The song is native to the master's house; but its production is the result of slave labor. The song's origins (as all origins) are irretrievable. What is clear, though, is the difference between the slave's vernacular and the master's literature. A traveling blues summoning as metaphor a network spanning hundreds of thousands of American miles draws into a single harmonica's breath dimensions of New World experience undreamed by a master literature. To transmute blues into a form overruling the American artistic firmament is the dream of the laborer (read: the Afro-American writer).

The Afro-American writer seeks to transform originless song—a poetic script always already extant—into a black (w)hole appropriating and graphing multiple dimensions of indigenous experience. In order to understand his endeavor, one must initially refigure American literary hisory and then discover AMERICA's relationship to various prior forms of literary-critical and literary-theoretical discourse. Only the trained critic who emerges on the far side of such educational enterprise can discover narrative transformations and inscriptions of low moans and hollers, whoops and rolling basses,

113

high-pitched laments and sassy condemnations in the work of Afro-American expressive craftsmen.

Blues energies assume strikingly diverse and subtle figurations in the efforts of Afro-American writers. A white, yellow journalist may serve a turn-of-the-century author's vernacular ends, for example, as well as an Alabama sharecropper or a Mississippi black boy burning with desire serve the ends of mid-twentieth-century writers. Efforts expended to discover the Afro-American writer's blues transformations are, however, meetly compensated by the realization that stunning success has been achieved in one quintessential American endeavor.

By writing experience in native (read: blues) as opposed to literary language, Afro-American writers have accomplished the American task of journeying from mastered existence to independent, national form. The subtle, parodic, inversive, complexly reflexive blues texts of black writers testify to the vitality of an Afro-American matrix as they fulfill the longstanding dream of an American Form.

Adequately inventive readings of Afro-American vernacular texts augur as well for informed cultural explanation in America as the legendary train board at the depot's junction: I went to the station, looked up at the bo'de/It said good times here, better times up the road. *Better times, baby, on up the road.)*

The "Limitless" Freedom of Myth: Paul Laurence Dunbar's *The Sport of the Gods* and the Criticism of Afro-American Literature

Well, you see, Mr. Skaggs, none are so dull as the people who think they think.

The Sport of the Gods

I

On the basis of blues or vernacular figurations in Afro-American expressive culture, one assumes with Stephen Henderson and Robert Stepto that the theme of black liberation manifests itself in any authentically creative Afro-American literary work of art. On the basis of practical-critical and ideological insights derived from the refiguration of American literary history, one assumes further that classic works of Afro-American expressive culture will reveal a negotiation of the economics of slavery leading to black expressive wholeness. In the past, however, certain periods and authors of Afro-American expression have simply been written off as "assimilationist." These

This section is a revised version of my essay that appeared in *The American Self: Myth, Ideology, and Popular Culture*, ed. Sam B. Girgus (Albuquerque: University of New Mexico Press, 1981), pp. 124–43.

"assimilationist" moments in Afro-American expressive culture (e.g., Booker T. Washington's *Up from Slavery*) have been categorized as slavishly imitative and metaphorically impoverished occurrences. Generally, a historical explanation has been offered for such failures: Rough and racist times prevented genuine artistry.

But if one can legitimately assume that a blues matrix is the productive network the present study claims, then one can also legitimately assume that what appear unlikely expressive spaces in Afro-America may well be charged with blues energies. Another way of stating the proposition is to say that a properly trained critic—one versed in the vernacular and unconstrained by traditional historical determinants—may well be able to discover blues inscriptions and liberating rhythms even in some familiarly neglected works of Afro-American expressive culture. Who, after all, has dismissed such works? Normally, they have been written off by commentators (black and white alike) constrained by a single standard of criticism. Who is to decipher such neglected expressive instances? Surely, the blues critic is the most likely agent.

A case in point is Paul Laurence Dunbar's *The Sport of the Gods*, a novel published in 1901. This turn-of-the-century narrative, written by one of the most extraordinary artists to have lived in the United States, should indeed manifest liberation themes and structures common to classic works of Afro-American narrative. Moreover, as the product of a brilliantly energetic craftsman of the vernacular, *The Sport of the Gods* might be expected to contribute positively to a quest for expressive liberation in America—that is, to initiate in certain formal ways *a dream of American form*. There is such an initiatory impulse in Dunbar's novel. It gestures toward what I call "a blues book most excellent." An interpretive strategy grounded in the study of myth and fictive discourse helps to clarify the nature of Dunbar's blues achievement. It also provides a critique of critical practices and propositions that have hindered due acknowledgment of the *The Sport of the Gods*' significance.

In "Myth and Symbol,"[1] Victor Turner oberves:

> Myths and liminal rites are not to be treated as models for secular behavior. Nor, on the other hand, are they to be regarded as cautionary tales, as negative models which should not be followed. Rather are they felt to be high or deep mysteries which put the initiand temporarily into close rapport with the primary or primordial generative powers of the cosmos, the acts of which transcend rather than transgress the norms of human secular society. In myth is a limitless freedom, a symbolic freedom of action which is denied to the normbound incumbent of a status in a social structure. [P. 577]

Under the terms suggested by this observation, myth—that is, narratives explaining the origin and nature of the world by reference to the acts and intentions of supernatural beings—is to be distinguished from history. While myth draws attention to the divine origins of things, the pragmatic constraints of history direct attention to discrete sets of human circumstances that mark determinate events. However, it is the "symbolic freedom" of myth that most sharply distinguishes it from a traditional historical universe of discourse. The boundaries of a historical universe are coextensive with communicative ends.

Literary criticism, as a case in point, constitutes a historical domain. To achieve status as an accepted and learned critic one must transmit readily comprehensible messages to a historical (i.e., human, and defined implicitly as possessing determinate needs, habits, customs, etc.) audience. The role of recommending or commending works of literary art is thus historically situated. It relies for social efficacy on the "ordinary language" and traditional historical grounding of a human community.

Myth by contrast, and its various performances are unbounded by such historical parameters. It finds its conditions of possibility in an ahistorical symbolic universe of discourse. Denoting myth as a "transitional phenomenon," as an occurrence lying between two distinct social statuses, Turner further observes:

> What the initiand seeks through rite and myth is not a moral *exemplum* so much as the power to transcend the limits of his previous status, although he knows he must accept the normative restraints of his new status. Liminality [a transitional or marginal state] is pure potency, where anything can happen, where immoderacy is normal, even normative, and where the elements of culture and society are released from their customary configurations and recombined in bizarre and terrifying imagery. [P. 577]

It is, finally, this inversion through imagery, this countermanding of social norms by symbolic means, that governs the mythic universe of discourse. A similar form of symbolic freedom characterizes the literary domain. Mythic and literary acts, defined as instances of symbolic inversion, comprise different orders of phenomena from traditional, historical acts of literary criticism.

The distinctions just set forth between the historical and other domains are not a prelude to a new defense of poesy. Rather they are propositions designed to clarify a long-standing difficulty in the study of Afro-American literature. This difficulty consists (as I shall demonstrate shortly) in the propensity of critics to apprehend Afro-American works of verbal art exclusively as historical acts of language. Given the foregoing stipulations on criticism's historical orientation, such an approach scarcely seems anomalous. When pursued in isolation, however, a traditional sociohistorical orientation toward black expressive culture is too myopic and inhibiting to render adequate accounts of black art. For such an orientation normally dismisses, or neglects, the creative symbolic potency of Afro-American literary works of art.

By invoking the example of Dunbar's *The Sport of the Gods*, I want to suggest in the discussion that follows that an analysis of works of Afro-American literature which privileges their "symbolic freedom" can dramatically (and profitably) alter critical perspectives on such works. My fundamental assumption is that although mythic/literary and sociohistorical domains *are distinguishable, they are not mutually exclusive*. A Venn diagram would properly represent their area of overlapping circularity as an intersection containing the historically grounded critic as a mediator— as an agent who summons and interprets for a human audience the symbolic force of literary or mythic narratives. Such an ideally projected mediation, however, is contingent on what might be called a certain "clarity of expectations." The sine qua non for the mediational prospect I have in mind is an expectation on the part of the critic that a novel like *The Sport of the Gods* is capable of generating a symbolic, mythic, distinctively literary force irreducible to simple historical explanations. In order to arrive at this blues certainty, one must postulate the kinds of heuristic distinctions that appear in my foregoing remarks. Subsequently, one must strive to make the interpretive intersection—the mediational juncture—a crossing where new meanings are stunningly generated. This qualification, which implies the willing suspension of critical consciousness between two realms, suggests the criticism of Afro-American literature as a liminal enterprise. Today's critic, that is to say, is betwixt and between. He is bound to engage terms of a traditional historical criticism in order to demonstrate its limitations. At the same time, he is free to move decisively beyond the inadequacies of a past historical criticism and engage Afro-American expressive texts in their full symbolic potency. In a sense that I will define and explore in the concluding section of my discussion, the critic at the present time has a "limitless," liminal freedom akin to authorial prerogatives possessed by the creator of *The Sport of the Gods*.

II

Like those of the eighteenth-century Afro-American poet Phillis Wheatley, Paul Laurence Dunbar's life and works have normally been interpreted by critics as documentary evidence in what can be termed an ongoing historico-critical discourse. This discourse, which has the effect of a "state of the race" address, defines Afro-American literary works of art as covariant signs of a historical, racial "progress." The fundamental notion generated by this correlation is that a critic of Afro-American literature will discover ever more sophisticated works of verbal art as he or she follows a historical path leading from Afro-American slavery to a proclaimed freedom. A further entailment of the correlation is that critics should expect to read in Afro-American expressive works of any given historical moment a report on the state of the race at that time.

The logic of this traditional historico-critical approach to Afro-American literature sharply curtails the attention that is granted to such writers as Wheatley and Dunbar. An implicit claim of this approach is that recent twentieth-century works of black literature (being farthest removed from slavery) are more "advanced" and hence more worthy of attention than historically earlier productions. The logic of socio-historical criticism also includes the propostion that Afro-American literary texts (in their supposed historical reflexivity) directly mirror social, political, and psychological conditions prevailing in Afro-American culture at any given time. Critical pronouncements on Wheatley and Dunbar governed by such logic at best have provided interesting descriptions and summaries.[2] At worst, they have bequeathed a distressing legacy of half-truths and tendentious clichés.[3]

Situated at some distance from the heroic couplets of Wheatley, critics have often begun with the assertion that the black Boston poet's art does not merit serious investigation because there was no articulate, Afro-American literary tradition (presumably one with which the critic sympathizes) and little social, political, or psychological freedom among Afro-Americans during her era. Similar assumptions have marked the evaluation of Dunbar. Some critics have almost automatically assumed that during the nadir of race relations in turn-of-the-century America and unaided by sophisticated literary influences and opportunities enjoyed by his successors, Dunbar *could not* have produced literary works that deserve serious attention by today's scholars. When historico-critical analysts have deemed it worthwhile to venture criticism of Dunbar and Wheatley, they have almost always ended by detailing historical reports that they believe such authors convey—"messages" their works are alleged to communicate about a determinate historical context of emergence.

The historico-critical discourse just described has endured for many reasons. But it seems to me that the grammar holding it intact includes two principal elements—the awesome history of slavery in the United States and the blatant racism of American social life. The force of these principal aspects of American history has been so quintessential in shaping Afro-American life and culture that critics are led to the inference that acts of historical interpretation and acts of literary criticism must be coterminous. The effects and meanings of a novel such as *The Sport of the Gods* thus become determinate, historical phenomena rounding out the critic's reading of history. Any facet of the work that appears to lie beyond a historical interpretive framework is ignored, minimized, or neglected by the critic as

a function of his very determination to explain the novel in terms of a
bedrock historicity. In sum, traditional socio-historical criticism of Afro-
American literature not only has felt the weight of a specific history on its
shoulders, but also has been driven by a compulsive urge to yoke together
unique interpretations of history and historically determinate analyses of
literary works of art. This observation becomes clearer in view of actual
historico-critical estimates of *The Sport of the Gods*.

Robert Bone, as a first case in point, is clearly governed by an a priori
interpretive stance on Afro-American history when he renders the following judgment on *The Sport of the Gods*:

> ... at the height of the post-Reconstruction repression, with the Great
> Migration already under way, Dunbar was urging Negroes to stay in
> the South, where they could provide a disciplined labor force for the
> new plantation economy. His only fear was that the stream of young
> Negro life would continue to flow Northward, a sacrifice to "false
> ideals and unreal ambitions."[4]

Between the 1880s and the second decade of the twentieth century, more
than 2 million Afro-Americans did leave the South and migrate to northern and western states. As a result, there were, indeed, at least two
geographical regions of black life in America when *The Sport of the Gods*
was published. Since both regions are represented in the novel, Bone is
driven to conclude that he not only must take an interpretive stance on a
historic demographic shift among Afro-Americans but also must press
Dunbar's narrative into the service of his historical interpretation. His
sociohistorical design sweeps all before it, implying in its roughshod
course that the meaning of *The Sport of the Gods* can be referred to a
historical dichotomy between northern and southern, industrial and agrarian modes of existence in turn-of-the-century Afro-American life. The
historical bias of another critic, Kenny Jackson Williams, is not so obvious
as Bone's.[5] She situates her interpretive intention in the terminology of a
critical debate that has exhausted most of the present century in its attempt
to determine whether Afro-American writers are, have been, or should be
protest writers.[6] Williams concludes that *The Sport of the Gods* proves
that Dunbar was a protest writer, supplying in his novel a critique of the
"evil influences" the city exerts on black life. We are, of course, back at
square one. Williams's discussion carries us no farther than Bone's historical reading.

A third variation of the historico-critical method—which obviously
presents itself in myriad guises—situates its argument in an ideological
context. Addison Gayle, Jr., argues that Dunbar merely imitated "the old
Plantation Tradition" in creating *The Sport of the Gods*.[7] The ideological
context conditioning his argument is a Black Aesthetic one which insists

that Afro-American authors should create "positive" images and symbols of black life in order to promote the social "progress" of Afro-Americans. Gayle assures readers that Dunbar was unable to contribute to such an endeavor because he failed to transcend negative stereotypes cast by white authors of his era. Then, by a deduction implicit in his underlying interpretive design, Gayle asserts that *The Sport of the Gods* documents the fact that Afro-American migrants to the North were destined for tragedy in the cities because they, like the author of the novel, were helpless without white support and influence. We are again confronted by an inhibiting fascination with historical context. Gayle is bent on answering the question: Was Dunbar's authorial response to a determinate set of historical circumstances in accord with *my* (Black Aesthetic) interpretation of Afro-American history?

When T. S. Eliot wrote of "cunning passages" and "contrived corridors" of history perhaps he had in mind the difficulty human beings face in resisting the allure of seemingly adequate historical explanations. Certainly the critics just discussed are so impelled by their desire to unravel the "supple confusions" of history that they repeatedly yoke history to their interpretive accounts of *The Sport of the Gods*. Their expectations of the novel are conditioned at a generative level by their assumption that it is at least implicitly a *historical* document. The irony of their expectations is that the historical allure is a priori justifying false expectations and resulting in critical accounts that seem to justify a desire for historical explanation. What one notes, therefore, is self-fulfilling prophecy—the solacing embrace of a tautological circle. A remark from Wittgenstein's lectures on aesthetics describes succinctly the type of cognitive activity at work among those who take *The Sport of the Gods* and other Afro-American expressive texts as narratives continuous with an historico-critical universe of discourse. Discussing Freud's theory of dreams—particularly the notion that all dreams are reducible to psychosexual explanation—Wittgenstein says:

> The attraction of certain kinds of explanation is overwhelming. At a given time the attraction of a certain kind of explanation is greater than you can conceive. In particular, explanation of the kind "This is really only this." There is strong tendency to say: "We can't get round the fact that this dream is really such and such." . . . If someone says: "Why do you say it is really this? Obviously it is not this at all," it is in fact even difficult to see it as something else.[8]

We can rephrase these remarks in terms of the present discussion to suggest that the claim that Afro-American literary texts are "really only" historical documents has an irresistible explanatory charm. It is extremely difficult—given this charm—for critics to regard such texts in any other way. Perceptions are always functions of hypotheses or theories that one finds persuasive. The only way one decides that an object, event, process (or novel) is not what one had taken it to be is by assuming a different hypothetical or theoretical orientation.

The first chapter of the present study suggests a possible alternative to the traditional historical orientation implied by the immediately foregoing remarks. Roland Barthes describes the primary effect of historical discourse as a *reality effect*, noting that the semantics of historical discourse are always confined to two terms *referent* and *expression*.[9] Confusion exists in the entire historical project, however, insofar as historians refuse to substitute *meaning* for referent. There is no such thing as an "objective" history whose windows open beyond discursive structures onto a meaningfully ordered sequence of human events. Instead, there is only meaningful discourse called "history"; it exists because human events—quite random, one supposes, in their occurrence—have been *meaningfully* ordered by a historical observer. Rather than as a *real* substrate on which literary critical analyses can be grounded, the critic should view history as a discourse conditioned by discoverable laws of formation. Further, any traditional historical discourse should be analyzed to determine precisely where its boundaries of exclusion lie. The enduring mistake of past critics of Afro-American verbal art such as *The Sport of the Gods* has been to reinscribe, at the very outset of their endeavors, the contours of a traditional American history.

Excluded from such history, of course, is the very possibility that sophisticated verbal art is an *always already present* feature of the Afro-American landscape. Traditional American literary history, as my earlier discussion in Chapter 1 makes clear, has repeatedly bracketed this always already present feature of Afro-America under the category "non-art." The Integrationist Poetics of Afro-American critics themselves have ironically validated such a categorization.

Hence, when recent critics like Bone, Williams, and Gayle have approached *The Sport of the Gods* from a *historical* orientation, there has been absolutely no opportunity for them to discover vibrant and inversive blues energies. The "realistic" grounding of their analyses excludes the possibility of such a discovery. Only a radically altered discursive prospect—one that dramatically dissociates itself from the "real"—can provide access to the blues artistry of Dunbar's novel. In a sense that will become clear in my subsequent discussion, what disappears in such an altered perspective is traditional history's trope of the simple-minded, passive, migratory, black victim hopelessly cut off from nurturing (though paradoxically subjugating) southern roots and inarticulately stranded in the urban North. The trope of an assimilationist northern Afro-American "coon singer" lamenting the loss of "old cotton fields back home" also fades. What replaces such figures is a vision of the liminal and inversive creator aware of a sharp dilemma and determined to express it in articulate form. A critical orientation that looks, not to real history, but to the limitless freedom of myth and fictive discourse offers the "unreal" prospect that I have in mind. This orientation gives rise to an intriguing trope of the *blues detective* in the course of its energetic work.

III

Mythic and literary acts of language are not intended or designed for communicative ends. Rather than informational or communicative utterances that assure harmonious normalcy in human cultures such linguistic acts are radically contingent events whose various readings or performances occasion inversive symbolic modes of cognition and other extraordinary human responses. Considered in these terms, *The Sport of the Gods* must be taken as a phenomenon different in kind from the communicative, historical document. The novel's conditions of existence under a mythic or fictive prospect are found, not in the determinate (or existentially determinable) circumstances of a historical moment, but in what Jonathan Culler calls "the institution of literature."[10] What is implied by Culler's phrase is not the treasured disjunction between "literature" and "life" of traditional aesthetics. An "institution" is a conventional or systematic behavioral pattern valued by a human community. To define literature as an institution, therefore, is to situate it directly "in life," focusing on the systematic linguistic behavior conventionally entailed among human beings by a particular kind of discourse. The justification for concentrating on language resides in the fact that literary works of art are inscribed in language. Additionally, the linguistic behaviors associated with literary discourse are, in my view, different from those surrounding speech in familiar everyday contexts. The manner in which performative speech acts function in ordinary discourse offers a case in point.[11]

When I say to a friend, "I promise that I will come to your party," I have performed a specific action. My utterance is historically determinate. When the party takes place my friend expects my attendance. When, however, a character in a novel, or the speaker of a poem or play says: "A distant relative of mine once had a great grief. I have never recovered from it," we do not assume that a historical action has been *performed*, nor do we go in search of a death certificate or a report of an actual disaster. We assume that the fictive or dramatic speaker's remarks (those of Sadness, a character in *The Sport of the Gods*, in this instance) offer a *representation* of the act of speaking and that the utterance, like the unfortunate relative, is historically indeterminate.[12]

In *The Theory of Literary Criticism*, John Ellis provides a broad description of what might be termed the audience expectations that surround literary language, or acts of literature:[13]

> When . . . we treat a piece of language as literature, we characteristically do something quite surprising: we no longer accept any information offered as something to act upon, nor do we act on its exhortations and imperatives. We do not generally concern ourselves with whether what it says is true or false, or regard it as relevant to any specific practical purpose. In sum we no longer respond to it as part of the immediate context we live in and as something to use in our normal way as a means of controlling that context; nor do we concern ourselves with the immediate context from which it emerged, and so [we] are not taking it up to learn, in our normal way, something about that actual everyday context. [P. 43]

Ellis's observations set literary texts apart both from the historical moment of their emergence and from the utilitarian, communicative ends of everyday language. They suggest, therefore, a sui generis institutional status for a work like Dunbar's *The Sport of the Gods*, a status that argues well for the analytical potential of a criticism that seeks the nonhistorical, mythic, or blues force of the narrative.

It would be a mistake of some magnitude, however, to allow the distinctions just adduced to stand unqualified by mention, at least, of the playfully brilliant critique of speech act philosophy rendered by Jacques Derrida in his engaging essay "Limited Inc."[14] Furthering the poststructuralist project's end of deconstructing Western philosophy's traditional privileging of *speech* and the speaker's *presence*, Derrida points out that a speech act in ordinary discourse (a performative) is only possible through reliance on already extant conventions of language. Hence, such an act is both a function of script (or "writing") *and* repeatable. The performative—an act in which speaker, intention, and voice all seem to be unequivocally present, determinate, and historically situated—is, in fact, an act parasitic upon a conventional script.

Since the "mark" (any instance of language use), according to Derrida, "*must be able* to function in the absence of the sender, the receiver, the context of production, etc., . . . [then] this *being able*, this *possibility* is *always* inscribed, hence *necessarily* inscribed *as possibility* in the functioning or the functional structure of the mark" (p. 184). The presence and historical determinacy of the performative are parasitic upon the iterability—the implicit function-in-"absence"—of the mark. To suggest, therefore, that performatives of ordinary discourse are distinct from utterances of fictive discourse on the grounds of presence and absence would be naive.

Instead I want to suggest an axiological division between the two types of utterances. Following Ellis's lead, I wish to claim for purposes of this discussion that the use value of performatives is *generally* a communicative one while that of fictive utterances is *generally* more ludic or mythic. The distinction between modes of discourse that I am seeking might be said to reside in the axiology of speaking rather than its ontology. But even here, it would be naive to define "communication" as a commonsense enterprise divorced from (rather than continuous with) ludic or fictive uses of language. Nonetheless, I think a profitably altered critical orientation results when Dunbar's work is situated in relation to a fictive or mythic mode of discourse that is heuristically held to stand in opposition to ordinary, historically conditioned modes of discourse. Such an orientation directs attention immediately to the title of the 1901 novel.

The title finds its meaning, not in the historically documented betrayals and confusions of American Reconstruction, but in the domain of literature. The blinded and deceived Gloucester of Shakespeare's drama *King Lear* remarks: "As flies to wanton boys are we to the Gods;/They kill us for their sport." The origin and nature of the world, this utterance implies, are functions of capricious supernaturals. The mythic universe of discourse is thus invoked in explanation of man's failings: Man is nothing special. He is a toy in the ludic world of the gods. While the title alone suggests *The Sport of the Gods'* association with Gloucester's mythic view of human events, the concluding line of the novel's narrator suggests an even more direct parallel. The novel ends as follows: "It was not a happy life [that of the black servant Berry Hamilton and his wife, who have returned to the South], but it was all that was left to them, and they took it up without complaint for they knew they were powerless against some Will infinitely stronger than their own."[15] An apotheosized Will "infinitely stronger" than human powers can only exist in a world of myth.

The "limitless" freedom of myth and its efficacy as a causal explanation in human affairs, however, exist in the works of both the Renaissance dramatist and the Afro-American novelist as ironic postulates. There may well be powerful, invisible beings in the wings, but the reader of *King Lear* is aware that the play's sufferings and deaths have more to do with distinctively human shortcomings than with the ludic wielding of authority by immortals. That Gloucester, whose incredible folly is matched only by that of his aged counterpart Lear, is the character who offers "the sport of the Gods" as explanation reinforces a reader's decision to concentrate on human agents and actions in understanding Shakespeare's drama. Similarly, having followed the controlling voice of the narrator from the first to the concluding line of *The Sport of the Gods*, a reader knows there is little need to summon incomprehensible supernatural powers to explain the human affairs represented in the novel.

The characters of Dunbar's work are, finally, victims of their own individual modes of processing reality. Their failings are paradoxical results of their peculiarly human ability (and inclination) to form theories of knowledge, to construct what Walter Pater calls in *The Renaissance* "habits of thought." The narrator's recourse to what seems a mythic dimension (an invincible "Will"), therefore, like Gloucester's evocation of the Gods in *Lear*, not only stands in ironic contrast to the novel's representations of a mundane reality but also suggests (as I shall discuss later) an authorial awareness on Dunbar's part crucial to a full, blues understanding of his narrative.

The Sport of the Gods is the story of a theft. During a social gathering in honor of Maurice Oakley's younger half-brother Francis, the latter reports that a substantial sum of money loaned him by Maurice and intended for his artistic education has disappeared. Oakley's black servant, Berry Hamilton, is accused of the theft, convicted, and sentenced to ten years at hard labor. His wife Fannie and his two children are forced to relocate in New York. His son Joe becomes involved with a Broadway chorus girl and finally murders her. His daughter Kit, meanwhile, rises to celebrity as a Broadway chorus girl. Fannie Hamilton enters an ill-fated bigamous marriage with a "race horse man" named Gibson. Oakley's world, in the interim, is shattered by a letter from Francis. The half-brother, and self-styled artist, confesses in the letter to having gambled away the money loaned by Maurice. In the name of "Southern honor" and to protect the reputation of his family, Frank reported the gambling loss as a theft. Prompted by the same code of honor, Oakley refuses to reveal Frank's confession to the world. He becomes an obsessed man, carrying the letter of confession inside his shirt, clutching to his bosom what he refers to as his "secret." It is Skaggs, a man described as a "monumental liar," who goes South, plays detective, wrests the secret from Oakley's bosom, and obtains Berry Hamilton's release. The black servant and his wife are reunited and returned to their former cottage on the Oakley estate. Maurice Oakley is now completely insane. His wild shrieks serve as sound effects for the novel's concluding tableau: the black couple sits alone forlornly clasping hands, listening to the cries of a white madman.

It is tempting, in view of this summary, to label Dunbar's novel a minor Southern romance, salvage what one can of historical import, and move on. I have already suggested, though, that such an approach forecloses the possibility of an adequate understanding of the work. The act of theft, which is central to the story, for example, cannot be comprehended in its textual implications unless one deciphers the narrative's implicit view of human understanding. *The Sport of the Gods* is essentially a discourse on the fallibility of human habits of thought. Maurice Oakley offers a case in point.

Considering himself a shrewd businessman beyond the reach of sentimentality, Oakley takes what he considers a rational position on his servant's alleged theft. He says: "I shall not condemn any one until I have proof positive of his guilt or such clear circumstantial evidence that my reason is satisfied" (p. 25). Only the flimsiest "circumstantial evidence"— the facts that Hamilton has more than the amount of the reported theft in a savings account and has easy access to the half-brother's bedroom—is available. Yet it is sufficient to convince the master of the servant's guilt. Indeed, Oakley's vaunted empiricism and proclaimed analytical bent are no more than linguistic masks. They are verbal shows concealing a sentimental and prejudiced ("no servant is beyond suspicion," he says; p. 25) fantast. Having received the envelope containing Frank's confession from Paris, he pauses before opening it to weave elaborate fantasies of his half-brother's triumphs:

> First, now, it might be a notice that Frank had received the badge of the Legion of Honour. No, no, that was too big, and he laughed aloud at his own folly, wondering the next minute, with half shame, why he laughed, for did he, after all, believe anything was too big for that brother of his? Well, let him begin, anyway, a way down. Let him say, for instance that the letter told of the completion and sale of a great picture. . . . His dreams were taking the shape of reality in his mind, and he was believing all that he wanted to believe. [Pp. 183–85]

When such musings are shattered by the contents of Frank's letter, Oakley has no way of processing reality. His mental operations are at an end. Bereft of a governing fancy, he goes completely mad, weeping "like a child whose last toy has been broken" (p. 194).

The black servant who suffers the consequences of Oakley's weak intellect is a man falsely accused. The text, however, does not grant Berry Hamilton the status of noble victim. Instead, the narrative implies that the servant has been as governed by illusion as his master. Berry has conducted his life based on an ideal of frugal, convivial Christian respectablity that he assumes is the moving force of the southern white world. He feels that by living in harmony with this ideal, he can transcend the limits that constrain black life in his community. He thus sets his goals and establishes his own "fictional finalisms."[16] However, he fails to take account of the nearly mindless state of Maurice Oakley and the class of ruling whites to which he belongs. In the servant's view, the world of the masters represents "quality." "It's de p'opah thing," he says, "fu' a man what waits on quality to have quality mannahs an' to waih quality clothes" (pp. 4–5). The paradoxical result of his idealism is that he is sentenced to ten years at hard labor in return for a life of industrious thrift. Ironically, the bank account that signals adherence to an ideal is the circumstantial evidence which condemns him.

The existence of the "theft" that disrupts the Oakley estate is contingent on a quite fragile southern psychological economy. A prejudicial fantasy and an infirm idealism supply its conditions of possibility. And Oakley's mode of processing experience is so prevalent among his fellow whites and so forceful as a mode of explanation that not a single person of "quality" is capable of realizing that Hamilton is not "really" a thief. The town readily concurs with Oakley that Hamilton could not have accumulated thirteen hundred dollars by honest means, even though the servant had "no rent to pay and no board to pay. His clothes came from his master, and Kitty and Fannie looked to their mistress for the larger number of their supplies. . . . Fannie herself made fifteen dollars a month, and . . . for two years Joe had been supporting himself" (p. 57). The narrator interjects that these aspects of Hamilton's situation did not "come up" in discussions of the alleged theft.

Later in the narrative, the narrator reflects on a clear and balanced empiricism's failure to prevail against the epistemologies of both the master's and the servant's communities. "In vain the lawyer whom he [Berry] had secured showed that the evidence against him proved nothing. In vain he produced proof of the slow accumulation of what the man had. In vain he pleaded the man's former good name. The judge and the jury saw otherwise. Berry was convicted" (pp. 61–62). The black townspeople respond in the manner of their white overlords. There is an immediate audit of the books Berry has kept as treasurer of his lodge, the Tribe of Benjamin. The black A.M.E. church expels him from membership. Finally, Berry's own response to events surrounding him is not unlike Oakley's to his brother's letter: "The shock had been too sudden for him, and it was as if his reason had been for the time unseated" (p. 58).

In the fictional world established by a theft in *The Sport of the Gods*, men and women are undone by limited and limiting modes of conception. They are incapable of seeing any object, person, or event steadily and whole because their cognitive strategies enable only a partial view. At its most absurd, this human inadequacy is represented by the denizens of the Continental Hotel. Horace Talbot, Beachfield Davis, and Colonel Saunders gather at the "Continental" (a devastatingly ironic label of sophistication in view of their discourse) to drink and discuss both current concerns and events of the southern past. The adequacy of their apprehension reveals itself in the three cronies' reflections on Afro-Americans. Talbot advances what he calls his "theory" that blacks are irrepressible children unprepared for "higher civilization." They have been mistakenly liberated from their bondage, according to Talbot, by well-intentioned northerners. "Why gentlemen," he intones, "I foresee the day when these people themselves shall come to us Southerners of their own and ask to be re-enslaved until such time as they shall be fit for freedom" (p. 57).

Beachfield Davis, by contrast, suggests that blacks suffer a condition of "total depravity." His evidence is the fact that one of his servants, on a fateful evening in the southern past, used Davis's finely bred hound for possum hunting. Finally, Colonel Saunders's epistemological mettle is displayed when he retracts even a speculative remark that Hamilton may be innocent. The three occupants of the Continental are parodic representations of "choice spirits of the old régime" (p. 220). They are men who pride themselves on a manner of ordering experience which, in fact, blinds them to their patent absurdity. Even Oakley, who is one of their number, refers to them as "a lot of muddle-pated fools" (p. 187).

The black counterparts of such unknowing whites are found in New York's "Banner Club." The establishment, as represented in *The Sport of the Gods*, is the white southern Continental Hotel's northern black analogue. Pretense, self-deception, masking, and indolence are normative behaviors at the Banner Club. It is here that Berry's son Joe meets Hattie Sterling, who is anything but "sterling." Hattie is an aging chorus girl, but her fast-disappearing physical beauty is sufficiently masked to attract the young man's idolatry: "nothing could keep her from being glorious in his eyes,—not even the grease-paint which adhered in unneat patches to her face, nor her taste for whiskey in its unreformed state. He gazed at her in ecstasy" (p. 125).

Joe has been primed for his ecstatic response to cosmetic beauty by experiences among young Southern whites of "quality": "Down home he had shaved the wild young bucks of the town, and while doing it drunk in eagerly their unguarded narrations of their gay exploits. So he had started out with false ideals as to what was fine and manly. He was afflicted by a sort of moral and mental astigmatism that made him see everything wrong" (p. 100).

Like his father, Joe is undone by his adoption of what he perceives as a suitable standard of conduct. When he finally realizes that naive enthusiasm and a sense of triumph in gaining Hattie's attention have played him false, he becomes a "Frankenstein." Having been manipulated and shaped by deceptive ideals, Joe is driven to murder. His state of mind when apprehended by the police is described: "there was no spirit or feeling left in him. He moved mechanically as if without sense or volition. The first impression he gave was that of a man over-acting insanity" (p. 210). When the boy's fragile world of illusion is shattered, he falls an easy victim to madness.

Kitty and Fannie Hamilton fare little better than Joe in their own habits of thought. The daughter's response to her first view of the New York stage is one of enchantment:

> The airily dressed women seemed to her like creatures from fairy-land. It is strange how the glare of the footlights succeeds in deceiving so

many people who are able to see through other delusions. The cheap dresses on the street had not fooled Kitty for an instant, but take the same cheese-cloth, put a little water starch in it, and put it on the stage, and she could only see chiffon. [P. 102]

Kitty's understanding is fixed in this narrative moment. Her vision and sympathies never extend beyond her own theatrical world. Her response to Joe's plight is ungenerous: "She felt the shame of it keenly, and some of the grief. To her, coming as it did just at a time when the company was being strengthened and she more importantly featured than ever, it was decidedly inopportune, for no one could help connecting her name with the affair" (p. 215). After a grudging gesture of support, she retreats entirely into a narcissistic world marked by her life as a chorus girl. She seems an ironic avatar of Hattie Sterling:

> Miss Kitty Hamilton had to be very careful about her nerves and her health. She had had experiences, and her voice was not as good as it used to be and her beauty had to be aided by cosmetics. So she went away from New York, and only read of all that happened [in Joe's trial and sentencing] when some one called her attention to it in the papers. [P. 217]

The matriarch of the Hamiltons, unlike her daughter, retains a staunch Christian faith that produces a charitable view of human events. The gullibility that this view occasions is almost unimaginable. She reports to Kitty the words of her suitor, Tom Gibson:

> He say dat I ain't noways ma'id [married] to my po' husban', dat a pen'tentiary sentence is de same as a divo'ce, an' if Be'y should live to git out, we'd have to ma'y [marry] ag'in. I would n't min' dat, Kit, but he say dat at Be'y's age dey ain't much chanst of his livin' to git out, an' heyeah I'll live all dis time alone, an' den have no one to tek keer o' me w'en I git ol'. [P. 168]

Fannie's dialect is but another means of representing her fidelity to the values of a provincial, black southern existence. The irony of her plight is that she sets these black, southern values and her Christian charity against a pressing economic necessity. Economics triumphs, hands down. That Fannie has no cognitive resources for anticipating the consequences of her choice of Gibson becomes clear in the penultimate scene of *The Sport of the Gods*: she describes her relationship with the man as one of fear and brutalization.

The unfortunate ends to which the characters come in Dunbar's novel are the logical outcome of their misguided modes of apprehending the world. The narrator of the novel, however, does not situate such human failing in a single geographical locale, nor does he suggest that it is solely a function of unalterable and determinate sets of historical events. Men and women in the city are as prone to misapprehension of experience as those in the country. The events of an implied historical progression (the "old days") may have left a legacy of inexact ideas and fragile ideals; nonetheless, human life is not helplessly shackled to these false historical constructs. Release from erroneous habits of thought can be secured in a realm that transcends an ordinary course of human affairs.

The redemptive area of transcendence is suggested by the first line of *The Sport of the Gods*, which offers the implicit subject of the entire narrative: "*Fiction* has said so much in regret of the old days when there were plantations and overseers and masters and slaves, that it was good to come upon such a household as Berry Hamilton's, if for no other reason than that it afforded a relief from the monotony of tiresome iteration" (p. 1, my emphasis). From the outset, one is alerted that Dunbar's text is a "fiction" whose implied goal is to avoid a monotonous iteration of traditional patterns of narrative. One might say, therefore, that the novel signals a subversive intent in its very first fictive utterance. The oft-repeated narrative pattern that it wishes to subvert has been called the "Plantation Tradition."[17]

Briefly, the Plantation Tradition consists of white American literary works that project a southern ideal based on a somewhat ad hoc model of the enlightened Greek city-state. In order to achieve the tradition's fictively projected ideal, southern society must be divided into discrete classes with white masters at the helm, black slaves in the galley, and all voyagers aware of the boundaries and duties of their respective positions. Shored up by Walter Scott's romantic chivalry, the plantation prospect produced literary narratives that represent kind masters, gracious manor houses, chastely elegant southern belles, and obediently happy dark servants who are given to a life of mindless labor and petty high jinks. The Plantation Tradition originated before the Civil War in the works of authors like James Kirke Paulding and John Pendleton Kennedy, and its products have found an enduring space in American letters.

The Sport of the Gods addresses itself to this tradition, representing it as a southern mode of cognition. Southern art and attitudes toward art are implicit evidence of American modes of processing reality. The interaction between Maurice Oakley and his brother Frank suggests a case in point. The relationship between the kinsmen implies an alliance between a naive southern capitalism and a romantic, European-oriented art that gives rise to fantastic readings of human events.

Frank, the younger half-brother, is repeatedly referred to as "the artist." His abilities, however, are always suspect in the narrator's view, and hence in the eyes of the reader as well. The young Frank is an inhabitant of Paris's Latin Quarter, and his immanent greatness is a matter of faith only to the

businessman Oakley and his wife Leslie. The following exchange captures
the relationship of the three characters:

> FRANK: Whether I fail or succeed, you will always think well of me,
> Maurice? And if I don't come up to your expectations, well—
> forgive me—that's all.

> MAURICE: You will always come up to my expectations, Frank. Won't
> he, Leslie?

> MRS. OAKLEY: He will always be our Frank, our good, generous-
> hearted, noble boy. God bless him! [P. 37]

The Oakleys expect their "generous-hearted" relation, who is off to study
in the bohemian schools of Paris, eventually to "settle in America" (p. 12)
and marry the southern heiress Claire Lessing. We are told by the narrator,
however, that "the artist," so revered by his kinsmen, is "always trembling
on the verge of a great success without quite plunging into it" (p. 10). And
the ironic undertone that marks this comment is heightened by the following description of Frank's physical bearing: "He had the face and brow of
a poet, a pallid face framed in a mass of dark hair. There was a touch of
weakness in his mouth, but this was shaded and half hidden by a full
mustache that made much forgiveable to beauty-loving eyes" (p. 11).

In sum, there are adequate reasons for distrusting the strength, ability,
and integrity of this artist named "Frank." As a man whose only product
so far is a picture above Oakley's mantle—a work combining a "woman's
soul and the strength of a man" (p. 186)—the half-brother reveals himself
as anything but ingenuous. The southern capitalist, Maurice, and the
southern heir to the type of capitalist fortune he represents, Claire Lessing
(diminishing light?), have simply been deceived by a charming surface
view which Frank presents to white southern society.

The artist, in fact, seems to represent for Oakley and his class the
elevation of southern, agrarian industry to the peaks of a European or
cultured acclaim. His confessional letter, however, reveals him as "a liar
and a thief" (p. 192). By inference, I want to suggest that the The Sport of
the Gods moves from its announced subject of "fiction" to an implicit
reductio ad absurdum of the Plantation Tradition. The desire of Oakley
and his confreres to elevate their provincial mode of life through art fosters
a pallid and deceptive southern romanticism. The reciprocal relationship
between the bourgeoisie of the South and the idealizing artist is ultimately
responsible for the true theft in the novel. And it is Berry Hamilton's
liberty and rightful earnings that are the genuine objects of theft. The
appropriation of these items by a bizarre system of southern justice is a

corollary of the distorted perception that both sanctions and gains support from a Plantation Tradition.

The "surplus value" accumulated by the black servant is seen by the South as a theft. Basing its conviction of the servant's guilt on prevailing stereotypes of an idealizing fiction, the town is incapable of perceiving a genuine American theft. Oakley offers a parodic illustration of the town's fictively conditioned myopia when he says:

> . . . as soon as a negro like Hamilton learns the value of money and begins to earn it, at the same time he begins to covet some easy and rapid way of securing it. The old negro knew nothing of the value of money. When he stole, he stole hams and bacon and chickens. These were his immediate necessities and things he valued. [P. 26]

The implication, of course, is that an Afro-American who honestly appropriates values that lie beyond subsistence—that lie beyond the "happy-servitor" status prescribed for blacks by the Plantation Tradition—is "unthinkable." The art in which Oakley and his class place their faith supports such a staunch southern ignorance. In a striking indictment, the black servant is represented as the hapless victim of *a fiction*. When he leaves prison, the extent of the novel's real theft is apparent: "All the higher part of him he [Berry] had left behind, dropping it off day after day through the wearisome years. He had put behind him the Berry Hamilton that laughed and joked and sang and believed, for even his faith had become only a numb fancy" (p. 243).

As integral to the narrative strategy of *The Sport of the Gods* as the work's indictment of the Plantation Tradition is its critique of Afro-American popular art in the North. On the day the Hamiltons arrive in New York, their landlady suggests an evening on the town. "Why, yes," says one of the occupants of the rooming house, "what's the matter with tomorrer night? There's a good coon show in town. Out o'sight. Let's all go" (p. 94). In *Black Magic: A Pictorial History of Black Entertainers in America*,[18] Langston Hughes and Milton Meltzer write:

> Slowly [at the turn of the twentieth century] the tradition of minstrel exaggerations began to give way to a non-blackface pattern in negro musicals which incorporated large choruses of pretty girls. At first, however, these shows were not termed musicals. They were called "coon shows" in contrast to the minstrels and Tom shows.

While Hughes and Meltzer consider such shows the "groundwork for public acceptance of Negro women and of the Negro male on the stage in other than bulresque fashion,"[19] the narrator of *The Sport of the Gods* characterizes them as theatricals combining "tawdry music and inane words" (p. 102). Their audiences are described as "swaggering, sporty young negroes" (p. 100) who move about as though they were "owners" of the shows. Kitty is represented in the novel as dropping "the simple old songs she knew to practise the detestable coon ditties which the stage demanded" (p. 130). The coon show, therefore, is finally as emblematic of black modes of perception in the North as the Plantation Tradition is of white understanding in the South.

At their first show, all the Hamiltons capitulate to the vision of life that it represents. Kitty gives way to the enchantment noted earlier. Joe is not only impressed by the pomp and swagger of the male audience, but also by the appearance of the chorus women: "His soul was floating on a sea of sense. He had eyes and ears and thoughts only for the stage. His nerves tingled and his hands twitched. Only to know one of those radiant creatures, to have her speak to him, smile at him. If ever a man was intoxicated, Joe was" (pp. 102–3). Mrs. Hamilton is at first reserved, but she gives way finally before the vigor of the performance:

> At first she was surprised at the enthusiasm over just such dancing as she could see any day from the loafers on the street corners down home, and then, like a good, sensible, humble woman, she came around to the idea that it was she who had always been wrong in putting too low a value on really worthy things. So she laughed and applauded with the rest, all the while trying to quiet something that was tugging at her away down in her heart. [Pp. 105–6]

The symbolic force of the coon show is reflected not only by the narrative careers of Joe and Kitty (a lover of a chorus girl and a chorus girl, respectively) but also by remarks of "sermonizers" on the plight of all blacks who migrate to New York. Such sermonizers, the narrator tells us, "wanted to preach to these people that good agriculture is better than bad art,—that it was better and nobler for them to sing to God across the Southern fields than to dance for rowdies in the Northern halls" (p. 213).

All northern black life, *The Sport of the Gods* implies, is a stage—the province of a gaudy coon show. And human lives guided by such a "tawdry" means of processing experience contrast markedly with lives governed by what the novel labels the "old teachings and old customs" (p. 152) of black southern life. The irony of the contrast is that "customs" and "teachings" associated with singing to God "across the Southern fields" have provided no security in the lives of the Hamiltons, nor have they in *any* sense enabled the family to withstand the allure of a northern coon show in all its gaudy deception. Even more ironic, of course, is the fact that the coon-show representations that so enchant the family are not substantially different from representations of the white Plantation Tradition. The opening scene of the show the Hamiltons attend presents jovial, energetic black picnickers on holiday, singing their tawdry contentment to the world's delight. The turn-of-the-century black theatrical, then, is hardly an art—a means of understanding life—that can redeem the theft sanctioned by plantation fiction.

What is needed to redeem the theft, *The Sport of the Gods* makes clear, is a new "idea," a new theory that will produce a dramatically different reading of life. Mr. Skaggs, the novel's yellow journalist, is the character who arrives at such an idea. Hearing Joe drunkenly speak of a theft, Skaggs "was all alert. He scented a story" (p. 204). When his hypothesis that Joe is a thief himself proves erroneous, he says to an inhabitant of the Banner Club: "I confess I am disappointed, but I've got an idea, just the same." His "idea" is that he can uncover the genuine theft and, in his role as a writer, set things right in print. He slowly nurtures this idea: ". . . that idea had stayed with him. . . . He thought and dreamed of it until he had made a working theory. Then one day, with a boldness that he seldom assumed when in the sacred Presence [of his editor at the New York *Universe*], he walked into the office and laid his plans before the editor" (p. 218).

What Skaggs's theory amounts to is a speculative ordering of bold propositions. The editor calls it "a rattle-brained, harum-scarum thing" (p. 219). Yet he is alert to the universe of discourse the reporter's idea represents and adds: "Yes, it [the theory] looks plausible, but so does all fiction" (p. 219). Earlier the narrator has commented that Skaggs has a penchant for the "bizarre" (p. 118). The yellow journalist is a person whose "saving quality . . . was that he calmly believed his own lies while he was telling them, so no one was hurt, for the deceiver was as much a victim as the deceived" (p. 122). The reporter, in fact, begins his relationship with Joe by telling the boy an elaborate lie about a white boyhood on a southern plantation. By the end of *The Sport of the Gods*, however, he has ferreted out the crime perpetrated by the Plantation Tradition and its businessmen and artists.

Skaggs's narrative progress involves the introduction of a new and revealing perspective into the universe of fictive discourse. He both represents (as a "monumental liar") and inhabits (given the text's strategies on the subject of "fiction") this new universe of discourse. He goes South, confronts Maurice Oakley, and demands that the "secret" of Frank's guilt be handed over. His procedure is largely speculative, one of trial and error.

In his speculative procedure, Skaggs offers a perfect example of the blues detective described by Albert Murray:

> . . . the detective-story hero may also be classified as a species of blues idiom hero, a *nada*-confrontation hero, which is also to say, a slapstick hero, not only because of the nature of his quest and certain characteristics of his sensibility, but also because his behavior is so compatible with his circumstances, which are nothing if not slapdash jam-session situation or predicament in the first place.[20]

Murray regards the blues detective as coextensive with the slapstick hero, who dedicates himself to the rectification of a specific wrong and employs whatever means come to hand to fill the "break" between, say, a secret crime and its successful solution. One might equate such a creatively improvisational hero with the *bricoleur*, or handyman, who assesses a problem and employs tools at hand to achieve nonce solutions. What is crucial to the work of the blues detective is his ability to break away from traditional concepts and to supply new and creative possibilities.

Dunbar's blues detective hero Skaggs is confronted by the type of riddle as old as Oedipus; he seeks to discover innovatively and energetically why things are the way they unequivocally are. He strives to decipher, that is, the mystery of origins. Only sharp, improvisationally creative skills can ensure his success. And the slapdash creativity of his enterprise—the rough-and-ready, "jamming" motion that carries him toward some newly expressive work—makes him equivalent to the artist seeking to bring forth some "nontraditional" product. In a sense that becomes quite important in the efforts of subsequent Afro-American writers such as Rudolph Fisher, Chester Himes, and Ishmael Reed, Dunbar conflates the aims and structures of the artistic novel (the *Künstlerroman*) and the detective novel in his 1901 narrative. In accord with the classic formulations of Ernst Bloch's essay "Philosophical View of the Detective Story—Philosophical View of the Novel of the Artist," Dunbar manages to merge successfully the corrective regressive impulses of the detective novel (its orientation toward righting/writing the past) and the prophetically utopian impulses of the novel of the artist.[21] *The Sport of the Gods* suggests that the energetically improvisational Skaggs can both solve the "crime" of the Plantation Tradition and provide a more adequate artistic perspective to take its place in an American universe of fictive discourse. What makes Skaggs such a likely candidate is his tenacious willingness to entertain seemingly aberrant, or novel, ideas.

The narrator of *The Sport of the Gods* remarks: "there was, perhaps, more depth to Mr. Skaggs than most people gave him credit for having. However it may be, when he got an idea into his head, whether it were insane or otherwise, he had a decidedly tenacious way of holding to it" (p. 218). One might say that the reporter—as a man willing to move beyond the surface of life, to entertain extraordinary propositions, and to commit himself to a new "theory" of experience—is the unlikely hero of *The Sport of the Gods*.

To be sure, Skaggs is the agent of a "yellow journal." But the narrator, who has so omnipresently shown us the manifold failings of plantation fictions and northern coon shows, seems willing to recommend even the reportage of yellow journalism if it offers conditions of possibility for a just means of apprehending the world: "The *Universe* was yellow. It was very so. But it had power and keenness and energy. It never lost an opportunity to crow, and if one was not forthcoming, it made one. In this way it managed to do a considerable amount of good, and its yellowness became forgivable, even commendable" (p. 237). The headline for Skaggs's story—which makes known Berry Hamilton's innocence and secures his release from prison—reads as follows: "A Burning Shame! A Poor and Innocent Negro Made to Suffer for a Rich Man's Crime!" (p. 238). The theft, in its economic and moral implications, is thus correctly (if sensationally) explained by the enterprising writer of a narrative that differs substantially from both the romance of plantation economics and the inane theatricals of a newly emergent black urban folk.

Finally, it is Skaggs's "theory," his fictive, indeed virtually mythic, mode of confronting reality, that fulfills the goal implied by the first line of *The Sport of the Gods*. A Plantation Tradition's "monotony of tiresome iteration" is transcended by the reporter's "clear, interesting, and strong" story. His narrative constitutes a vivid perspective: "One could see it all as if every phrase of it were being enacted before one's own eyes" (p. 236).

IV

The final sentence of *The Sport of the Gods*, as I have previously mentioned, invokes an unseen "Will" before which human beings are powerless. I suggested earlier that this invocation signals authorial awareness on Dunbar's part. I want to hypothesize now that given the framework of the fictive text in which it appears, the narrator's concluding line implies that the causal explanations and theories human beings employ to organize their experience are generally half-truths or, worse, palpably distorted frames of reference. When such modal epistemologies are overthrown by "shocking," "bizarre," or "unthinkable" events, men and women give way to the impotence of madness. Every man is thus, in the narrator's implicit terms, his own Lear.

Art's role in this drama of human fallibility can be that of an abettor ceaselessly confirming and reiterating a traditional and partial view. On the other hand, a properly oriented "fiction" growing out of an idea or theory that looks beyond traditional modes of understanding can open the way for a just conceptualization of the world. After such a fiction has been completed, however, men may still feel powerless. For the fresh propositions and persuasive, symbolic reorderings of life represented by such a fiction may so alter customary ways of perceiving experience that familiar social norms are destroyed. In the fictive world of *The Sport of the Gods*, Skaggs's work has just this effect. It undercuts, disrupts, indeed destroys, both the stale monotony of the Plantation Tradition and the gay triviality of the northern coon show. Since these artistic constructs are but extensions of the false or partial epistemologies of Maurice and Leslie Oakley, Berry and Fannie Hamilton, and most of the other characters in the novel, human beings are logically represented as "powerless" after Skaggs's story had done its work. "After such knowledge, what forgiveness?"

The "Will" referred to in the narrative's final tableau, therefore, must be understood as the force that generates a new mode of fictive discourse. Dunbar, however, seems patently aware that his representation of the redemptive potential of fiction is in itself but one propostion *in a fiction*. His narrator, after all, does self-consciously announce "fiction" as his subject at the very outset of the novel. What I am suggesting is that Dunbar knew there was no such thing in the world of actual human events as a "limitless" freedom—mythic or otherwise. He knew that his own novel would not have the type of immediate effect on the context in which it emerged that Skaggs's story has on a novel's world of southern governors and northern readers. Dunbar realized, in short, that actual fictions operate within the "institution of literature," and, like myths, are marked by institutional constraints. Turner notes:

> ... this boundlessness [of the mythic performance] is restricted ... by the knowledge that this is a unique situation and by a definition of the situation which states that the rites and myths must be told in a prescribed order and in a symbolic rather than a literal form. The very symbol that expresses at the same time restrains; through mimesis there is an acting out—rather than the acting—of an impulse that is biologically motivated but socially and morally reprehended.[22]

The Sport of the Gods, viewed in terms of Turner's observation, is Dunbar's symbolic "acting out" of the effects on American life and letters of a supreme, revelatory fiction that will enable human beings to see life steadily and whole, enabling them to break free from both their "artistic" and "ordinary" modes of structuring experience. The novel thus captures in subtly energetic ways a dream of American form. It specifically explores the proposition that a literary tradition governed by plantation and coonshow images of Afro-Americans can be altered through an ironic, symbolic, fictive (blues) manipulation of such images and the tradition of which they are a formative part.

The Plantation Tradition and its images (like the coon show) did not spring, ab nihilo, from Dunbar's mind. Both were intrinsic to the world of artistic discourse institutionalized in the society of his era. Hence, while he was at liberty to suggest in *The Sport of the Gods* a radical alteration of the prevailing universe of fictive discourse, Dunbar was at the same time hedged round by the conventions—the social existence, as it were—of that very universe. His own fictive discourse could imply a nontraditional fiction, but since his novel was not intended or designed as a utilitarian, communicative, documentary, or historical text, he knew that it was not likely to be taken as an injunction to act. He could propose a shattering of old icons, and he could even represent such iconoclasm in literary form. Ultimately, however, it was men and women governed by traditional images who had the power to dispose.

Though Dunbar's freedom in creating *The Sport of the Gods* was shaped by the conventions of the "institution of literature," his novel's rich implications suggest a need for modes of interpretation that go beyond traditional historico-social critical approaches to narrative. In order to apprehend the turn-of-the-century Afro-American narrative as an act of fictive discourse which initiates, in energetic blues ways, a dream of American form, one must engage the freedom of an adequate critical mythology. One's mode of explaining the novel's meanings (and, indeed, the meanings of Afro-American literary texts in general) must transcend, that is to say, a customary, sharply limiting critical strategy that yokes the analysis of works of verbal art to acts of historical interpretation.

I have tried to suggest that a new "theory" or idea in the investigation of even a much-neglected narrative like *The Sport of the Gods* offers striking possibilities for understanding Afro-American expressive culture. If a single point of discussion deserves emphasis, it is that one need not stand "powerless" before a novel like Dunbar's; neither is one compelled to continue repeating, with "tiresome iteration," the partial truths of a flawed critical past. The symbolic freedom of action that accompanies adequate investigative methods assures for Afro-American literary criticism a kind of blues liberation.

While the critic may still find himself compelled to address conventions and shortcomings of a traditional, historico-critical approach, his awareness of the manifold range of literary theoretical insights available to today's blues critic should lead him to discover (and explore) dimensions of Afro-American expressive culture that have long been ignored. Like Dunbar himself, today's critic is bound on one hand by an institutional world of discourse, yet he is free, on the other, to hypothesize and represent meanings that have previously been "unthinkable." This speculative freedom, it seems to me, suggests a "limitless" freedom of myth and is essential for the task of revealing successful achievements toward the fulfillment of a dream of form in America.

Reassessing (W)right: A Meditation on the Black (W)hole

I strove to master words, to make them disappear.
                              Wright, *American Hunger*

What is to be avoided above all is the reestablishing of "Society"
as an abstraction vis-à-vis the individual. The individual *is the social being*. His life, even if it may not appear in the direct form of
a *communal* life carried out together with others—is therefore an
expression and confirmation of *social life*.
                    Marx, *Economic and Philosophical Manuscripts*

I tried to find the usual ladder that leads out of such holes, but
there was none.
                              Ellison, *Invisible Man*

                              I

The reassessment of *The Sport of the Gods* which yields the foregoing
interpretation of the novel is simply an instant—one blues moment, as it
were—in the project of deciphering an American form. Dunbar's effort
was early, and its inscriptions of the vernacular matrix are revealed only
through subtle analysis.

   The same does not hold for a mid-twentieth-century black author like
Richard Wright. For the blues energies of theme and narrative structure
that Dunbar preserved and passed on in *The Sport of the Gods* were
magnified by the efforts of the Harlem Renaissance of the 1920s—a time
of extraordinary production in Afro-American writing.

   When he commenced his autobiography *Black Boy* (1945), in fact,
enough narrative instances existed to make available for Wright options
that are implied in his essay "How Bigger Was Born." In this interpretive
essay, Wright insists that he might have followed a genteel, integrationist
line in the novel *Native Son* (1940), endearing himself thereby to the
Afro-American middle class and amusing Anglo-America with polite
observations on life among the black lowly. To have followed such a line
would have been to rank himself with a great many Afro-American
predecessors. Instead, he chose to take the lid completely off the seething
cauldron of Afro-American vernacular culture and show the indigenous
folk in both their glory and their squalor—but, certainly, in their resonantly energetic capability for disruptive expressive action. In this latter
course, too, Wright followed a classic line in Afro-American expression, a
line suggested, for example, by *Narrative of the Life of Frederick Douglass*
with its uncompromising protrayals of vernacular dimensions in the life of
the "slave community."

   The point, surely, is that Dunbar and the Harlem Renaissance—as well
as writers of the thirties such as Zora Hurston and Waters Turpin—
provided options for Wright vis-à-vis a dream of American form. And like

his more energetic predecessors who absorbed into their conscious lives and creative styles the rhythms of train-wheels-over-track-junctures, he chose to provide yet another installment in the project of achieving a blues book most excellent. Wright's place in the project, however, can be understood only through the deconstruction of quite familiar (and lamentably narrow) modes of assessing his corpus that have held sway for decades. Tropological energy is de rigueur if one would comprehend the signal black (w)holeness of Richard Wright.

The word "reassessment" implies a shift in axiological determinants that prompts reconsideration of the type and amount of use one hopes to extract from familiar objects and events. To reassess Richard Wright, therefore, would be to alter prevailing conceptions of the value to be extracted from such characteristic fictions as, say, "Big Boy Leaves Home" and "The Man Who Lived Underground." Such an alteration would constitute a beneficial cognitive shift, for traditional evaluative accounts of Wright and his corpus have been grounded on a theoretical model that has generated a quite limited set of explanatory terms. This well-rehearsed model is a discourse predicated on *lack*. It is, in fact, a model which proceeds almost entirely in terms of a capitalistic economics' "need" and "lack." And it inscribes, in each evaluative instance, the effects of a decidedly bourgeois orientation. The polarization that it privileges, as my subsequent discussion will make clear, stands in marked contrast to Wright's own iconography of "absence" and "desire."

In such classic instances of traditional evaluation as James Baldwin's controversial essays[23] and Ralph Ellison's engaging "The World and the Jug,"[24] the author of *Native Son* is adjudged a rebellious Southerner psychologically deprived by the Jim Crow ethics of a Mississippi upbringing and intellectually denied by the vagaries of an incomplete formal education. Baldwin insists, for example, in an extraordinarily derogatory postmortem entitled "Alas, Poor Richard" that Wright's "notions of society, politics, and history . . . seemed . . . utterly fanciful" (p. 184). Only at the close of his life, asserts Baldwin, did Wright begin to acquire "a less uncertain esthetic distance, and a new depth" (p. 183). Yet he never achieved, in his successor's venomous accounting, an informed, artistic comprehension of the modern world, remaining through all his days "a Mississippi pickaninny, mischievous, cunning, and tough" (p. 184). Baldwin's evaluation of Wright is incomparably more malevolent than Ellison's. The latter merely refuses to grant Wright the status of "artist," insisting that his predecessor adopted a fixed, ideological perspective before he had achieved the technical mastery requisite for genuine creativity.

Wright's own creative self-portrait in *Black Boy* is to some extent responsible for the assessments of Baldwin and Ellison. The narrator of the autobiography depicts himself as largely autodidactic, attracted to "words as weapons," and uncommonly fierce in his appropriation of literature as a form of social action. Wright's successors seem to read this portrait, not as a figuration of the deconstructive writer at work or as an implicit condemnation of the shortcomings of a warped system of southern injustice. Rather, both Ellison and Baldwin interpret the autobiography's portrait of denial, lack, and fierce appropriation as an inscription of the artist *manqué*. Wright's successors see him as a writer bereft of rich intellectual endowments and committed to a limiting form of engaged literary action. The craftsman of "The Man Who Lived Underground" is characterized in traditional evaluative discourse as a "protest" writer. "Lack," thus, generates "protest" in the familiar discourse. And "protest" stands as both an indictment and a levy, signaling to the initiated a realm of quite problematic expressive value. James Baldwin provides the classic formulation of the charge of "protest" in "Many Thousands Gone."[25]

The protest writer, according to Baldwin, is less a creator of cultural texts than a victim. He lacks the informed *individuality* (a term to which we shall return shortly) that would allow him to escape the effects of cultural imperialism. He never, in Baldwin's view, transcends the peculiar status of Caliban, whose response to language's largesse is always either passive compliance in the restrictive, linguistic terms meted out for his existence or a bitter curse. In "Everybody's Protest Novel," this prospect on protest is illustrated by the following homology: Richard Wright is to the agit-prop naturalism of protest writing as the pagan African is to the crude salvifics of missionary Christianity.

> Thus, the African, exile, pagan, hurried off the auction block and into the fields, fell on his knees before that God in Whom he must now believe; who had made him, but not in His image. This tableau, this impossibility, is the heritage of the Negro in America: *Wash me*, cried the slave to his Maker, *and I shall be whiter, whiter than snow!* . . . [and] Bigger's tragedy [Wright's failure in his protest writing in *Native Son*] is not that he is cold or black or hungry, not even that he is American, black; but that he [Wright] has accepted a theology [linguistic code of social protest] that denies him life, that he admits the possibility of his being sub-human and feels constrained, therefore, to battle for his humanity according to those brutal criteria bequeathed him at his birth. [Pp. 16–17]

The metaphor's terms imply—in the case of both Wright and the analogical African—a primitive, artisanal consciousness incapable of avoiding the constraints and codes of cultural oppression. The productive results of such a consciousness—one perennially shaped by the scripted texts of the cultural "other"—are always imitative, flatly rebellious, metaphorically impoverished. Protest writing is, therefore, in Baldwin's view, only a pale shadow of the cultural missionary's (or cultural arbiter's) resonant acts of language. And insofar as men's and women's needs vis-à-vis art include intellectually charged and symbolically rich texts, they are destined to frustration if they place a sizable levy on the efforts of Richard Wright.

A reassessment of Wright must begin with a rereading of the traditional discourse's *lack*. This predicate cannot be taken as a mark of "objective" truth about the life and works of an "artisan of protest." Rather, it must be read as a symptom of the traditional discourse's unposed, but nevertheless answered, question.

Analyzing Marx's relationship to the texts of classical economics, Louis Althusser asserts that Marx's comprehension and revision of the classical texts resulted from his ability to "read the illegible," to measure the theoretical framework initially visible in such texts "against the invisible problematic contained in the paradox of *an answer which does not correspond to any question posed*."[26] I want to suggest, in the interest of (W)right reassessment, that the answer *lack* in classical texts of Wright analysis is a response to the "illegible" problematic constituted by bourgeois aesthetic theory.[27] The un-inscribed question is, "What is art?" And the answer proposed by bourgeois aesthetics is a response that necessarily finds Wright *lacking*.

II

If we recur for a moment to Baldwin's protest writer and African pagan, we find that both metaphorical entities in "Everybody's Protest Novel" recapitulate one pole of a familiar antinomy. The writer and the savage represent helpless *social* victims juxtaposed with resolutely *individualistic* creators. Baldwin elaborates a contradistinction between *individual* and *society* as though the division possesses the force of natural law, when, in fact, it carries only the reinscribed, metaphorical force of an old problematic. The power of the distinction is contingent upon a model of perceiving "reality" that emerges from a peculiar, cultural ordering of existence. And its very delineation, perforce, implies that the person reinscribing its antinomies is superior to all merely *social* determinants.

If Baldwin's essays are paradigm instances, then traditional evaluative discourse assessing Wright assuredly constitutes a theoretical framework in direct opposition to the well-known Marxian dictate that reads: "It is not the consciousness of men that determines their being, but, on the contrary, their social being that determines their consciousness." Bourgeois aesthetics is an axiological extension of a bourgeois society's privileging of "consciousness" in the domain of expressive culture. The theory is coextensive with the emergence of an industrial society that commodified life and reduced value to a cash nexus. Bourgeois aesthetics postulates an artistically transcendent realm of experience, production, and value as a "cultural" preserve, a domain where individual creativity ("consciousness") secures itself against corruptions of industrialism ("social being"). The British Marxist Raymond Williams aptly summarizes the contours of bourgeois aesthetic theory in his study *Marxism and Literature.*[28] He suggests that such a theory produces: "specializing abstractions of 'art' and 'the aesthetic' " which represent "a particular stage of the division of labour" (p. 153). He further asserts:

> 'Art' is [defined in bourgeois aesthetic theory as] a kind of production which has to be seen as separate from the dominant bourgeois productive norm: the making of commodities. ['Art'] has then, in fantasy, to be separated from 'production' altogether; described by the new term 'creation'; distinguished from its own material processes; distinguished, finally, from other products of its own kind or closely related kinds—'art' from 'non-art'; 'literature' from 'para-literature' or 'popular literature'; 'culture' from 'mass culture'. The narrowing abstraction ['Art'] is then so powerful that, in its name, we find ways of neglecting (or of dismissing as peripheral) that relentless transformation of art works into commodities, within the dominant forms of capitalist society. *Art and thinking about art have to separate themselves, by ever more absolute abstraction, from the social processes within which they are still contained. Aesthetic theory is the main instrument of this evasion.* In its concentration on receptive states, on psychological responses of an abstractly differentiated kind, it [aesthetic theory] represents the division of labour in consumption corresponding to the abstraction of art as the division of labour in production. [Pp. 153–54, my emphasis]

In the well-rehearsed evaluative discourse devoted to Wright, certain features of the author's career are inescapable. He was certainly a writer of *socially ordained* fictions. His success in the marketplace is a matter of record. (His income in the year after *Native Son*'s publication was in excess of $30,000—a not inconsiderable sum in 1941.) Taken together, these features of Wright's career identify him—under a bourgeois aesthetic prospect—as an artist *manqué*. In Ellison's account in "The World and the Jug," the author of *Native Son* suffers the fullest condemnations of a dichotomizing, bourgeois aesthetic code.[29] Ellison, as previously mentioned, laments that "Wright found the facile answers of Marxism before he learned to use *literature* as a means for discovering the forms of American Negro humanity" (p. 120, my emphasis). Extending a cautionary aesthetic wisdom, Ellison goes on to suggest that Wright's artistic failures in a novel like *The Long Dream* may constitute a form of "artistic immorality" leading to "chaos" (p. 134).

Wright and his productions are consigned by Ellison to a simplistic, sociological field of *nonart*. The highest "creativity" of symbolic production and the deepest affectivity of "aesthetic" response that are characteristic of "art" are held to be always *lacking* in his career. He is defined, therefore, as inadequately symbolic and metaphorical—that is, as an artistically lacking artisan of protest. The signal misfortune of such a traditional reading of Wright is that it prevents access to the ample symbolic content of such works as "Big Boy Leaves Home" and "The Man Who Lived Underground."

The question, therefore, becomes, How, once a "symptomatic" reading has revealed the unposed query and latent problematic of traditional evaluative discourse, does one institute a forcefully reevaluative investigation? My response is that one begins with a signifying device sufficiently unusual in its connotations to shatter familiar conceptual determinations. (W)right reasoning begins in tropological thought.

III

In suggesting a tropological perspective on Wright, I will appropriate once again the interpretive modes detailed by Hayden White.[30] The introduction of unusual metaphors (or tropes) where objects of traditional knowledge are concerned generates new conceptual images. The trope is equivalent in effect to a symbol, providing neither icon nor description, but suggesting instead how we should both constitute *and* feel about an object of knowledge.[31] In my subsequent discussion, I want to summon what is known to physics as a "black hole" as a useful trope for a reevaluation of Richard Wright. To meditate on the *black hole* is to understand how tropic thought, as a device of reassessment, serves toward a realignment of conceptual economies. First, however, a definition in answer to the question: What is a *black hole*?

A black hole is "an area of space which appears absolutely black because the gravitation there is so intense that not even light can escape into the surrounding areas."[32] Such areas are posited by the General Theory of Relativity as unimaginably dense remains of stars. They may be only a few miles in diameter yet contain the entire mass of a star three times larger than the sun. The area marked by the black hole is dark because an initially luminescent star has, in its burning, converted energy to mass. (It has become a "massive concentration," one might say, invoking the term *Mascon*, first appropriated to Afro-American literary criticism by Stephen Henderson.[33])

But while the black hole is darkly invisible, it is detectable by the energy field resulting from its attraction of hydrogen atoms, cosmic particles, and other objects. As these objects move through the black hole's gravitational field they approach the velocity of light, creating an intense field of electromagnetic radiation. The gravitation is so forceful that it not only attracts cosmic particles but also may hold another massive, luminous star in a binary system.

Black holes are not, however, as simply fathomable as the foregoing implies. They are surrounded by an "event horizon," a membrane that prevents the unaltered escape of anything which passes through. Light shone into a black hole disappears. And at the center of the hole—at what is called its "singularity"—all objects are "squeezed" to zero volume. Space and time disappear.

The black hole as a trope presents an invisible, attractive force—a massive concentration of energy that draws all objects to its center. It reduces matter that passes its event horizon to zero sum. Richard Wright and this trope come together in meditation if *Black Boy* is allowed to serve as a mediating textual ground.[34]

IV

First there is the luminescent star, burning with furious energy, ravenously consuming. It is like a massive, cosmic furnace of desire. The light produced is that which can be dispensed. The mass is sharply concentrated.

Richard Wright in the intense passion of autodidactic illumination is figured in *Black Boy* as a center of ravenous desire. He is like the Red Giant burning toward fulfilled concentration. He seeks to consume:

> I hungered for books, new ways of looking and seeing. It was not a matter of believing or disbelieving what I read, but of feeling something new, of being affected by something that made the look of the world different. . . . Reading grew into a passion. . . . The plots and stories in the novels did not interest me so much as the point of view revealed. . . . Reading was like a drug, a dope. [Pp. 272–73]

The fuel consumed by Wright is the work of H. L. Mencken, Sinclair Lewis, Theodore Dreiser, whose relationship to the quotidian, to "everyday reality," is less mediated by beautifying literary conventions than the works of their contemporaries. But it would not have mattered whether Wright fueled his hunger with Flaubert or Frank Norris, because he was not in search of literary *lights*. As with the black hole, so with Wright: the light is that which can be dispensed (with). The mass remains.

The search presented in *Black Boy* is a quest for a correlative, an articulated set of relationships that will make sense of desire. It is not an expedition in discovery of literary, or "artistic," mastery. Hence the narrator's initial reading of Mencken ends, not with a paean to "literary" genius, but with a statement of absence: "I concluded the book with the conviction that I had somehow overlooked something terribly important in life. I had once tried to write, had once reveled in feeling, had let my crude imagination roam, but the impulse to dream *had been slowly beaten*

out of me by experience" (p. 272, my emphasis). The matter consumed by
Wright to fuel desire—to secure an "overlooked" *something* that is "terribly important" for the amelioration of absence—is naturalistic and
realistic fiction.

Reading *Black Boy* under the trope of the black hole, one might say that
Wright "burns" novels to fuel *his own concentration*. He is unconcerned
with novels' truth value ("It was not a matter of believing or disbelieving
what I read . . ."), and their literary techniques are of no importance ("The
plots and stories in the novels did not interest me . . ."). Rather, he
consumes them ravenously, voraciously. "I gave myself over to each novel
without reserve, without trying to criticize it; it was enough for me to see
and feel something different" (p. 272). Wright's quest is ultimately to
achieve articulate structures of vision and feeling that constitute a correlative, supplying an equivalent to that "terribly important" *something*
found absent. What he seeks, one might say, is a *difference* that will fulfill
desire.

Vision and feeling are primary functions of writing for Wright; the
malleability of words before *individualistic* "literary artistry" is a matter
of indifference. Words are commodities, a necessary fuel in the meaningful
structuring of a concentratedly *different* experience.

The experience that is at issue is squeezed to an unimaginably dense
point in *Black Boy*. In the autobiography, the mother's suffering absence
becomes a figure gathering to itself all lineaments of a black "blues life."[35]
In a single instant of recall, it suggests the foundational image in the
repertoire of human desire: "Once, in the night, my mother called me to
her bed and told me that she could not endure the pain, that she wanted to
die. I held her hand and begged her to be quiet. That night I ceased to react
to my mother; my feelings were frozen" (p. 111). "Frozen" means *fixed* as
in a stop-action photograph which serves as a set point of significant
emotional reference.

The mother's suffering—generalized, internalized, "frozen" as framed
image—becomes, for Wright: "a symbol . . . gathering to itself all the
poverty, the ignorance, the helplessness; the painful, baffling, hunger-
ridden days and hours; the restless moving, the futile seeking, the uncertainty, the fear, the dread; the meaningless pain and the endless suffering"
(p. 111). From this long chorus emerges the litany of a lean blues life in
black America: a life of "poverty . . . baffling . . . hunger-ridden days . . .
restless moving . . . meaningless pain and . . . endless suffering." What is
coextensive with this litany (providing, as it were, its brilliant symbolic
generality) is the primary image of human desire. Roland Barthes delineates the relationship of absence, desire, and language as follows in *A
Lover's Discourse*:[36]

Absence persists—I must endure it. Hence I will *manipulate* it: trans-form the distortion of time into oscillation, produce rhythm, make an entrance onto the stage of language (language is born of absence: the child has made himself a doll out of a spool, throws it away and picks it up again, miming the mother's departure and return: a paradigm is created). . . . This staging of language postpones the other's death: a very short interval, we are told, separates the time during which the child still believes his mother to be absent and the time during which he believes her to be already dead. To manipulate absence is to extend this interval, to delay as long as possible the moment when the other might topple sharply from absence into death. Absence is the figure of privation; simultaneouly, I desire and I need. Desire is squashed against need: that is the obsessive phenomenon of all amorous senti-ment. [P. 16]

In the autobiographical instant materializing his mother's suffering absence, Wright linguistically structures desire—the vision and feeling of a *black blues life*—as universal symbol. There occurs a striking conflation of motive, event, and goal when the narrator reports (subsequent to the image's presentation) that the quest is "to wring a meaning out of meaningless suffering" (p. 112). The meaning (appearing *for itself*) is, in fact, the mother's image. It is *always already there* in the text of human life *in general*, and has just been *textualized* in writing by Wright's autobio-graphical voice of desire.

Novels are depicted by *Black Boy* as the fuel that allows the narrator (at age nineteen) to take a first step in the achievement of the kind of signifi-cant structure that is represented by the image of the mother's suffering absence itself. Novels' words fuel, that is to say, an internalized, half-beaten-down-by-experience image of the black blues life's desire. And the "literariness" of such words can be dispensed (with).

The conventions that condition literary "artistry," Wright's narrator implies, maintain life's surfaces. By reducing "literariness" to the concen-trated image of *my* mother's suffering absence as symbol, the narrator institutes a descent toward the "meaningless suffering" that is, in his view, the very engine of class division and embittering absence in the segregated society of America.

One way of phrasing the implied expressive-productive norms of *Black Boy* is to say that the narrator's presentation of the desire of a black blues life—one almost under erasure by experience's "slow" beatings—is ontogenetic, symbolized by *my* (Wright's) mother's suffering absence. Yet this desire is also concentratedly phylogenetic—signified by the mother's suffering absence as an image of that primitive form of human conscious-ness (desire) that strives to annul surfaces (objects). In a Hegelian sense,

Evicted tenants in Poinsett County, Arkansas, 1935. Photo from the Howard A. Kester Papers (#3834). Courtesy Southern Historical Collection, Library of the University of North Carolina at Chapel Hill.

the phylogenetic desire implied by *Black Boy* is a form of consciousness that achieves—through suffering and "unhappiness"—a recognition that genuine self-certainty consists in community.[37] Only through the intersubjectivity of community can consciousness become *self-consciousness*. In *Black Boy*, words are, finally, objects annulled by a desirous consciousness in order to achieve the communality of "point of view." The narrator, in a passage from the autobiography already cited, says: "The plots and stories in the novels did not interest me so much as the point of view revealed." The phylogenetic "trace" of consciousness' journeyings is thus discovered as "point of view" in realistic and naturalistic fiction. "Point of view," one might say, defined not as subjective intention but as trace of human desire, is the subjective correlative required for (W)right self-consciousness.

A beautifying, "literary" language is a restrictive array of conventions preserving class division, maintaining the status quo surfaces of life, *creating desire* rather than elaborating its transcendence. What is required for the *social* (intersubjective) project comprised by desire's existence, expression, and transcendence is an adequate, expressive vehicle.

The trope of the black hole suggests a "squeezing" of matter to zero sum. Wright, as voracious center of desire—seeking desire's trace as "point of view"—reduces literary language to zero sum. *Black Boy*, in fact, is utterly relentless in its representations of what might be termed a "code of desire" that reduces conventional discourse to zero. Inversive language is repeatedly represented as nullifying fixed discursive norms in the autobiography.

The narrator reports, for example, on a day's encounter during his sixth year with "the blues people" of Memphis, Tennessee: "Toward early evening, they let me go. I staggered along the pavements, drunk, repeating obscenities to the horror of the women I passed and to the amusement of the men en route to their homes from work" (p. 28). The quotidian expectations of street exchange are shockingly voided. Expectations encoded by theological fundamentalism fare no better in the face of the narrator's reductive code of desire. When the young man who lives across the street from his grandmother attempts to set scriptures against the narrator's own articulations, the results are described as follows:

> During our talk I made a hypothetical statement that summed up my attitude toward God and the suffering in the world, a statement that stemmed from my knowledge of life as I had lived, seen, felt, and suffered it in terms of dread, fear, hunger, terror, and loneliness. "If laying down my life could stop the suffering in the world, I'd do it. But I don't believe anything can stop it," I told him. Frightened and baffled, he left me. I felt sorry for him. [Pp. 127-28]

And the holy, matriarchal center of the Wilson clan herself finds church norms scandalously reduced in an instant by the narrator's words. Grandmother Wilson is drying the young Wright after a bath:

> "Bend over," she ordered. I stooped and she scrubbed my anus. My mind was in a sort of daze, midway between daydreaming and thinking [the province of desire?]. Then, before I knew it, words—words whose meaning I did not fully know—had slipped out of my mouth. "When you get through, kiss back there," I said, the words rolling softly but unpremeditatedly.... Granny rose slowly and lifted the wet towel high above her head and brought it down across my naked body. [Pp. 49–50]

The examples can be multiplied: the narrator's reduction of the discourse of black southern education to zero sum in his unshakable determination to deliver his own commencement speech, the reduction of a white woman employer's text of vocational expectations for the Negro to zero through his assertion that he wants to be a writer, the "unpremeditated" nullification of bourgeois social exchange at the home of Uncle Clark and Aunt Jody, the inversive countermanding of numinous discourse in his crafting of desirous fiction (tales of Indian maidens and "hellish" voodoo) in the moments designated for prayer at his grandmother's house.

The narrator's reported youthful relationship to Christian discourse in *Black Boy* serves as a shorthand for all his zero-sum reductions of conventional discourse:

> Some of the Bible stories were interesting in themselves, but we always twisted them, secularized them to the level of our street life, rejecting all meanings that did not fit into our environment. And we did the same to the beautiful hymns. When the preacher intoned: *Amazing grace, how sweet it sounds*, we would wink at one another and hum under our breath: *A bulldog ran my grandma down*. [Pp. 92–93]

Rejecting "all meanings" that do not fit into the environment means, for the narrator, shaping a code that accords with the lean life of a black blues people's intense desire. The "flat" speech and "vague" gestures of convention are incommensurate with a world that has imprinted the narrator with its desire—a world, "a plane of living," marked by "swinging doors of saloons, the railroad yard, the roundhouses, the street gangs, the river levees, an orphan home." This imprinting existence found him "shifted from town to town," mingling with "grownups more than perhaps was good for me" (pp. 115–16). And it is finally the determinate influence of such an existence that motivates the narrator's refusal to "curb . . . [his] habit of cursing" (p. 116)—to restrain his propensity for engaging in reductively inversive and shocking discursive acts conditioned by a blues life's desire. Such inversive discourse is precisely where Richard Wright's attractive singularity resides.

From one analytical perspective, Wright and his autobiographical narrator are forerunners of Roland Barthes's project in *Writing Degree Zero*.[38] Like Barthes's idealized writer, Wright confounds the "literariness" expected of "novelists," of "literary autobiographers," by inversively inscribing desire into what the Russian formalism of Mikhail Bakhtin describes as "carnivalesque" discourse.[39] *Literature*, reduced to "zero degree writing," becomes in Wright's canon a language in which "ambivalent" words such as obscenities, parodic utterances, inversive or ironical phrases function as reductive junctures.[40] The conventional orders of language are reduced to dialogical (two discourse "yoked," sometimes "violently," together) symbolic occasions. The result is language of startling misalliances, sacreligious punnings, scandalous repudiations.

Following the lead of Julia Kristeva in *Desire in Language*, one might say that zero degree, nonliterary language results when desire "adds itself to the linear order of language"[41] through the types of displacement, arch condensation, and festive inversions witnessed in the writing of Richard Wright. A definition of "carnivalesque discourse" provides an apt characterization of Wright's discursive practice: "Carnivalesque discourse breaks through the laws of language censored by grammar and semantics and, at the same time, is a social and political protest. There is no equivalence, but rather, identity between challenging official linguistic codes and challenging official law" (p. 65). Just as matter crossing the black hole's event horizon is compressed to zero, so conventional, literary language indrawn by Wright's blues life's black desire is forced to "bare its devices."[42] The time and space of conventional bourgeois aesthetic theory break down at desire's signal (w)holeness. Within the black (w)hole's force-field, old laws of "literature" no longer operate.

The paradox in Wright assessment is that traditional evaluative accounts bracket the author of *Black Boy* as an artisan of social protest, charging that he failed to transcend the *social* in order to arrive at *art*. Baldwin, for example, writes as follows in "Many Thousands Gone":

> [Wright's] work, from its beginning, is most clearly committed to the social struggle. Leaving aside the considerable question of what relationship precisely the artist bears to the revolutionary, the reality of man as a social being is not his only reality and that artist is strangled who is forced to deal with human beings solely in social terms. [P. 25]

From the perspective of the black hole as trope, however, one recognizes what paradoxes can arise from an inadequate theory. For Wright incontestably drew all of *art* into his own singularity and employed it to fuel his project of articulating a black blues life's pressing desire. He thus became an irreducibly dark, powerful, and invisible core at the very center of the Afro-American expressive ("artistic"?) universe. The manifest "unevenness" of his prose, its pastiche, shards of theological, philosophical, and sociological discourse, sparse (sometimes mechanical) stichomythia are fragments of a "literature" that *was*—a discursive order reduced to zero in the interest of the black (w)hole's blues desire.

V

Invisible, massive in its energies, erasing old law, nullifying time and space in its singularity, the black hole metaphorically suggests the proportions of Wright's achievement—his space, as it were, in the tradition of Afro-American expressive culture. The implications of the trope's suggestiveness for practical criticism and evaluative reassessment are not far to seek. To derive the metaphor's productiveness, one need only play on rich imagistic possibilities that it reveals.

Transliterated in letters of Afro-America, the *black hole* assumes the subsurface force of the black underground. It graphs, that is to say, the subterranean *hole* where the trickster has his ludic, deconstructive being. Further, in the script of Afro-America, the hole is the domain of *Wholeness*, an achieved relationality of black community in which desire recollects experience and sends it forth as blues. To be *Black* and *(W)hole* is to escape incarcerating restraints of a white world (i.e., a *black hole*) and to engage the concentrated, underground singularity of experience that results in a blues desire's expressive fullness.

The symbolic content of Afro-American expressive culture can thus be formulated in terms of the *black hole* conceived as a subcultural (underground, marginal, or liminal) region in which a dominant, white culture's representations are squeezed to zero volume, producing a new expressive order. As Richard Wright's work brilliantly demonstrates, there is a set pattern of rites marking this Afro-American underground experience. Wright knew that in any black life, in any white-dominated society, a "life-crisis" of black identity—an event equivalent to such other life crises as birth, social puberty, and death—was an inevitable event. The scholarship of Belgian anthropologist Arnold Van Gennep is suggestive where such life crises are concerned.[43]

Van Gennep insists that a person's departure from one stage of social life in order to enter another marks a time of critical transformation, creating cultural instability and requiring appropriate ceremonies. The purpose of such ceremonies, according to Van Gennep, is to enable the individual to pass "safely" and profitably from one defined social position to another. The circumcision rites that initiate West African males into manhood might be offered as instances of a ceremonial movement from one stage of social life to another.

Van Gennep persuasively demonstrates in his classic work *The Rites of Passage* that ceremonies accompanying social transisition share the tripartite form common to *rites of passage*. Such ceremonies are characterized by the following phases: (1) separation from a fixed social position, (2) movement through a "timeless" and "statusless" marginality, and (3) reincorporation into a new, fixed social state with a new status. A diagram of passage rites borrowed from Edmund Leach's work *Culture and Communication*[44] provides a clarifying graphic for Van Gennep's scheme.

The life crisis of black identity in a white society is instituted by the black person's sudden awareness that he or she represents what Carolyn Fowler calls a "zero image" in the perceptual schemes of the white, dominant culture.[45] Zora Neale Hurston's Janie, the protagonist of *Their Eyes Were Watching God*,[46] offers a striking narrative instance of a black person's encounter with the "zero image." Janie is perplexed and dismayed when she surveys the photograph that an itinerant photographer has taken of her and her childhood playmates: "Where is me? Ah don't see me," she says (p. 22). Recalling the event in later years, a mature Janie says: "Before Ah seen de picture Ah thought Ah wuz like de rest." Once she "gets the picture," however, Hurston's protagonist reflexively understands that her status is that of an alien, a "nigger," a "zero" in the white world's structures of perception.

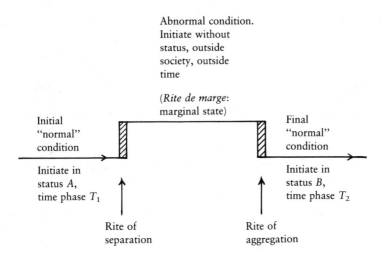

Abnormal condition.
Initiate without
status, outside
society, outside
time

(*Rite de marge*:
marginal state)

Initial
"normal"
condition

Final
"normal"
condition

Initiate in
status *A*,
time phase T_1

Initiate in
status *B*,
time phase T_2

Rite of
separation

Rite of
aggregation

One might well think of Janie's encounter with the "zero image" as identical to Richard Wright's narrator's sudden realization that his internal (*essential*) self is "under erasure." Such a realization is always followed in black narratives by passage rites—by what might be termed *rites of the black (w)hole.* The first stage in such rites involves the black person's separation from a dominant, white society. The act of withdrawal is equivalent to a conflagrational retreat in which the mass of old edicts is reduced to a light that can be dispensed (with).

Ellison's invisible man making his *underground* retreat, reports as follows: "I tried to find the usual ladder that leads out of such holes, but there was none. I had to have a light. . . . I started searching for paper to make a torch, feeling about slowly over the coal pile. . . . I'd have to open my brief case. In it were the only papers I had. I started with my high school diploma, applying one precious match with a feeling of remote irony, even smiling as I saw the swift but feeble light push back the gloom."[47] And in the moment of autodidactic passion, Wright's narrator in *Black Boy* fuels desire with naturalistic and realistic novels. The result of such burning separations is a new, forceful, and dense black mass that signals the second stage of an underground ritual.

This second stage of the rites of the black (w)hole commences with a renewal of desire. Mythic images of experiences internalized by active black culture bearers are brilliantly summoned, expressed, and passed on as an educational experience. The black initiand in the second or liminal phase enters a period of instruction that is "betwixt and between" anything approximating fixed social status. The timelessness and spaceless- -ness of this period outside history are characterized by receipt of "ancestral" wisdom. The initiand, in fact, learns to employ the internalized images of a black blues life's desire in peculiarly Afro-American ways. Through inversion and deconstructive parody he sets conventional wisdom on its head—that is, at zero sum. Achieving what might be termed an "ahistorical," "metaphorical" sense of the black self's *historicity* or placement within a diachronic series of Afro-American events, the initiand, in the liminal phase, effects a negation of negation. Grasping his own black timely timelessness through receipt of ancestral wisdom, he negates a dominant society's perceptual schemes by re-(w)riting (and righting) history. What results is his recognition of the irreversibility of rites of the black (w)hole. He becomes aware that he can never "reintegrate" into a dominantly white society with a "socially responsible" status. And here begins the final stage of the ritual.

The third, and final, phase of conventional *rites of passage* is aggregation. The marginal initiand is reintegrated, with a new status, into the society from which he has separated. It is at this stage of conventional rites that the suggestiveness of the black hole trope becomes fully manifest. In the rites of the black underground, there is *no return* to a renewed plenitude of "origins." The rites are irreversible. Having passed the event horizon into the singularity of *(W)holeness*, the initiand and his experience are irretrievably transformed.

Another way of phrasing this irreversibility is to say that once liminality has been accomplished in the rites of the black (w)hole, an enduring *Black Difference* is the only world available to the initiand. For the historicization of the black self in liminal regions of desire—the constitution, as it were, of a concentrated, *mass* Afro-American identity—renders reintegration into "white" society impossible. The achievement of *Black (W)holeness* means that accepted and acceptable roles meted out for blacks by a dominantly white society are no longer feasible.

What is possible is *entry* into the singularity at the black (W)hole's center. This *singularity* consists of an initiated, expressive black *community* that has "gotten the [white world's] picture," used it to fuel retreat, found the center of its own singular desire, and given expressive form to a new and meaningful *Black (W)holeness*. If one were to invoke René Girard's *Deceit, Desire, and the Novel*, one might say that what ultimately occurs in black (w)hole rites is the installation of a black expressive community at the tip of the triangle of desire as a substitute for the perceptual schemes and modes of discourse of white society in a premarginal phase of black existence.[48]

The expressive community at the center of the black hole is always conceived as "marginal" because its members never "return" to the affective and perceptual structures of an old, white dispensation. In actuality, the expressive community of the black (w)hole, as Richard Wright understood so well, is the center of a new order of existence. Invisible, charged with extraordinary attractive force, it draws all events and objects into its horizon; (w)rites a new order of discourse. A graphic presentation like the figure that follows provides some notion of the structure of black (w)hole rites and indicates (in its contrast with Leach's previously adduced illustration) the way in which such rites comprise a re-(w)rite.[49]

The black center in rites of the black (w)hole transforms old matter into new light. It "gives birth," in Sherley Anne Williams's apt phrase, "to brightness."[50] For a black hole's intense attraction is responsible for the incredibly brilliant energy sources that physicists call "quasars"—quasi-stellar radio sources—which may be several times the diameter of our own solar system, emitting more energy than a galaxy of a hundred and fifty billion stars. The incredible light of the black underground's "invisible" space (say, 1,369 bulbs multiplied by wattage) finds its expressive fullness in liminality, in the margins. Questions of inside and outside, central ("centered") and marginal become extraordinarily complex in the tropic province of the black hole—the domain of the outside/elsewhere identity of *Black Wholeness*. Who (including Ellison's Mr. Norton) would not want to be at the blue-black singularity's "center" when experience and desire converge to give birth to light billions of times brighter than the sun?

Examples from Richard Wright's fiction provide an idea of the immensely dense symbolic action that occurs at the center of the black (w)hole. Big Boy, in the short story that bears his name in its title, having slain the white man who murderously seeks to reduce him to a "zero image," tells his parents: "Theres some holes big enough fer me to git in n stay till Will comes erlong."[51] "Will," of course, is simply a proper name in the fiction, but its conjunction with the protagonist's strategy of retreat is significant in a delineation of the rites of the black (w)hole. In successive acts of "will," Big Boy escapes a white world's murderous conception of blackness. The hole into which he enters to avoid a lynch mob in hot pursuit is—in any blue/black reading of Afro-American experience— clearly a *singularly* black route of escape.

Several days prior to their disastrous encounter with the white world's "zero image," Big Boy and his youthful companions have turned a southern hillside into a highballing train, a blues-whistle locomotive of liberation. By digging kiln holes into southern earth and setting tin cans of water in the holes to boiling, the black boys have turned dirt, the earth itself, into an instrument of freedom's desire:

> The train [heard by Big Boy secure in one of the kiln holes] made him remember how they had dug these kilns on long, hot summer days, how they had made boilers out of big tin cans, filled them with water, fixed stoppers for steam, cemented them in holes with wet clay, and built fires under them. He recalled how they had danced and yelled when a stopper blew out of a boiler, letting out a big spout of steam

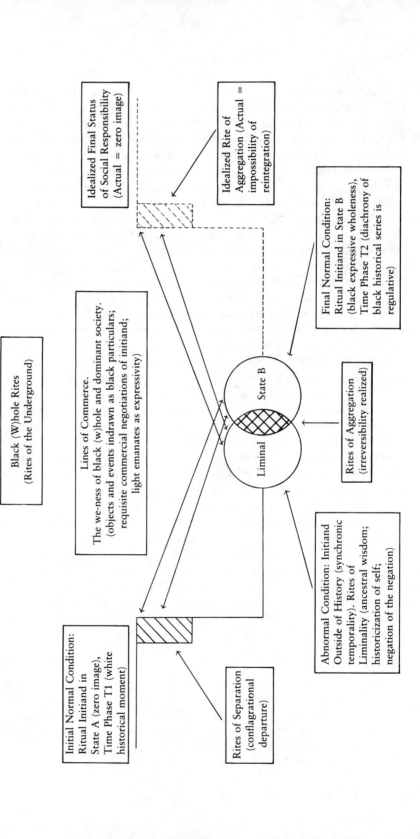

Black (W)hole Rites
(Rites of the Underground)

Lines of Commerce.
The we-ness of black (w)hole and dominant society.
(objects and events indrawn as black particulars;
requisite commercial negotiations of initiand;
light emanates as expressivity)

Idealized Final Status
of Social Responsibility
(Actual = zero image)

Idealized Rite of
Aggregation (Actual =
impossibility of
reintegration)

Final Normal Condition:
Ritual Initiand in State B
(black expressive wholeness),
Time Phase T2 (diachrony of
black historical series is
regulative)

State B

Liminal

Rites of Aggregation
(irreversibility realized)

Abnormal Condition: Initiand
Outside of History (synchronic
temporality). Rites of
Liminality (ancestral wisdom;
historicization of self;
negation of the negation)

Initial Normal Condition:
Ritual Initiand in
State A (zero image),
Time Phase T1 (white
historical moment)

Rites of
Separation
(conflagrational
departure)

> and a shrill whistle. There were times when they had the whole hillside blazing and smoking. Yeah, yuh see, Big Boy wuz Casey Jones n wuz speedin down the gleamin rails of the Southern Pacific . . . [P. 42]

Indeed, Big Boy in the marginal black hole of escape not only assumes figurative dimensions of the railroad hero Casey Jones, but also metaphorical resonances of Afro-America's arch trickster—Brer Rabbit himself. The agon of "Big Boy Leaves Home" is, finally, that of the wily hare Big Boy against the ferocious white hounds seeking to drive him out of existence—to "beat" his desire down to zero. "Gawddam them white folks!" the protagonist reflects bitterly, "Thas all they wuz good fer, t run a nigger down like a rabbit. Yeah, they git yuh in a corner n then they let yuh have it" (p. 44). But oppression's traditional scenario is thwarted in Big Boy's case. No one lets *him* have it. He violently confronts the green-eyed hound that threatens his (w)hole. Strangling the dog to death, he escapes to the universe of the North when "Will comes erlong" in the morning. The rabbit hole, black hole, train-whistle-heroic domain of Afro-American underground expressive *Will* results in self-defense and escape.

VI

But a black boy violently initiated into manhood is not, according to Wright's short fiction, presented with substantially altered prospects in the North. "The Man Who Lived Underground," a novella published in 1944, is set in the North and signals what might be termed a "black-hole intentionality" in its very title.[52] When the work's protagonist "gets the picture," he discovers that he—like many thousands gone before—is always/already "guilty." Escaping from a trumped-up murder charge down a city sewer system manhole, he proceeds to construct an inversively expressive text with the shattered instrumentalities of the white-owned aboveground world.

The story of "The Man Who Lived Underground" is one of Wright's more striking presentations of the crime-magazine plot in a form designed for an implied audience of symbolically aware readers.[53] It presents a system of actions familiar to readers of detective fiction and traces, at this interpretive level, events in the life of Fred Daniels, who is arrested, charged with the murder of Mrs. Peabody, and forced by three white policemen to sign a confession. Daniels escapes the police station and takes refuge in a dry place in an old sewer beneath the city. In this underground world, he comes to a new and authentic consciousness of his own and society's essential condition and eventually ascends to share his new knowledge.

The conjunctions between this sequence of actions and Feodor Dostoevsky's "Notes from Underground" have been remarked by past critics.[54] A descent to a new level of comprehension followed by an emergent desire for dialogue with one's judges brings Wright's work into archetypal accord with that of his Slavic predecessor. Daniels's acts of fleeing the police station and establishing a voluntary underground exile, moreover, seem to imply a central propostition articulated by Dostoevsky. The narrator of "Notes from Underground" says to the judges:

> You see, you gentlemen have, to the best of my knowledge, taken your whole register of human advantages from the averages of statistical figures and politico-economical formulas. Your advantages are prosperity, wealth, freedom, peace—and so on, and so on. So that the man who should, for instance, go openly and knowingly in opposition to all that list would, to your thinking, and indeed mine too, of course, be an obscurantist or an absolute madman: would not he? But, you know, this is what is surprising: why does it so happen that all these statisticians, sages and lovers of humanity, when they reckon up human advantages invariably leave one out? They don't even take it into their reckoning in the form in which it should be taken and the whole reckoning depends upon that. . . . One's own free unfettered choice, one's own caprice—however wild it may be, one's own fancy worked up at times to a frenzy—is that very "most advantageous advantage" which we have overlooked, which comes under no classification and against which all systems and theories are continually being shattered to atoms.[55]

Fred Daniels's "anti-system" acts and the point of view that motivates them, however, do not find a responsive audience aboveground. When he is again in the custody of Johnson, Murphy, and Lawson—the three policemen who first extract his confession—he is taken back to the man-hole where he first descended. As he summons the officers to his underground cave, promising them the reward of enlightenment, Lawson shoots him in the chest. The novella concludes as the black man's eyes close and he becomes "a whirling object rushing alone in the darkness, veering, tossing, lost in the heart of the earth."

From the perspective of rites of the black (w)hole, Wright's simply described plot becomes an occasion for an exceedingly rich representation of the encounter with a zero image. Like Kafka's Joseph K, Wright's protagonist finds himself under arrest and charged with crime by the authorities for no apparent reason. Daniels, an employee of Mrs. Wooten (Mrs. Peabody's next-door neighbor) and a contentedly married man, is suddenly subjected to brutal and arbitrary constraints of the state. To end his pain he signs a confession he has not even read. His condition is one of uncomprehending guilt. His initial status in the eyes of white society, therefore, is that of a "branded" man. Separation from this status begins when he leaps from the police station's window. Through an act of will, he moves decisively away from a passive and guilty subjugation.

The sirens (an ironical word given the role of Sirens in Western mythology) that mark the opening of "The Man Who Lived Underground" serve as an audible boundary separating Daniels from the aboveground: " A police car swished by through the rain, its siren rising sharply. They're looking for me all over. . . . He crept to the door and squinted through the fogged plate glass. He stiffened as the siren rose and died in the distance. Yes, he had to hide, but where?" (p. 22). The answer to his query comes when tiny columns of water "snake into the air from the perforations of a manhole cover." The columns are a sign of underground currents, and they draw Daniels to the manhole from which they arise. The audible boundary of the sirens and a spatial boundary marked by the manhole's cover converge as Daniels descends into darkness: "He heard a prolonged scream of brakes and the siren broke off. Oh, God! They had found him. Looming above his head in the rain a white face hovered over the hole" (p. 23). The policeman peering into the underground, however, is only interested in replacing the cover: "The cover clanged into place, muffling the sights and sounds of the upper world" (p. 23).

The rite of separation is complete; the opposition between "aboveground" and "underground" is firmly established. Daniels becomes a liminal figure hovering "between two worlds" (p. 39). His isolation from prevailing classifications aboveground is reflected by the disappearance of time and the loss of social designation that occur in his new existence: "In this darkness the only notion he had of time was when a match flared and measured time by its fleeting light" (p. 26). After stealing a typewriter on one of his excursions through the underground, he "inserted a piece of paper and poised his fingers to write. But what was his name? He stared, trying to remember. He stood and glared about the dirt cave, his name on the tip of his lips. But it would not come to him" (p. 49). Later when he ascends from underground a policeman inquires: "What is your name?" Daniels opens his lips to respond, and "no words came. He had forgotten. But what did it matter if he had? It was not important" (p. 63).

As a nameless figure in a realm of social timelessness, Wright's protagonist is a quintessentially liminal being. His actions include negation, trespass, parody, burlesque, theft, and mockery. He is the agent of dream-visions that are radically inversive in their symbology. And his ironically imaginative creative acts lead ultimately to a transvaluation of value in which guilt is figured as the founding condition of a new order of existence.

The Christian import of Daniels's paradoxical transvaluation of aboveground values is implied by the relationship between the narrative pattern of the novella and the passion and resurrection of Christ. Daniels descends into darkness and the cover is placed on his "tomb" on Friday at dusk. He emerges the following Sunday to the "spirited singing" of a black congregation:

> The Lamb, the Lamb, the Lamb
> I hear thy voice a-calling
> The Lamb, the Lamb, the Lamb
> I feel thy grace a-falling.
> [P. 60]

These messianic lyrics of a second coming are represented as the backdrop for ascent. The aboveground world, however, rejects its new "Savior" by hurling epithets such as "filthy," "rowdy," "drunk," and "crazy" (p. 61). The worshipers forcefully (and with an inversive vehemence worthy of the medieval "feast of fools") eject Daniels.

The conflict between aboveground Christianity and the radical christology represented by an ascendant Daniels begins almost immediately on the protagonist's descent. One of his first subsurface acts is to say an ambivalent no to the proceedings of traditional Christian worshipers whose singing he overhears. When he listens to the religious community enjoining: "Jesus, take me to your home above/And fold me in the bosom of Thy love," Daniels is suddenly aware that he has experienced feelings of guilt like those which prompt the community to enjoin its song. Yet, peering through a small slit in the wall that separates him from the singers in a subbasement, he sees the white robes and shabbily tattered song books and responds as follows: "he shook his head, disagreeing in spite of himself. They oughtn't do that he thought. . . . He felt that he was gazing upon something abysmally obscene" (p. 26).

The singing has first seemed to Daniels like a "siren" or "a baby crying"—hence, it is marked as both a sign of guilt and infantilism. In effect, its subbasement ceremonial context gives it the character of a basic, or primordial, social action in the mediation of guilt. It is, in effect, "primitive" religion designed to "socialize" guilt. Daniels's hesitant negation is directed toward religion conceived in such terms. He thinks of the worshipers' actions as "grovelling" and "begging," reflecting that "those people should stand unrepentant and yield no quarter in singing and praying, yet *he* had run away from the police, had pleaded with them to believe *his* innocence. He shook his head, bewildered" (p. 26).

Thus begins a visual, emotional, and reflective underground encounter with images perceived from what can be called a "threshold perspective." Wily and resourceful, like the trickster of black folklore, Daniels tunnels his way through the earth, transgressing all boundaries in order to secure a distinctive outsider's point of view. He is the unseen seer, the tabula rasa, in fact, for an illicitly gained and radically revisionist comprehension of aboveground existence.

Daniels's perspective is far from a comforting one. The relief provided by a primitive church's "socializing" of guilt is immediately counteracted in the novella by the emotional effects that derive from a "strangely familiar image" which both attracts and repels the protagonist (p. 27). The vague light of a manhole cover reveals:

> a tiny nude body of a baby snagged by debris and half-submerged in water. Thinking that the baby was alive, he moved impulsively to save it, but his aroused feelings told him that it was dead, cold, nothing, the same nothingness he had felt while watching the men and woman singing in the church. Water blossomed about the tiny legs, the tiny arms, the tiny head, and rushed onward. The eyes were closed, as though in sleep; the fists were clenched, as though in protest; and the mouth gaped black in a soundless cry. [P. 27]

The emotional effect of this percept is a sense of "nothingness." The implicit connection between the percept and religious acts of men and women occurs for Daniels at the level of "feeling."

The distinguishing qualities of the baby are its nudity, its "soundless" (and hence *vain*) protest, and its mortality. An array of images complementing this initial representation in the novella allow one (as I shall demonstrate shortly) to infer that the "strangely familiar" image signals the human condition in general. Life is a vast, uncharted sea onto which man is cast naked remaining half-submerged for a breathing instant before sinking to death.

Finitude and nudity (an absence of inherent, or "natural," shelters against an indifferent world) are existentially perceived as distinctive features of man's fate. Philosophies of existence summarize this perspective in the dictum: "Man is nothing special."[56] The defining human act according to such philosophies is to die. The manifest absence of divine, supreme, or holy "essence" that such a determinant mortality signals leads to human feelings of condemnation, imperfection, and guilt. On encountering the dead baby, Daniels feels as "condemned as when the policemen had accused him" (p. 27). The desire for human atonement implied by religious singing such as that he overheard before seeing the baby is a function of men's and women's sense of *nothingness*—of a separation from grace and supreme essence that results from naked mortality.

The protagonist does not comprehend the full significance of the baby's image until a later stage in his underground sojourn, after his consciousness has been shaped by a series of variations of the initial image. When he has tunneled through a brick wall and ascended basement stairs of a building beyond the church, for example, he peeps through a keyhole and sees "the nude waxen figure of a man stretched out upon a white table" (p. 29). He has surfaced at an undertaking establishment, and the image of naked finitude that he encounters is rendered additionally haunting by the presence of a chuckling "invisible voice" in the room where the corpse is lying. The voice seems to imply an unseen, cosmic joker hovering above man's hapless mortality. Only an "empty sky" and "sea," however, mark the scene when Daniels dreams that "his body was washed by cold water . . . and swept out to sea" (p. 33). As he dreams of miraculously walking upon the cold seawater of human existence, he sees himself encountering

> a nude woman holding a nude baby in her arms and the woman was sinking into the water holding the baby above her head and screaming *help* and he ran over the water to the woman and he reached her just before she went down and took the baby from her hands and stood watching the breaking bubbles where the woman sank and he called *lady*. [P. 34]

Receiving no answer, he lays the baby on the water (where it miraculously floats) and dives below to rescue the woman. His attempt fails, and on surfacing he finds the baby gone. He searches the surface and then "he began to doubt that he could stand upon the water and then he was sinking and as he struggled the water rushed him downward spinning dizzily" (p. 37).

The dream recapitulates the images of the dead baby and the waxen figure at the undertaking establishment. Man is born for death; after a brief attempt at altruistic interaction he submerges in the "gloomy volume" of an impassive sea. The fact of man's condemnation to death as the condition of his existence leads to a sense of imperfection. This sense translates as chronic anxiety that one has fallen from (or been abandoned by) a more perfect Other.

The "Other" (what Kierkegaard calls the "Wholly Other")[57] is envisaged by man as an authority unlimited by death and capable of providing happiness on the far side of human atonement. Forgiveness and eternal life are guarantees for such a religious point of view. Daniels achieves his own perspective on guilt through the power of underground images of mortality. When he again views black worshipers near the conclusion of the novella, he understands that their songs express—at an emotional level—a primal human drive to shed the burden of guilt that seems "innate" to men and women (p. 55). Thoughts of transcendent authority (some "Wholly Other" such as Jesus) lead the religious community to "search for a happiness they [the black congregation] could never find" (p. 57). And the comunity's sacred meditations lead, in turn, to its feelings that it "had committed some dreadful offense" (p. 57). From a newly achieved perspective on guilt and mortality, however, Daniels is able to postulate that the sole "offense" committed by man is being born: "it seemed that one was always trying to remember [he thought] a gigantic shock that had left a haunting impression upon one's body which one could not forget or shake off, but which had been forgotten by the conscious mind, creating in one's life a state of eternal anxiety" (p. 55).

Daniels's reflection here suggests the Freudian notion of a birth trauma[58]—a "gigantic shock" that occurs on leaving behind the warm instinctual world in utero. The notion of such a trauma serves to synthesize and bring to the level of coherent thought the implicit meanings of images the protagonist has encountered. His experiences with the dead have taught him, as it were, at least one consoling and liberating interpretation of guilt's functioning in the life of man. The images of the dead and dying in his subsurface world provide him with a fruitfully altered conception of the animate regions aboveground. The interpretive homology resulting from his revised view reads as follows: religious worshipers seek to make known their guilt to God, just as accused black men confess their guilt to white policemen. The irreducible fact of human mortality prompts human subservience—its groveling and begging before an authority from which man hopes to gain enduring reprieve. Daniels both generalizes his own guilt and, by the novella's conclusion, contemplates his own *death* as transcendence.[59] He dreams that he stands

> in a room watching over his own nude body lying stiff and cold upon a white table. At the far end of the room he saw a crowd of people huddled in a corner, afraid of his body. Though lying dead upon the table, he was standing in some mysterious way at his side, warding off the people, guarding his body, and laughing to himself as he observed the situation. They're scared of me, he thought. [Pp. 53–54]

Guardianship over his own death is the signal of Daniels's acceptance of the condition of human finitude. This acceptance forecloses the possibilities of fear and obviates the necessity to plead innocence before authority. Penitent confession becomes a needless act.

The dream revery of guardianship over his own death follows immediately on another dream in which Daniels "saw himself rising, wading again in the sweeping water of the sewer; he came to a manhole and climbed out and was amazed to discover that he had hoisted himself into a room filled with armed policemen who were watching him intently" (p. 53). There is no need for, nor fear of, the authority figures in this dream. *Authority* only has power over those whose instinctual fear of death and resultant feelings of guilt make them incapable of transcending aboveground institutions established to socialize their anxieties. By abandoning the confessional structure of the police station and descending to an emotional level where guilt's earliest traces are embedded, Daniels therapeutically transcends aboveground arrangements. His readings of images of mortality return him to himself as a limited—but responsible—agent of his own destiny.

The implicit message of the protagonists's progress is not: "If God is dead, then all things are possible." Rather, his underground encounters

lead him to infer: If mankind is mortal and born without inherent shelter-
ing norms, then existential freedom is the founding condition of human
existence. Jean-Paul Sartre's realization that "Man is condemned to be
free" is identical to the discovery of Wright's progatonist.[60]

In order to arrive at the view of man's fate attained by Daniels, "The
Man Who Lived Underground" implies that one must tunnel through
walls, trespass sacred religious precincts, peep through keyholes of the
unsuspecting, and secure to oneself the boundless and mythical freedom of
dreams. One must move in the unsocial ways of the ludic trickster in order
to effect the type of transvaluation of values represented by Daniels's
actions during one of his forays aboveground. As he prepares to leave the
aboveground, he

> [scrubs and rinses] his hands meticulously, then . . . [hunts] for a
> towel; there was none. He shut off the water, pulled off his shirt, dried
> his hands on it . . . he turned on the faucet again . . . drank in long slow
> swallows. His bladder grew tight; he . . . faced the wall, bent his head,
> and watched a stream strike the floor. His nostrils wrinkled against
> acrid wisps of vapor; though he had tramped in the waters of the
> sewer, he stepped back from the wall so that his shoes, wet with sewer
> slime, would not touch his urine. [P. 31]

Daniels's actions imply a striking transvaluation. He washes *before* descending into the sewer. He protects slimy shoes from the touch of urine.
The scene suggests that what might be defined as a "polluted" world
underground has become a sacred territory.

The employment of the word "polluted" here is meant to extend my
earlier definitions of the "zero image" to include striking insights on
pollution beliefs and social categories represented by Mary Douglas's
study *Purity and Danger*.[61] Douglas, in a stunning account of "The Abom-
inations of Leviticus," demonstrates that the "unclean" items abhorred by
the culinary code of Leviticus are, in fact, anomalies. They are not unclean
in themselves, but merely as the negative and anomalous side of what are
defined as *pure* items. Douglas summarizes her conclusions as follows: "a
rule of avoiding anomalous things affirms and strengthens the definitions
to which they do not conform. So where Leviticus abhors crawling things,
we should see the abomination as the negative side of the pattern of things
approved" (p. 39). The proposition might be introduced that the abhor-
rent is that which does not *fit*; "dirt" is matter out of place (or unplaceable
matter). Ironically, the very negative, anomalous, and ambiguous character of the "polluted" gives it suprarational efficacy in cultural rituals. The
"tainted" (such as twins in some traditional societies) may bespeak the
intervention of the divine. "Dirt" and "danger" may thus exist in the same
matrix with the sacred and the divine.

We can speak of holy anomalies that mark a boundary between the sacred and the secular—the world of man and the intervention of the gods. The uncategorical nature of the polluted, however, makes it a cause of grave cultural anxiety which society always attempts to ameliorate through the manipulation of verbal categories. In a suggestive essay entitled "Anthropological Aspects of Language: Animal Categories and Verbal Abuse," Edmund Leach persuasively argues that "our world is a representation of our language categories and not vice versa."[62] *Between* such categories, however—in the interstices, as it were, between *p* and ~*p*—lies an ambiguous region subject to taboo. In a conventional, white American field of cultural perception, the Afro-American falls between categories into a suppressed, "unnameable," taboo. He is thus a *tertium quid*, a "third thing" giving forth neither human nor animal image. From the perspective of Douglas's analysis of pollution beliefs, the Afro-American—in the white American perceptual scheme—is a threat to order. The physiological avoidances of blacks reflected by "color bars" and "caste barriers" are "symbolic expressions of other undesirable contacts which would have repercussions on the structure of [American] social or cosmological ideas."[63]

The extensions to language categories and social boundaries implied here suggest that a "zero image" is a deeply embedded taboo of white American cultural life, a symbolic mode of processing reality that forestalls even physical proximity with blacks in its attempt to preserve and promote a distinctively white ordering of reality. The black speaking subject who attempts to invert the negative ontology that whites promote as a "natural" entry in American discourse becomes a heroic figure. By separating himself from the white, perceptual void, the inversive black subject achieves new status. His actions contribute to the institution of a new "interstitial" cultural discourse and both substantiate and materialize a distinctively black mode of constituting "reality."

Immediately before washing his hands at the sink, Daniels views with compassion a sea of laughing faces watching the "jerking shadows" of the screen in a moviehouse. The notion of art as illusion,[64] as a means of socializing the instinctual life of man, implied by this encounter leads the protagonist to conclude: "these people [the theater audience] were children sleeping in their living, awake in their dying" (p. 31). He envisions stepping out "upon thin air" and walking "on down to the audience; and, hovering in the air just above them" to awaken them to consciousness. But he judges that such a course would be of little avail. Like the messianic dream journey on the sea previously discussed, Daniels's moviehouse reverie suggests that even a miraculous and saving walk by an altruistic messiah cannot rescue man from his fate. Only by transmuting normative values—by manipulating the boundaries between purity and danger—can man engage emotional experiences that enable him to cast off illusion. Hence the protagonist washes his hands of aboveground experience, descending once more to a sacred, subsurface domain of intense emotional existence.

The emotional, socially uncategorized constructs that Wright's liminal and seemingly inarticulate hero encounters suggest the possibility of a productive phenomenological consideration of "The Man Who Lived Underground."[65] According to Edmund Husserl, the human sense of identity is the result of human consciousness acting in a straightforward manner.[66] A person's sense of himself is formed, therefore, without his being actively aware of its formation. Hence, our identity, or our sense of precisely who we are, is never, as a matter of course, genuine, or "authentic" (to employ Husserl's term) because the origins of identity remain unclear.

The phenomenological act par excellence is to reflectively meditate on the development of the sense of identity as a "specific theme." The mental operations represented by Wright's "The Man Who Lived Underground" constitute such a meditation. Daniels moves beyond an always/already formed sense of identity as a *guilty* social being to a comprehension of the constitutive activities of human consciousness itself. His trespassing of social boundaries and his subverting of social norms enable him, one might say, to grasp the phylogeny of human culture. In effect, he recapitulates in his own descrete meditation the experience of the entire species. The generative images of this recapitulation are ones of economic exploitation and war. The protagonist's formative actions are those of thief and clown.

The most forceful symbolic structure in Daniels's reflections on the constitution of human consciousness is Peer's—Manufacturing Jewelers, the factory that he robs. This factory is an icon of human transformation of the world into commodities with cultural value. Manufacturing cultural value involves such processes as the conversion of *stones* into "diamonds" and the conversion of minerals into watches to serve as instruments of cultural time. An anthropological reading of man's development to a stage of cultural manufacture suggests that he moves from a status as a simple tool-user to an industrial order of society in which valuables and values are factory produced. It is not the *labor* of tradesmen who work at factory benches and machines, however, that Daniels discovers in his liminal observations of Peer's. Rather, he gazes in fascination at a disembodied white hand twirling the dial of the factory safe:

> He [Daniels] held his breath; an eerie white hand, seemingly detached from its arm, touched the metal knob and whirled it, first to the left, then to the right. It's a safe! . . . Suddenly he could see the dial no more; a huge metal door swung slowly toward him and he was looking into a safe filled with green wads of paper money, rows of coins wrapped in brown paper, and glass jars and boxes of various sizes. [P. 35]

This image eventually comes to signal the absolute absurdity of above-ground values.

The safe, in fact, is a repository of surplus value. This Marxian concept, which I discussed at length in my first chapter, seems an apt description of the safe's contents. It holds the profitable residue resulting from a discrepancy between subsistence wages paid to the worker for labor power and the increase in store derived from actual labor by managers of the factory. The surplus achieved is *of value*, however, only because an aboveground community has entered into patterns of evaluation that give rise to the factory in the first instance.

The upper world's *estimate* and *use* of products viewed in the safe gives these products value. From an underground, or "primitive" apprehension, such items are no more than toys. And in the most daringly inversive act of his liminal existence, Daniels—who has climbed up a rain pipe (thus reversing the downward path of dirt and debris into the sewer) to oversee the acts of the "white hand"—*steals* the combination to the factory safe.

The sound of a typewriter is the audible sign of the factory world—the world of business—and it is opposed by the crude petroglyph which Daniels scratches into the brick wall of Peer's—Manufacturing Jewelers (p. 42). With a stolen screwdriver he etches the safe's combination in order to rob the factory. At the time of his robbery, his scratchings on the wall have been transferred to memory as a lesson learned—if not yet fully understood: "He turned the dial to the figures he saw on the blackboard of his memory; it was so easy that he felt that the safe had not been locked at all" (p. 44).

Before effecting his bold theft, Daniels has undergone an experience that brings together in his mind the processes of slaughter—the butchery of the living by the living—and economic change. Attempting to tunnel into Peer's, he finds himself instead in an icebox where "halves and quarters of hogs and lambs and steers [hang from] metal hooks on the low ceiling, red meat encased in folds of cold white fat" (p. 37). A butcher enters the freezer, and Daniels watches as he uses a cleaver to cut away a portion of meat. The man's actions are described in sanguinary terms:

> Each time he lifted the cleaver and brought it down upon the meat, he let out a short, deep-chested grunt. After he had cut the meat, he wiped the blood off the wooden block with a sticky wad of gunny sack and hung the cleaver on a hook. His face was proud as he placed the chunk of meat in the crook of his elbow and left. [P. 37]

A moment later, the man says: "Forty-eight cents a pound, ma'am," as the cash register rings with a "vibrating, musical tingle." Daniels's mind is fixed all the while on the meat cleaver's "sharp edge smeared with cold blood" (pp. 37–38). The associative union between butchery and economics as distinctive features of aboveground existence is not fully realized until later in the narrative when the cleaver merges with images of war broadcast by Daniels's stolen radio.

From his situation inside Nick's Fruits and Meats (an establishment that also converts items of the natural world into cultural commodities), Daniels is driven to a burlesque parody of aboveground's mercantile enterprise. Prying open the door of the delicatessen with his screwdriver, he becomes a clown of commerce. He is the gluttonous trickster who consumes the owner's fruits and then sells grapes to a white woman who has come into the store. Finally, he rejects the economics of the upper world by flinging a coin the woman has paid him "to the pavement with a gesture of contempt" (p. 40). His actions are only the first in a series of inversive gestures in the protagonist's spiraling imagistic meditation on economic and aggressive dimensions of the development of human consciousness.

During his robbery of the factory, he straps on a gun and cartridge belt and clowns at the role of lawman. And when he returns to his underground cave with stolen bounty, he mockingly imitates a businessman and clowns before a typewriter. "Yes," he parodically says to empty walls of his cave, "I'll have the contracts ready to go tomorrow" (p. 49). He then burlesques the role of "a rich man who lived aboveground in the obscene sunshine" (p. 51). Strolling past the mound of stolen diamonds in his cave, he only casually touches them with his foot until the moment when "his right foot smashed into the heap and diamonds lay scattered in all directions" (p. 51).

The fullest realization of such mockeries of aboveground values and evaluation comes when Daniels begins a radical and scandalous act of deconstruction. At the moment of his theft, he has meditatively reduced paper money to essential qualities: "He rubbed the money with his fingers, as though expecting it to reveal hidden qualities. He lifted the wad to his nose and smelled the fresh odor of ink. Just like any other paper, he mumbled" (p. 44). Back in his underground cave, he proceeds to reduce all the items stolen from Peer's to a primitive state in order to reveal their implicit qualities and to subvert their aboveground meanings. The stolen items seem to promise—if they can be properly decoded—an *authentic* understanding of human culture and consciousness. That is, they seem to offer keys to a coherent interpretation of the myriad images that have marked his underground journeyings:

> He saw these items hovering before his eyes and felt that some dim meaning linked them together, that some magical relationship made them kin. He stared with vacant eyes, convinced that all of these images, with their tongueless reality, were striving to tell him something. [P. 47]

In order to seize a meaningful "something" and transform a "tongueless reality" into an articulate message, Daniels converts stolen coins into "a glowing mound of shimmering copper and silver" (p. 49). Hundred-dollar bills become wallpaper for his cave. Watches are textually reduced to "metal . . . casing," then "golden disks," and finally "blobs of liquid yellow" (p. 50). Diamond rings are decomposed into "golden bands," "blue and white sparks," and finally "brittle laughter" (p. 50). Diamonds are pressed back as *stones*, into elemental earth. And after he has driven nails into the wall and hung rings, watches, a stolen meat cleaver and a gun, the protagonist has, in fact, effectively produced a *countertext* to the cultural discourse of the upper world.

His willful creation is a striking and ironic inversion of Plato's classical epistemology.[67] The cave dweller of *The Republic* must leave the underground and ascend to a world of "higher intelligence" before he can attain true knowledge. Daniels, by contrast, makes the walls of his underground cave into a knowledgeable statement of essential forms of reality.

His text invokes an image of conflict between "natural" harmony and "cultural" acts of economic production and global warfare: "Brooding over the diamonds on the floor was like looking up into a sky full of stars; the illusion turned into its opposite: he was high up in the air looking down at the twinkling lights of a sprawling city" (p. 52). The reflexive, natural order of phenomena stands opposed to cities of man. The voice of a radio broadcast tells of "cities . . . razed," "planes scattering death," and "troops with fixed bayonets charging in waves against other troops who held fixed bayonets and men groaned as steel ripped into their bodies and they went down to die" (p. 52–53). The bloody meat cleaver and industrial processes that convert natural phenomena into surplus value merge, receiving a coherent, interpretive description in graphic visions of war. Sky, sea, and earth are polluted by mankind's acts of butchery: "steel tanks" rumble "across fields of ripe wheat," and warships draw "near each other over wastes of water." The machine has come crashing indisputably into the garden; cultural mechanics have disrupted nature's fundamental harmony. Supporting the senseless arrival and perpetration is a man-made arsenal of commercial values symbolized by items that Daniels has stolen from Nick's and Peer's—Manufacturing Jewelers.

The aboveground world appears as a "wild forest filled with death." And if the aboveground is, in fact, an untamed wilderness, then the underground text created by Daniels as a counterstatement to norms of the social world can serve as a revised logos—a new "Word" transforming chaos and death into a humane order of existence. A life of responsible human freedom can be predicated, that is to say, on the achieved and authentic consciousness implied by Daniels's text.

The fundamental narrative pattern of "The Man Who Lived Underground" suggests a conversion of "instrumental value" of aboveground objects into expressive, underground, textual value. Stolen goods become expressive signs when the protagonist "reads" their implicit message of false values and cultural bloodshed. The understanding that Daniels derives from his emotional transactions, however, is, in actuality, a wordless phenomenon. His new consciousness, in fact, seems far less "discursive" than *ludic*. It has the expressive character of play or a game.

Both during and immediately after his acts of theft, he plays "games." Further, he refers to his bounty as "serious toys" of the upper world. The watchman's gun is like "a memento from a county fair" (p. 47). And the typewriter is not used to compose serious messages, but to manipulate words "merely for the ritual of performing" an *act* of composition (p. 49). The victory obtained in his phenomenological *meditation on consciousness*, therefore is a ludic triumph. It writes itself at the level of emotions and serves as an idealistic palimpsest covering old cultural tracings. While his new consciousness and the text that it makes available alter irrevocably his definitions of guilt and prompt him to act, they still comprise, in their initial instance, an "inarticulate" victory.

After he has contemplated his own death (in the scene discussed earlier), Daniels arrives at what Heidegger calls a stage of "resolute decision."[68] He decides to ascend and share his liminally attained understanding with aboveground society. Upon his emergence, he has the burlesque appearance of a seedy clown. In a men's clothing store (a cultural establishment designed to cloak man's fundamental nudity) he regards himself in a long mirror and sees "his cheekbones protruded from a hairy black face; his greasy cap. . . perched askew upon his head and his eyes . . . were red and glassy. His shirt and trousers were caked with mud and hung loosely. His hands were gummed with a black stickiness" (p. 60).

Daniels is "dirt" appearing in a world that seeks "purity," a world that conceals nakedness through commercial manufacture and sale of social "clothes." As he moves across the threshold of a black church in the messianic scene referred to earlier, he is summarily rejected. And when he appears, in all of his polluted glory, at the police station where he tendered his earlier confession, the entire establishment is thrown into confusion. For he is not only "polluted" but also culturally inarticulate, a citizen from an underground *mundus inversus*—a world upside down.

The aboveground seeks to contain Daniels with negative verbal epithets—"nuts," "psycho," "Fifth Columnist," "fool" (pp. 63–68). But he is existentially beyond words: "he could no longer think with his mind; he thought with his feelings and no words came" (p. 64). His inversion of cultural norms has left him wordless. And his possible reentry into society with a new and responsible role is blocked by the revised rules that constitute his own new "game." Officer Lawson (son of cultural laws) says in response to the protagonist's assertion that he stole valuables from Peer's in order to "play" with them: "What's your game, boy?" (p. 68). And after a further exchange between the two, Lawson proclaims: "He's playing a game and I wish to God I knew what it was" (p. 68).

Daniels is a ludic clown; he is representative of a revised human emotional and expressive understanding of guilt and innocence, the naturally harmonious and the culturally disruptive, the inherently free-and-limited condition of man and his social grovelings before authority. The protagonist has returned, like the Messiah, from underground, compelled by a sense of compassion and love: "Mister, when I looked through all those holes and saw how people were living, I loved em . . . " (p. 69). But his drive toward community is thwarted by an uncomprehending and conventional aggressiveness of aboveground society. He cannot effect dialogue, *communitas*, or change because the social world fears and rejects an authentic consciousness that he represents.

Like the textualized wall of his cave, therefore, Daniels is only comprehensible at an expressive level that aboveground citizens are unwilling to survey. Finally, his very confession of guilt—the documentary signal of his initial *social* status—is burned by Lawson in an attempt to drive away this parodic representation of man in an untrammeled condition of expressive freedom.

Daniels is "thunderstruck" by the destruction of his confession. For his underground message is significant only insofar as it marks the conclusive phase of rites of transition that began in an initial, confessional relationship. Still optimistic about reentry, however, he allows himself to be manipulated by the white policemen as they feign a desire to share his underground wisdom. Daniels leads the officers to the manhole. He descends the steps as a willing guide. But at this hopeful juncture, which portends a new order of existence for the world, Lawson fires a bullet into his chest. Aggregation is violently denied.

The protagonist's decoding—indeed, his destruction—of instrumentalities of aboveground life leads to a comprehension of an essential humanness (an intersubjectivity) in which all men and women are not only guilty but also condemned to die. Mortality makes a mockery of the acquisitively brutal existence of aboveground life. This text with its implicit antinomian and egalitarian underground norms is violently repudiated by aboveground authority. Daniels's murder transforms immediate revisional textual possibility into "a whirling object rushing along in the darkness" of the sewer's currents.

It is necessary, however, to regard the demise of Wright's protagonist within its black (w)hole ceremonial context, as a *ritual act*. As Daniels whirls into underground darkness, he returns to the singularity of the black (w)hole's expressive cluster. He rejoins, that is, his radically deconstructive text—the "words" through which he became incarnate in the first instance: the signs by which he came to *live* underground. As a primal, expressive Logos, or Word, he is no more dead at the conclusion of the novella than his Judeo-Christian archetype.

VII

Freed from limiting terms of a traditional evaluative discourse, guided by the trope of the black (w)hole, and aware of the densely attractive symbolic action at the core of his fiction, a literary critic should be prepared to acknowledge the singular expressive achievement of Richard Wright. With such enabling conditions in force, the critic should be fully equipped to transcend outmoded terms of an old problematic and to appreciate carnivalesque transformations worked by Wright on the devices of traditional literary discourse. Finally, from a symbolic reading of characteristic fictions such as "Big Boy Leaves Home" and "The Man Who Lived Underground," a critic should feel compelled to designate Wright as the very center of that dark (and powerfully invisible) area of Afro-American life that constitutes its underground expressive (w)holeness.

Richard Wright's translation of the desire of a black blues life into an irresistible *difference* makes him undisputed master of Black Wholeness. If a tradition of modern Afro-American narrative exists, it is only possible because Wright achieved the concentrated power of a Black Whole that attracts all nearby stars and gives birth to the quasi-stellar brightness of successors. Wright is the Black Symbolist par excellence. His "entrance onto the stage of language" marked a daring conversion of a uniquely black blues desire into Afro-American fictions—into expressive (w)holes—that present a culture's social being for itself. In the final analysis, Wright's singular force makes all of us his "assessors" in a key sense of that term. Ultimately, we have no choice but to situate ourselves and our expressive traditions *beside* him.

To Move without Moving: Creativity and Commerce in Ralph Ellison's Trueblood Episode

> Them boss quails is like a good man, what he got to do he *do*.
>
> Trueblood

I

In such close alliance with his predecessor of blue-black, inversive rites of the black underground—indeed, a protégé—yet so anxious to scandalize the name of Wright, Ralph Ellison suggests the agonizing dues extracted

Permission to reprint my essay, "To Move without Moving," *Publications of the Modern Language Association* 98 (October 1983): 828–45, is gratefully acknowledged.

from the author who writes the blues book most excellent—who fitly and brilliantly achieves a form that fulfills the American dream. Dunbar's dilemma and Wright's magnificent expressive strategies in creating authoritative rites that mark a modern Afro-American narrative tradition combine in the career of the author of *Invisible Man*. The combination provides extraordinarily rich and subtle texture for that career. Appearing to mediate between a consuming desire for "literary" form and an overwhelming attraction to the expressive desires of a black blues life, Ellison sometimes seems suspended just above a bedrock ground whose touch would renew him, make him whole. Yet this suspension, like all acts of levitation, is merely an appearance—part of the magic of the crafty blues artist who knows which way the bad wind is blowing. Under blues analysis, Ellison's career emerges as a productive reconciliation of Dunbar's dilemma and Wright's achievement. *Invisible Man* reflexively and nimbly negotiates not only the economics of slavery, but also the *break* held to obtain between "the forms of things unknown" and the "evolved" forms of English and American literatures. The novel not only discovers AMERICA in a stunningly energetic blues manner, but also sets that idea singing in ways unheard before its production and unequaled since its first appearance in 1952. To study the fulfillment of a dream of American form is to read *Invisible Man* as a brilliant expressive moment that achieves both the limitless freedom of myth and the remarkably efficacious passage through rites of the blue-black, underground (w)hole.

In his essay "Richard Wright's Blues,"[69] Ralph Ellison states one of his cherished distinctions: "The function, the psychology, of artistic selectivity is to eliminate from art form all those elements of experience which contain no compelling significance. Life is as the sea, art a ship in which man conquers life's crushing formlessness, reducing it to a course, a series of swells, tides and wind currents inscribed on a chart" (p. 94). The distinction between nonsignificant life experiences and their inscribed, artistic significance (i.e., the meaning induced by form) leads Ellison to concur with André Malraux that artistic significance alone "enables man to conquer chaos and to master destiny" (p. 94).

Artistic "technique," according to Ellison, is the agency through which artistic meaning and form are achieved. In "Hidden Name and Complex Fate"[70] he writes:

> It is a matter of outrageous irony, perhaps, but in literature the great social clashes of history no less than the painful experience of the individual are secondary to the meaning which they take on through the skill, the talent, the imagination and personal vision of the writer who transforms them into art. Here they are reduced to more manageable proportions; here they are imbued with humane value; here, injustice and catastrophe become less important in themselves than what the writer makes of them. [Pp. 148–49]

Even the thing-in-itself of lived, historical experience is thus seen as devoid of "humane value" before its sea change under the artist's transforming technique.

Since Ellison focuses his interest on the literary, the inscribed, work of art, he regards even folklore as part of that realm of life "elements . . . which contain no compelling significance" in themselves. In "Change the Joke and Slip the Yoke,"[71] he asserts:

> the Negro American writer is also an heir to the human experience which is literature, and this might well be more important to him than his living folk tradition. For me, at least, in the discontinuous, swiftly changing and diverse American culture, the stability of the Negro folk tradition became precious as a result of an act of literary discovery. . . . For those who are able to translate [the folk tradition's] meanings into wider, more precise vocabularies it has much to offer indeed. [Pp. 72–73]

During a BBC program recorded in May 1982 and entitled "Garrulous Ghosts: The Literature of the American South," Ellison stated that the fiction writer, to achieve proper resonance, must go beyond the blues—a primary and tragically eloquent form of American expression:

> The blues are very important to me. I think of them as the closest approach to tragedy that we have in American art forms. And I'm not talking about black or white, I mean just American. Because they do combine the tragic and the comic in a very subtle way and, yes, they are very important to me. But they are also limited. And if you are going to write fiction there is a level of consciousness which you move toward which I would think transcends the blues.

Thus Ellison seems to regard Afro-American folklore, before its translation into "more precise vocabularies," as part of lived experience. Art and chaos appear to be homologous with literature and folklore.

To infer such a homology from one or two critical remarks, however, is to risk the abyss of "false distinction," especially when one is faced with a canon as rich as Ralph Ellison's. It is certainly true that the disparagement of folk expression suggested by these remarks can be qualified by the praise of folklore implicit in Ellison's assertion that Afro-American expressive folk projections are a group's symbolically "profound" attempts to "humanize" the world.[72] Such projections, even in their crudest forms, constitute the "humble base" on which "great literature" is erected.

It does seem accurate, however, to say that Ellison's criticism repeatedly implies an extant, identifiable tradition of literary art—a tradition consisting of masters of form and technique who must be read, studied, emulated, and (if one is lucky and eloquent) equaled. This tradition stands as the signal, vital repository of "humane value." And for Ellison the sphere that it describes is equivalent to the primum mobile, lending force and significance to all actions of the descending heavens and earth.

Hence, while the division between folk and artistic may be only discursive, having no more factual reality than any other such division, it seems to matter to Ellison, who never, as far as I know, refers to himself as a folk artist. Moreover, in our era of sophisticated "folkloristics," it seems mere evasion to shy from the assertion that Ellison's criticism ranks folklore below literary art on a total scale of value. What I argue is that the distinction between folklore and literary art evident in Ellison's critical practice collapses in his creative practice in *Invisible Man*'s Trueblood episode. Further, I suggest that an exacting analysis of this episode illuminates the relation not only between Ellison's critical and creative practices but also between what might be called the public and private commerce of black art in America.

The main character in the Trueblood episode, which occupies chapter 2 of *Invisible Man*, is a country blues singer (a tenor of "crude, high, plaintively animal sounds") who is also a virtuoso prose narrator. To understand the disjunctiveness between Ellison's somewhat disparaging critical pronouncements on "raw" folklore and his striking fictional representation of folk character in chapter 2, one must first comprehend, I think, the sharecropper Trueblood's dual manifestation as trickster and merchant, as creative and commercial man. Blues and narration, as modes of expression, conjoin and divide in harmony with these dichotomies. And the episode in its entirety is—as I demonstrate—a metaexpressive commentary on the incumbencies of Afro-American artists and the effects of their distinctive modes of expression.

In an essay that gives a brilliant ethnographic reading of the Balinese cockfight, Clifford Geertz asserts:

> Like any art form—for that, finally, is what we are dealing with—the cockfight renders ordinary, everyday experience comprehensible by presenting it in terms of acts and objects which have had their practical consequences removed and been reduced (or, if you prefer, raised) to the level of sheer appearances, where their meaning can be more powerfully articulated and more exactly perceived.[73]

Catching up the themes of Balinese society in symbolic form, the cockfight thus represents, in Geertz's words, "a metasocial commentary . . . a Balinese reading of Balinese experience, a story they tell themselves about themselves" (p. 448). This implies that the various symbolic (or "semiotic") systems of a culture—religion, politics, economics—can themselves be "raised" to a metasymbolic level by the orderings and processes of "ritual interactions" like the Balinese cockfight.

The coming together of semiotic systems in ways that enlarge and enhance the world of human meanings is the subject of Barbara Babcock-Abrahams's insightful essay "The Novel and the Carnival World."[74] Following the lead of Julia Kristeva, Babcock-Abrahams asserts that a "metalanguage" is a symbolic system that treats of symbolic systems; for example, *Don Quixote* "openly discusses other works of literature and takes the writing and reading of literature as its subject" (p. 912). Both social rituals and novels, since they "embed" other semiotic systems within their "texture," are "multivocal," "polyvalent," or "polysemous"—that is, capable of speaking in a variety of mutually reflexive voices at once.

The multiple narrative frames and voices in Ellison's Trueblood episode include the novel *Invisible Man*, the protagonist's fictive autobiographical account, Norton's story recalled as part of the fictive autobiography, Trueblood's story as framed by the fictive autobiography, the sharecropper's own autobiographical recall, and the dream narrative within that autobiographical recall. All these stories reflect, or "objectify," one another in ways that complicate their individual and composite meanings. Further, the symbolic systems suggested by the stories are not confined to (though they may implicitly comment on) such familiar social configurations as education, economics, politics, and religion. Subsuming these manifestations is the outer symbolic enterprise constituted by the novel itself. Moreover, the Trueblood episode heightens the multivocal character of the novel from within, acting as a metacommentary on the literary and artistic system out of which the work is generated. Further enriching the burden of meanings in the episode are the Christian myth of the Fall and Sigmund Freud's mythic incest "narrative," which are both connoted (summoned as signifiers, in Babcock-Abrahams's terms) and parodied, or inverted. I analyze the text's play on these myths later in my discussion.

For the moment, I am primarily interested in suggesting that the Trueblood episode, like other systematic symbolic phenomena, gains and generates its meanings in a dialogic relation with various systems of signs. As a text this chapter derives its logic from its intertextual relation with surrounding and encompassing texts and in turn complicates their meanings. The Balinese cockfight, according to Geertz, can only tell a "metastory" because it is intertextually implicated in a world that is itself constituted by a repertoire of "stories" (e.g., those of economics and politics) that the Balinese tell themselves.

As a story that the author of *Invisible Man* tells himself about his own practice, the Trueblood episode clarifies distinctions that must be made between Ellison as critic and Ellison as artist. To elucidate its metaexpressive function, one must summon analytical instruments from areas that Ellison sharply debunks in his own criticism.

For example, at the outset of "The World and the Jug,"[75] a masterfully instructive essay on the criticism of Afro-American creativity, Ellison asks:

> Why is it so often true that when critics confront the American as *Negro* they suddenly drop their advanced critical armament and revert with an air of confident superiority to quite primitive modes of analysis? Why is it that sociology-oriented critics seem to rate literature so far below politics and ideology that they would rather kill a novel than modify their presumptions concerning a given reality which it seeks in its own terms to project? [Pp. 115–16]

What I take these questions to imply is that a given artistic reality designed to represent "Negro-American" experience should not be analyzed by "primitive" methods, which Ellison leaves unspecified but seems to associate with sociological, ideological, and political modes of analysis. In the following discussion I hope to demonstrate that sociology, anthropology, economics, politics, and ideology all provide models essential for the explication of the Trueblood episode. The first step, however, is to evoke the theater of Trueblood's performance.

II

Trueblood's narration has an unusual audience, but to the farmer and his Afro-American cohorts the physical setting is as familiar as train whistles in the Alabama night. The sharecropper, a white millionaire, and a naive undergraduate from a nearby black college have arranged themselves in a semicircle of camp chairs in the sharecropper's yard. They occupy a swath of shade cast by the porch of a log cabin that has survived the ravages of climate since the hard times of slavery. The millionaire asks, "How are you faring now? . . . Perhaps I could help."[76] The sharecropper responds, "We ain't doing so bad, suh. 'Fore they heard 'bout what happen to us out here I couldn't get no help from nobody. Now lotta folks is curious and go outta their way to help" (p. 52). What has occurred "out here"—in what the millionaire Mr. Norton refers to as "new territory for me" (p. 45) and what the narrator describes as "a desert" that "almost took [his] breath away" (p. 45)—is Jim Trueblood's impregnation of both his wife and his daughter. The event has brought disgrace on the sharecropper and has mightily embarrassed officials at the nearby black college.

The whites in the neighboring town and countryside, however, are scarcely outraged or perturbed by Trueblood's situation. Rather, they want to keep the sharecropper among them; they warn the college officials not to harass him or his family; and they provide money, provisions, and abundant work. "White folks," says Trueblood, even "took to coming out here to see us and talk with us. Some of 'em was big white folks, too, from the big school way cross the State. Asked me lots 'bout what I thought 'bout things, and 'bout my folks and the kids, and wrote it all down in a book" (p. 53). Hence, when the farmer begins to recount the story of his incestuous act with his daughter Matty Lou, he does so as a man who has thoroughly rehearsed his tale and who has carefully refined his knowledge of his audience: "He cleared his throat, his eyes gleaming and his voice taking on a deep, incantatory quality, as though he had told the story many, many times" (p. 53).

The art of storytelling is not a gift that Trueblood has acquired recently. He is introduced in *Invisible Man* as one who "told the old stories with a sense of humor and a magic that made them come alive" (p. 46). A master storyteller, then, he recounts his provocative exploits to an audience that is by turns shamed, indignant, envious, humiliated, and enthralled.

The tale begins on a cold winter evening in the sharecropper's cabin. The smell of fat meat hangs in the air, and the last kindling crackles in the dying flames of the stove. Trueblood's daughter, in bed between her father and mother, sleepily whispers, "Daddy." At the story's close, the share-cropper reports his resolution to prevent Aunt Cloe the midwife from aborting his incestuous issue. At the conclusion of his tale, he reiterates his judgment that he and his family "ain't doing so bad" in the wake of their ordeal.

Certainly the content and mode of narration the sharecropper chooses reflect his knowledge of what a white audience expects of the Afro-American. Mr. Norton is not only a "teller of polite Negro stories" (p. 37) but also a man who sees nothing unusual about the pregnant Matty Lou's not having a husband. "But that shouldn't be so strange," he remarks (p. 49). The white man's belief in the promiscuity of blacks is further suggested by Mr. Broadnax, the figure in Trueblood's dream who looks at the sharecropper and his daughter engaged in incest and says, "They just nigguhs, leave 'em do it" (p. 58). In conformity with audience expecta-tions, the sharecropper's narrative is aggressively sexual in its representa-tions.

Beginning with an account of the feel of his daughter's naked arm pressed against him in bed, the farmer proceeds to reminisce about bygone days in Mobile when he would lie in bed in the evenings with a woman named Margaret and listen to the music from steamboats passing on the river. Next, he introduces the metaphor of the woman in a red dress "goin' past you down a lane . . . and kinda switchin' her tail 'cause she knows you watchin'" (p. 56). From this evocative picture, he turns to a detailed account of his dream on the night of his incestuous act.

The dream is a parodic allegory in which Trueblood goes in quest of "fat meat." In this episode the name "Mr. Broadnax" (Mr. Broad-in-acts) captures the general concepts that mark any narrative as allegory. The man whose house is on the hill is a philanthropist who gives poor blacks (true bloods) sustaining gifts as "fat meat." The model implied by this conceptualization certainly fits one turn-of-the-century American typology, recalling the structural arrangement by which black, southern colleges were able to sustain themselves. In one sense, the entire Trueblood episode can be read as a pejorative commentary on the castrating effects of white philanthropy. Trueblood's dream narrative is parodic because it reveals the crippling assumptions (the castrating import) of the philanthropic model suggested in "Broadnax." The man who is broad-in-acts in the dream is the one who refers to the sharecropper and his daughter as "just nigguhs." Further, his philanthropy—like Mr. Norton's—has a carnal undercurrent: it is dangerously and confusingly connected with the sexuality of Mrs. Broadnax. What he dispenses as sustaining "fat meat" may only be the temporarily satisfying thrill of sexual gratification. The "pilgrim," or quester, in Trueblood's dream allegory flees from the dangers and limitations of such deceptive philanthropy. And the general exposé effected by the narrative offers a devastating critique of that typography which saw white men on the hill (northern industrialists) as genuinely and philanthropically responsive to the needs of those in the valley (southern blacks).

Instructed to inquire at Mr. Broadnax's house, Trueblood finds himself violating a series of southern taboos and fleeing for his life. He enters the front door of the home, wanders into a woman's bedroom, and winds up trapped in the embraces of a scantily clad white woman. The gastronomic and sexual appetites surely converge at this juncture, and the phrase "fat meat" takes on a dangerous burden of significance. The dreamer breaks free, however, and escapes into the darkness and machinery of a grandfather clock. He runs until a bright electric light bursts over him, and he awakens to find himself engaged in sexual intercourse with his daughter.

In *Totem and Taboo*, Freud advances the hypothesis that the two taboos of totemism—the interdictions against slaying the totem animal and against incest—result from events in human prehistory.[77] Following Darwin's speculations, Freud claims that human beings first lived in small hordes in which one strong, jealous man took all women to himself, exiling the sons to protect his own exclusive sexual privileges. On one occasion, however, Freud suggests, the exiled sons arose, slew and ate the father, and then, in remorse, established the taboo against such slaughter. To prevent discord among themselves and to ensure the survival of their new form of social organization, they also established a taboo against sexual intercourse with the women of their own clan. Exogamy, Freud concludes, is based on a prehistorical advance from a lower to a higher stage of social organization.

From Freud's point of view, Trueblood's dream and subsequent incest seem to represent a historical regression. The sharecropper's dreamed violations of southern social and sexual taboos are equivalent to a slaughter of the white patriarch represented by Mr. Broadnax, who does, indeed, control the "fat" and "fat meat" of the land. To eat fat meat is to partake of the totemic animal. And having run backward in time through the grandfather clock, Trueblood becomes the primal father, assuming all sexual prerogatives unto himself. He has warned away "the boy" (representing the tumultuous mob of exiled sons) who wanted to take away his daughter, and as the sexual partner of both Matty Lou and Kate, he reveals his own firm possession of all his "womenfolks"—his status, that is to say, as a sexual producer secure against the wrath of his displaced "sons." Insofar as Freud's notions of totemism represent a myth of progressive social evolution, the farmer's story acts as a countermyth of inversive social dissolution. It breaks society down into components and reveals man in what might be called his presocial and unaccommodated state.

One reason for the sharecropper's singular sexual prerogatives is that the other Afro-Americans in his area are either so constrained or so battered by their encounters with society that they are incapable of a legitimate and productive sexuality. The sharecropper's territory is bounded on one side by the black college where the "sons" are indoctrinated in a course of instruction that leaves them impotent. On the other side lie the insane asylum and the veterans' home, residences of black men driven mad—or at least rendered psychologically and physically crippled—by their encounters with America. These "disabled veterans" are scarcely "family men" like Trueblood. Rather, they are listless souls who visit the whores in "the sun-shrunk shacks at the railroad crossing . . . hobbling down the tracks on crutches and canes; sometimes pushing the legless, thighless one in a red wheelchair" (p. 35). In such male company Trueblood seems the only person capable of ensuring an authentic Afro-American lineage. When he finds himself atop Matty Lou, therefore, both the survival of the clan and the sharecropper's aversion to pain require him to reject the fate that has been physically or psychologically imposed on his male cohorts. He says, "There was only one way I can figger that I could git out: that was with a knife. But I didn't have no knife, and if you'all ever seen them geld them young boar pigs in the fall, you know I knowed that was too much to pay to keep from sinnin' " (p. 59). In this reflection, he brings forward one of the dominant themes of *Invisible Man*. This theme—one frequently slighted, or omitted, in discussions of the novel—is black male sexuality.

Perhaps critical prudery prevents commentators from acknowledging the black male phallus as a dominant symbol in much of the ritual interaction of *Invisible Man*. In *The Forest of Symbols: Aspects of Ndembu Ritual*,[78] Victor Turner provides suggestive definitions for both "ritual" and "dominant symbols." He describes ritual as "prescribed formal behavior for occasions not given over to technological routine, having reference to beliefs in mystical beings or powers. The symbol is the smallest unit of ritual which still retains the specific properties of ritual behavior; it is the ultimate unit of specific structure in a ritual context" (p. 19). For Turner, the most prominent—the "senior," as it were—symbols in any ritual are dominant symbols (p. 20); they fall into a class of their own. The important characteristic of such symbols is that they bring together disparate meanings, serving as a kind of semiotic shorthand. Further, they can have both ideological and sensuous associations; the mudyi tree of Ndembu ritual, for example, refers both to the breast milk of the mother and to the axiomatic values of the matrilineal Ndembu society (p. 28).

Ellison's *Invisible Man* is certainly an instance of "prescribed formal behavior" insofar as the novel is governed by the conventions of the artistic system in which it is situated, a system that resides ludically outside "technological routine" and promotes the cognitive exploration of all systems of "being" and "power," whether mystical or not. The black phallus is a dominant symbol in the novel's formal patterns of behavior, as its manifold recurrence attests. In "The Art of Fiction: An Interview," Ellison writes, "People rationalize what they shun or are incapable of dealing with; these superstitions and their rationalizations become rituals as they govern behavior. The rituals become social forms, and it is one of the functions of the artist to recognize them and raise them to the level of art" (p. 175). Stated in slightly different terms, Ellison's comment suggests an intertextual (indeed, a connoted) relation between the prescribed formal social behaviors or American racial interaction and the text of the novel. Insofar as Jim Crow social laws and the desperate mob exorcism of lynchings (with their attendant castrations) describe a formal pattern of Anglo-American behavior toward black men, this pattern offers an instance of ritual in which the black phallus gathers an extraordinary burden of disparate connotations, both sensuous and ideological. It should come as no surprise that an artist as perceptive as Ellison recognizes the black phallus as a dominant symbol of the sometimes bizarre social rituals of America and incorporates it into the text of a novel. In "The Art of Fiction," in fact, Ellison calls the battle-royal episode of *Invisible Man* "a ritual in preservation of caste lines, a keeping of taboo to appease the gods and ward off bad luck" (p. 175). He did not have to invent the ritual, he says; all he had to do was to provide "a broader context of meaning" for the patterns the episode represents.

The black phallus, then, does seem an implicit major symbol in Ellison's text, and there are venerable precedents for the discussion of male sexual symbols in ritual. For example, in "Deep Play" Geertz writes:

> To anyone who has been in Bali any length of time, the deep psychological identification of Balinese men with their cocks is unmistakable. The double entendre here is deliberate. It works in exactly the same

way in Balinese as it does in English, even to producing the same tired
jokes, strained pun, and uninventive obscenities. [Gregory] Bateson
and [Margaret] Mead have even suggested that, in line with the
Balinese conception of the body as a set of separately animated parts,
cocks are viewed as detachable, self-operating penises, ambulent
genitals with a life of their own. [P. 417]

Certainly, the notion of "ambulent genitals" figures in the tales of the
roguish trickster as recorded in Paul Radin's classic work *The Trickster*.[79]
In tale sixteen of the Winnebago trickster cycle, Wakdjunkaga the trickster
sends his penis across the waters of a lake to have intercourse with a chief's
daughter.

The black phallus as a symbol of unconstrained force that white men
contradictorily envy and seek to destroy appears first in the opening
chapter of *Invisible Man*. The influential white men of a small southern
town force the protagonist and his fellow black boxers in the battle royal
to gaze on "a magnificent blonde—stark naked" (p. 18). The boys are
threatened both for looking and for not looking, and the white men smile
at their obvious fear and discomfiture. The boys know the bizarre consequences that accompany the white men's ascription of an animal-like
and voracious sexuality to black males. Hence, they respond in biologi-
cally normal but socially fearful (and justifiably embarrassed) ways. One
boy strives to hide his erection with his boxing gloves, pleading desper-
ately to go home. In this opening scene, the white woman as a parodic
version of American ideals ("a small American flag tattooed upon her
belly," p. 19), is forced into tantalizing interaction with the mythically
potent force of the black phallus. But because the town's white males
exercise total control of the situation, the scene is akin to a castration,
excision, or lynching.

Castration is one function of the elaborate electrically wired glass box
that incarcerates the protagonist in the factory-hospital episode: " 'Why
not castration, doctor?' a voice asked waggishly" (p. 231). In the Brotherhood, the class struggle is rather devastatingly transformed into the "ass
struggle" when the protagonist's penis displaces his oratory as ideological
agent. A white woman who hears him deliver a speech and invites him
home seizes his biceps passionately and says, "Teach me, talk to me. Teach
me the beautiful ideology of Brotherhood" (p. 405). And the protagonist
admits that suddenly he "was lost" as "the conflict between the ideological
and the biological, duty and desire," became too subtly confused (p. 406).
Finally, in the nightmare that concludes the novel, the invisible man sees
his own bloody testes, like those of the castrated Uranus of Greek myth,
floating above the waters underneath a bridge's high arc (p. 557). In the
dream, he tells his inquisitors that his testes dripping blood on the black
waters are not only his "generations wasting upon the water" but also the

"sun" and the "moon"—and, indeed, the very "world"—of their own human existence (p. 558). The black phallus—in its creative, ambulent, generative power, even when castrated—is like the cosmos itself, a self-sustaining and self-renewing source of life, provoking both envy and fear in Anglo-American society.

While a number of episodes in *Invisible Man* (including Trueblood's dream) suggest the illusory freedoms and taboo-induced fears accompanying interaction between the black phallus and white women, only the Trueblood encounter reveals the phallus as producing Afro-American generations rather than wasting its seed upon the water. The cosmic force of the phallus thus becomes, in the ritual action of the Trueblood episode, symbolic of a type of royal paternity, an aristocratic procreativity turned inward to ensure the royalty (the "truth," "legitimacy," or "authenticity") of an enduring black line of descent. In his outgoing phallic energy, therefore, the sharecropper is (as we learn on his first appearance in *Invisible Man*) a "hard worker" who takes care of "his family's needs" (p. 46). His family may, in a very real sense, be construed as the entire clan, or tribe, of Afro-America.

As cosmic creator, Trueblood is not bound by ordinary codes of restraint. He ventures chaos in an outrageously sexual manner—and survives. Like the Winnebago trickster Wakdjunkaga, he offers an inversive play on social norms. He is the violator of boundaries who—unlike the scapegoat—eludes banishment.[80] Indeed, he is so essential to whites in his sexual role that, after demonstrating his enviable ability to survive chaos, he and his family acquire new clothes and shoes, abundant food and work, long-needed eyeglasses, and even the means to reshingle their cabin. "I looks up at the mornin' sun," says the farmer, describing the aftermath of his incestuous act, "and expects somehow for it to thunder. But it's already bright and clear. . . . I yells, 'Have mercy lawd!' and waits. And there's nothin' but the clear bright mornin' sun" (pp. 64–65).

Noting that most tricksters "have an uncertain sexual status," Victor Turner points out that on some occasions

> tricksters appear with exaggerated phallic characteristics: Hermes is symbolized by the herm or pillar, the club, and the ithyphallic statue; Wakdjunkaga has a very long penis which has to be wrapped around him and put over his shoulder in a box; Eshu is represented in sculpture as having a long curved hairdress carved as a phallus.[81]

Such phallic figures are, for Turner, representatives of "liminality"[82]—that "betwixt and between" phase of rites of passage when an individual has left one fixed social status but has not yet been incorporated into another. When African boys are secluded in the forest during circumcision rites, for example, they are in a liminal phase between childhood and adulthood.

During this seclusion they receive mythic instruction in the origin and structures of their society. This instruction serves not only to "deconstruct" the components of the ordered social world they have left behind but also to reveal these elements recombined into new and powerful composites. The phallic trickster aptly represents the duality of this process. In his radically antinomian activities—incest, murder, and the destruction of sacred property—he symbolically captures what Turner describes as the "amoral and nonlogical" rhythms and outcomes of human biology and of meteorological climate, that is, the uncontrollable rhythms of nature.[83] But the trickster is also a cultural gift bearer. Turner emphasizes that "the Winnebago trickster transforms the pieces of his broken phallus into plants and flowers for men."[84] Hermes enriches human culture with dreams and music. In a sense, therefore, the phallic trickster is a force that is, paradoxially, both anticonventional and culturally benevolent. The paradox is dissolved in the definition of the trickster as the "*prima materia*—as undifferentiated raw material" from which all things derive.[85] Trueblood's sexual energies, antinomian acts, productive issue, and resonant expressivity make him—in his incestuous, liminal moments and their immediate aftermath—the quintessential trickster.

In his sexual manifestation, Ellison's sharecropper challenges not only the mundane restraints of his environment but also the fundamental Judeo-Christian categories on which they are founded. As I have already noted, he quickly abandons the notion of the knife—of casting out, in Mr. Norton's indignant (and wonderfully ironic) phrase, "the offending eye." His virtual parodies of the notions of sin and sacrifice lend comic point to his latitudinarian challenge to Christian orthodoxy. When his wife brings the sharpened ax down on his head, Trueblood recalls, "I sees it, Lawd, yes! I sees it and seein' it I twists my head aside. Couldn't help it . . . I moves. Though I meant to keep still, I moves! Anybody but Jesus Christ hisself woulda moved" (p. 63). So much for repentance and salvation through the bloody sacrifice of one's life. But Trueblood goes on to indicate why such sacrifice may not have been required of him: with the skill of a revisionist theologian, he distinguishes between "blood-sin" and "dream-sin" (p. 62) and claims, with unshakable certainty, that only the dream of his encounter at the Broadnax household led to his sexual arousal and subsequent incest.

But while this casuistic claim suffices in the farmer's interaction with the social world, his earlier appraisal of the event suggests his role as a cosmically rebellious trickster. He says that when he awoke to discover himself atop Matty Lou, he felt that the act might not be sinful, because it happened in his sleep. But then he adds "although maybe sometimes a man can look at a little old pigtail gal and see him a whore" (p. 59). The naturalness, and the natural unpredictability, of sexual arousal implied by "although" seem more in keeping with the sharecropper's manifestation as black phallic energy.

Trueblood's sexual energies are not without complement in the arid regions where the sharecropper and his family eke out their existence. His wife, Kate, is an awesome force of both new life and outgoing socioreligious fury. His yard is filled with the children she has borne, and his oldest child, Matty Lou, is Kate's double—a woman fully grown and sexually mature who looks just like her mother. Kate and Matty Lou—both moving with the "full-fronted motions of far-gone pregnancy" (p. 47)— are the first human figures Mr. Norton sees as he approaches the Trueblood property. The two bearers of new black life are engaged in a rite of purification, a workaday ritual of washing clothes in a huge boiling cauldron, which takes on significance as the men situate themselves in a semicircle near the porch where the "earth . . . was hard and white from where wash water had long been thrown" (p. 51). In a sense the women (who flee behind the house at Norton's approach) are present, by ironic implication, as the sharecropper once more confessionally purges himself—as he, in vernacular terms, again "washes his dirty linen" before a white audience. Further, Matty Lou, as the object of Trueblood's incestuous desire, and Kate, as the irate agent of his punishment for fulfilling his desire, assume significant roles in his narrative.

The reversal of a traditional Freudian typology represented by Trueblood's dream encounter at the Broadnax Big House is reinforced by an implied parody of the Christian myth of the Fall.[86] For if the white Mrs. Broadnax serves as the temptress Eve in the dream, then Matty Lou becomes an ersatz Eve, the paradoxical recipient of the farmer's lust. Similarly, if Mr. Broadnax—an inhabitant of the sanctuary-like precincts of a house of "lighted candles and shiny furniture, and pictures on the walls, and soft stuff on the floor"—is the avenging father, or patriarch, of the dream, then the matriarchal Kate replaces him in exacting vengeance. The "fall" of Trueblood is thus enacted on two planes— on a dream level of Christian myth and on a quotidian level of southern black actuality. In its most intensely conscious and secular interpretation, the incestuous act is a rank violation that drives Kate to blind and murderous rage: "I heard Kate scream. It was a scream to make your blood run cold. It sounds like a woman who was watching a team of wild horses run down her baby chile and she caint move. . . . She screams and starts to pickin' up the first thing that comes to her hand and throwin' it" (p. 61).

The "doubleness" of Kate and Matty Lou is felt in the older woman's destructive and avenging energies, which elevate her to almost legendary proportions. Her woman's wrath at the sharecropper's illicit violation of "my chile!" spirals, inflating Kate to the metaphorical stature of an implacable executioner: "Then I sees her right up on me, big. She's swingin' her arms like a man swingin' a ten-pound sledge and I sees the knuckles of her hand is bruised and bleedin . . . and I sees her swing and I smells her sweat and . . . I sees that ax" (p 63). Trueblood tries to forestall Kate's punishing blow but, he says, he "might as well been pleadin' with a switch engine" (p. 63). The ax falls, and the farmer receives the wound whose blood spills on Matty Lou. The wound becomes the "raw and moist" scar the protagonist notices when he first moves "up close" on the sharecropper (p. 50).

Kate becomes not only an awesome agent of vengeance in the sharecropper's account but also the prime mover of the parodic ritual drama enacted in the chilly southern cabin. It is Kate's secular rage that results in the substitute castration-crucifixion represented by Trueblood's wound. She is the priestess who bestows the scarifying lines of passage, of initiation—the marks that forever brand the farmer as a "dirty lowdown wicked dog" (p. 66). At her most severe, she is the moral, or socioreligious, agent of both Trueblood's "marking" and his exile. She banishes him from the community that rallies to support her in her sorrow. In keeping with her role as purifier—as supervisor of the wash—she cleans up the pollution, the dirt and danger, represented by Tueblood's taboo act.

It is important to bear in mind, however, that while Kate is a figure of moral outrage, she is also a fertile woman who, like her husband, provides "cultural gifts" in the form of new life. In her family manifestation, she is less a secular agent of moral justice than a sensitive, practical parent who turns away in sick disgust at the wound she inflicts on Trueblood. And though she first banishes the farmer, she also accepts his return, obeys his interdiction against abortions for herself and Matty Lou, and welcomes the material gains that ironically accrue after Trueblood's fall from grace. The sharecropper says, "Except that my wife an' daughter won't speak to me, I'm better off than I ever been before. And even if Kate won't speak to me she took the new clothes I brought her from up in town and now she's gettin' some eyeglasses made what she been needin' for so long" (p. 67).

As a woman possessed of a practical (one might say a "blues") sensibility, Kate knows that men are, indeed, sometimes "dirty lowdown wicked" dogs who can perceive a whore in a pigtailed girl. She is scarcely resigned to such a state of affairs where her own daughter is concerned, but like the black mother so aptly described in Carolyn Rodgers's poem "It Is Deep,"[87] Kate knows that being "religiously girdled in her god" (p. 11) will not pay the bills. She thus brings together the sacred and the secular, the moral and the practical, in a manner that makes her both a complement for Trueblood and (again in the words of Rodgers) a woman who "having waded through a storm, is very obviously, a sturdy Black bridge" (p. 12).

To freight Trueblood's sexual manifestation and its complement in Kate with more significance than they can legitimately bear would be as much a critical disservice as were previous failures, or refusals, even to acknowledge these aspects. For while it is true that sexuality burdens the content of his narrative, it is also true that Trueblood himself metaphorically transforms his incestuous act into a single, symbolic instance of his total life situation:

> There I was [atop Matty Lou] trying to git away with all my might, yet having to move *without* movin'. I flew in but I had to walk out. I had to move without movin'. I done thought 'bout it since a heap, and when you think right hard you see that that's the way things is always been with me. That's just about been my life. [P. 59]

Like the formidable task of the invisible man's grandfather, who gave up his gun during the Reconstruction but still had to fight a war, Trueblood's problem is that of getting out of a tight spot without undue motion—without perceptibly moving. The grandfather adopted a strategy of extrication by indirection, pretending to affirm the designs of the dominant white society around him. Having relinquished his gun, he became "a spy in the enemy's country," a man overcoming his adversaries with yeses. He represents the trickster as subtle deceiver. Trueblood, in contrast, claims that to "move without movin' " means to take a refractory situation uncompromisingly in hand: "You got holt to it," he says, "and you caint let go even though you want to" (p. 60). He conceives of himself in the throes of his incestuous ecstasies as "like that fellow . . . down in Birmingham. That one what locked hisself in his house and shot [with a gun that he had *refused to give up*] at them police until they set fire to the house and burned him up. I was lost" (p. 60). An energetic, compulsive, even ecstatically expressive response is required:

> Like that fellow [in Birmingham], I stayed. . . . He mighta died, but I suspects now that he got a heapa satisfaction before he went. I *know* there ain't nothin' like what I went through, I caint tell how it was. It's like when a real drinkin' man gets drunk, or like a real sanctified religious woman gits so worked up she jumps outta her clothes, or when a real gamblin' man keeps on gamblin' when he's losing. [P. 60]

In his energetic response, Trueblood says a resounding no to all the castratingly tight spots of his existence as a poor black farmer in the undemocratic south.[88]

The most discursively developed *expressive* form of this no is, of course, the narrative that Trueblood relates. But he has come to this narrative by way of music. He has fasted and reflected on his guilt or innocence until he thinks his "brain go'n bust," and then he recalls, "one night, way early in the mornin', I looks up and sees the stars and I starts singin'. I don't know what it was, some kinda church song, I guess. All I know is I *ends up* singin' the blues. I sings me some blues that night ain't never been sang before" (pp. 65–66). The first unpremeditated expression that Trueblood summons is a religious song. But the religious system that gives birth to the song is, presumably, one in which the term "incest" carries pejorative force. Hence, the sharecropper moves on, spontaneously, to the blues.

III

In *The Legacy of the Blues*, Samuel Charters writes:

> Whatever else the blues was it was a language; a rich, vital, expressive language that stripped away the misconception that the black society in the United States was simply a poor, discouraged version of the white. It was impossible not to hear the differences. No one could listen to the blues without realizing that there are two Americas.[89]

On the origins of this blues language, Giles Oakley quotes the blues singer Booker White: "You want to know where did the blues come from. The blues come from behind the mule. Well now, you can have the blues sitting at the table eating. But the foundation of the blues is walking behind the mule way back in slavery time."[90] The language that Trueblood summons to contain his act grows out of the soil he works, a soil that has witnessed the unrecompensed labor of many thousand blacks walking "behind the mule," realizing, as they negotiated the long furrows, the absurdity of working from "can-to-caint" for the profit of others.

Born on a farm in Alabama and working, at the time of his incestuous act, as an impoverished, cold, poorly provisioned sharecropper, Trueblood has the inherent blues capacity of a songster like Lightnin' Hopkins, who asserts, "I had the one thing you need to be a blues singer. I was born with the blues."[91] Originating in the field hollers and work songs of the agrarian South and becoming codified as stable forms by the second decade of the twentieth century, the blues offer a language that connotes a world of transience, instability, hard luck, brutalizing work, lost love, minimal security, and enduring human wit and resourcefulness in the face of disaster. The blues enjoin one to accept hard luck because, without it, there is "no luck at all." The lyrics are often charged with a surreal humor that wonders if "a match box will hold my clothes." In short, the "other America" signaled is a world of common labor, spare circumstances, and grimly lusty lyrical challenges to a bleak fate.

In the system of the blues Trueblood finds the meet symbolic code for expressing the negativity of his own act. Since he is both a magical storyteller and a blues singer par excellence, he can incorporate the lean economics and fateful intransience of the blues world into his autobiographical narrative. His metaphorical talent, which transforms a steamboat's musicians into a boss quail's whistle and then likens the quail's actions to those of a good man who "do" what he "got to do," reflects a basic understanding of the earthy resonances of blues. He says of his evenings listening to boats in Mobile:

Plowing, at Gee's Bend, Alabama, 1937. Photo by Arthur Rothstein, Farm Security Administration. Reproduced from the collections of the Library of Congress, Washington, D.C.

> They used to have musicianers on them boats, and sometimes I used to wake her [Margaret] up to hear the music when they come up the river. I'd be layin' there and it would be quiet and I could hear it comin' from way, way off. Like when you quail huntin' and it's getting dark and you can hear the boss bird whistlin' tryin' to get the covey together again, and he's coming toward you slow and whistlin' soft, 'cause he knows you somewhere around with your gun. Still he got to round them up, so he keeps on comin'. Them boss quails is like a good man, what he got to do he *do*. [P. 55]

The farmer begins his story by describing his desperate economic straits, like those frequently recorded in blues—that is, no wood for fuel and no work or aid to be found (p. 53)—and then traces the outcome of his plight. Matty Lou is in bed with her mother and father because it is freezing: "It was so cold all of us had to sleep together; me, the ole lady and the gal. That's how it started" (p. 53). It seems appropriate—even natural—that the act resulting from such bitter black agrarian circumstances should be expressively framed by blues. And it is, in fact, a blues affirmation of human identity in the face of dehumanizing circumstance that resonates through the sharecropper's triumphant penultimate utterance: "I make up my mind that I ain't nobody but myself and ain't nothin' I can do but let whatever is gonna happen, happen" (p. 66).

The farmer's statement is not an expression of transcendence. It is, instead, an affirmation of a still recognizable humanity by a singer who has incorporated his personal disaster into a code of blues meanings emanating from an unpredictably chaotic world. In translating his tragedy into the vocabulary and semantics of the blues and, subsequently, into the electrifying expression of his narrative, Trueblood realizes that he is not so changed by catastrophe that he must condemn, mortify, or redefine his essential self. This self, as the preceding discussion indicates, is in many ways the obverse of the stable, predictable, puritanical, productive, law-abiding ideal self of the American industrial-capitalist society.

The words the sharecropper issues from "behind the mule" provide a moral opposition (if not a moral corrective) to the confident expressions of control emanating from Mr. Norton's technological world. From a pluralistic perspective, the counteractive patterns represented by the sharecropper and the millionaire point to a positive homeostasis in American life. In the southern regions represented by Trueblood, an oppositional model might suggest the duty-bound but enfeebled rationalist of northern industry can always achieve renewal and a kind of shamanistic cure for the ills of civilization. But the millionaire in the narrative episode hardly appears to represent a rejuvenated Fisher King. At the close of the sharecropper's story, in fact, he seems paralyzed by the ghostly torpor of a stunned Benito Cereno or a horrified Mr. Kurtz. Thus a pluralistic model that projects revivifying opposition as the relation between sharecropper and millionaire does not adequately explain the Norton-Trueblood interaction. Some of the more significant implications of the episode, in fact, seem to reside not in the opposition between industrial technocrat and agrarian farmer but in the commercial consensus the two sectors reach on Afro-American expressive culture. Eshu and Hermes are not only figures of powerful creative instinct. They are also gods of the marketplace. Two analytical reflections on the study of literature and ideology, one by Fredric Jameson (already cited in chap. 1) and the other by Hayden White, elucidate the commercial consensus achieved by Trueblood and his millionaire auditor.

Fredric Jameson writes:

> The term "ideology" stands as the sign for a problem yet to be solved, a mental operation which remains to be executed. It does not presuppose cut-and-dried sociological stereotypes like the notion of the "bourgeois" or the "petty bourgeois" but is rather a mediatory concept: that is, it is an imperative to reinvent a relationship between the linguistic or aesthetic or conceptual fact in question and its social ground.... Ideological analysis may ... be described as the rewriting of a particular narrative trait or seme as a function of its social, historical, or political context.[92]

Jameson's interest in a reinvented relation between linguistic fact and social ground, as I made clear in my first chapter, is a function of his conviction that all acts of narration contain, within their very form, the inscription of social ideologies. In other words, there is always a historical, or ideological, subtext in a literary work of art. Since history is accessible to us only through texts, the literary work of art has to either "rewrite" the historical texts of its time or "textualize" the uninscribed events of its day in order to "contextualize" itself. What Jameson calls the "ideology of form" White calls, as I indicated earlier, "reflection theory."[93]

If literary art can indeed be said to reflect, through inscription, the social ground from which it originates, at what level of a specifically social domain, asks White, does such reflection occur? White's answer is that ideological analysis must begin with a society's exchange system and must regard the literary work as "merely one commodity among others and moreover as a commodity that has to be considered as not different in kind form any other" (pp. 376–77). To adopt such an analytical strategy, according to White, is to comprehend "not only the alienation of the artist which the representation of the value of his product in terms of money alone might foster, but also the tendency of the artist to fetishize his own produce as being itself the universal sign and incarnation of value in a given social system" (p. 378).

White could justifiably summon Ellison's previously quoted remarks on the transformative powers of art to illustrate the "fetishizing" of art as the incarnation of value. In Ellison's view, however, artistic value is not a sign or incarnation in a given social system but rather a sign of humane value in toto. What is pertinent about White's remarks for the present discussion, however, is that the relation Jameson would reinvent is for White an economic one involving challenging questions of axiology.

To apply Jameson's and White's reflections in analyzing the Trueblood episode, we can begin by recognizing that the sharecropper's achievement of expressive narrative form is immediately bracketed by the exchange system of Anglo-American society. Recalling his first narration of his story to a group of whites, the sharecropper remembers that Sheriff Barbour asked him to tell what happened:

> ... and I tole him and he called in some more men and they made me tell it again. They wanted to hear about the gal lots of times and they gimme somethin' to eat and drink and some tobacco. Surprised me, 'cause I was scared and spectin' somethin' different. Why, I guess there ain't a colored man in the county who ever got to take so much of the white folkses' time as I did. [P. 52]

Food, drink, tobacco, and audience time are commodities the sharecropper receives in barter for the commodity he delivers—his story. The narrative of incest, after its first telling, accrues an ever-spiraling exchange value. The Truebloods receive all the items enumerated earlier, as well as a hundred-dollar bill from Mr. Norton's Moroccan leather wallet. The exchange value of the story thus moves from a system of barter to a money economy overseen by northern industrialists. The status of the farmer's story as a commodity cannot be ignored.

As an artistic form incorporating the historical and ideological subtexts of American industrial society, the sharecropper's tale represents a supreme capitalist fantasy. The family, as the fundamental social unit of middle-class society, is governed by the property concept. A man marries—takes a wife as his exclusive "property"—to produce legitimate heirs who will keep their father's wealth (i.e., his property) in the family. Among royalty or the aristocracy such marriages may describe an exclusive circle of exchange. Only certain women are eligible as royal or aristocratic wives. And in the tightest of all circumstances, incest may be justified as the sole available means of preserving intact the family heritage—the nobleman's or aristocrat's property and propriety. An unfettered, incestuous procreativity that results not only in new and legitimate heirs but also in a marked increase in property (e.g., Trueblood's situation) can be viewed as a capitalist dream. And if such results can be achieved without fear of holy sanction, then procreation becomes a secular feat of human engineering.

Mr. Norton reflects that his "real life's work" has been, not his banking or his researches, but his "first-hand organizing of human life" (p. 42). What more exacting control could this millionaire New Englander have exercised than the incestuous domination of his own human family as a productive unit, eternally giving birth to new profits? Only terror of dreadful heavenly retribution, of punishment for "impropriety," had prevented him from attempting such a construction of life with his pathetically idealized only child, now deceased. Part of his stupefaction at the conclusion of the sharecropper's narrative results from his realization that he might have safely effected such a productive arrangement of life. One need not belabor the capitalist-fantasy aspect of Trueblood's narrative, however, to comprehend his story's commodity status in an industrial-capitalist system of exchange. What the farmer is ultimately merchandizing is an image of himself that is itself a product—a bizarre product—of the slave trade that made industrial America possible.

Africans became slaves through a "commercial deportation" overseen by the white West.[94] In America, Africans were classified as "chattel personal" and turned into commodities. To forestall the moral guilt associated with this aberrant, mercantile transformation, white Americans conceptualized a degraded, subhuman animal as a substitute for the actual African. This categorical parody found its public, physical embodiment in the mask of the minstrel theatrical. As Ellison writes in "Change the Joke and Slip the Yoke," the African in America was thus reduced to a "negative sign":[95] "the [minstrel] mask was the thing (the 'thing' in more ways than one) and its function was to veil the humanity of Negroes thus reduced to a sign, and to repress the white audience's awareness of its moral identification with its own acts and with the human ambiguities pushed behind the mask" (p. 64). Following the lead of Constance Rourke, Ellison asserts that the minstrel show is, in fact, a "ritual of exorcism."[96] But what of the minstrel performance given by the Afro-American who dons the mask? In such performances, writes Ellison,

> Motives of race, status, economics and guilt are always clustered. . . . The comic point is inseparable from the racial identity of the performer . . . who by assuming the group-debasing role for gain not only substantiates the audience's belief in the "blackness" of things black, but relieves it, with dreamlike efficiency, of its guilt by accepting the very profit motive that was involved in the designation of the Negro as national scapegoat in the first place. There are all kinds of comedy; here one is reminded of the tribesman in *Green Hills of Africa* who hid his laughing face in shame at the sight of a gut-shot hyena jerking out its own intestines and eating them, in Hemingway's words, "with relish." [Pp. 64–65]

Trueblood, who assumes the minstrel mask to the utter chagrin of the invisible man ("How can he tell this to white men, I thought, when he knows they'll say that all Negroes do such things?"), has indeed accepted the profit motive that gave birth to that mask in the first place. He tells his tale with relish: "He talked willingly now, with a kind of satisfaction and no trace of hesitancy or shame" (p. 53). The firm lines of capitalist economics are, therefore, not the only ideological inscriptions in the sharecropper's narrative. The story also contains the distorting contours of that mask constructed by the directors of the economic system to subsume their guilt. The rambunctiously sexual, lyrical, and sin-adoring "darky" is an image dear to the hearts of white America.

Ideologically, then, there is every reason to regard the sharecropper's story as a commodity in harmony with its social ground—with the system of exchange sanctioned by the dominant Anglo-American society. Though Trueblood has been denied "book learning" by the nearby black college, he has not failed to garner some knowledge of marketing. Just as the college officials peddle the sharecropper's "primitive spirituals" to the white millionaires who descend every spring, so Trueblood sells his own expressive product—a carefully constructed narrative, framed to fit market demands. His actions as a merchant seem to compromise his status as a blues artist, as a character of undeniable folk authenticity. And his delineation as an untrammeled and energetic prime mover singing a deep blues no to social constraints appears to collapse under the impress of ideological analysis. The complexities of American culture, however, enable him to reconcile a merchandizing role as oral storyteller with his position as an antinomian trickster. For the Afro-American blues manifest an effective, expressive duality that Samuel Charters captures as follows:

> The blues has always had a duality to it. One of its sides is its personal creativity—the consciousness of a creative individual using it as a form of expression. The other side is the blues as entertainment. Someone like Memphis Slim is a professional blues entertainer. But the blues is a style of music that emphasizes integrity—so how does a singer change his style without losing his credibility as a blues artist?[97]

As entertainment, the blues, whether classic or country, were sung professionally in theaters.[98] And their public theatricality is analogous to the Afro-American's donning of the minstrel mask. There is, perhaps, something obscenely—though profitably—gut wrenching about Afro-Americans delivering up carefully modified versions of their essential expressive selves for the entertainment of their Anglo-American oppressors. And, as Charters implies, the question of integrity looms large. But the most appropriate inquiry in the wake of his comment is, Integrity *as what*?

To deliver the blues as entertainment—if one is an entertainer—is to maintain a fidelity to one's role. Again, if the performance required is that of a minstrel and one is a genuine performer, then donning the mask is an act consistent with one's stature. There are always fundamental economic questions involved in such uneasy Afro-American public postures. As Ellison suggests, Afro-Americans, in their guise as entertainers, season the possum of black expressive culture to the taste of their Anglo-American audience, maintaining, in the process, their integrity as performers. But in private sessions—in the closed circle of their own community (such as that represented by store-porch inhabitants in Hurston's novel)—everybody knows that the punch line to the recipe and the proper response to the performer's constrictive dilemma is, "Damn the possum! That sho' is some good gravy!" It is just possible that the "gravy" is the inimitable technique of the Afro-American artist, a technique (derived from lived blues experience) as capable of "playing possum" as of presenting one.

A further question, however, has to do with the artist's affective response to being treated as a commodity. And with this query, White's and Jameson's global formulations prove less valuable than a closer inspection of the self-reflexive expressivity of Afro-American spokespersons in general. Ellison's Trueblood episode, for example, suggests that the angst assumed to accompany commodity status is greatly alleviated when that status constitutes a sole means of securing power in a hegemonic system.

In the Trueblood episode, blacks who inhabit the southern college's terrain assume that they have transcended the peasant rank of sharecroppers and their cohorts. In fact, both the college's inhabitants and Trueblood's agrarian fellows are but constituencies of a single underclass. When the college authorities threaten the farmer with exile or arrest, he has only to turn to the white Mr. Buchanan, "the boss man," to secure immunity and a favorable audience before Sheriff Barbour, "the white law" (p. 52). The imperious fiats of whites relegate all blacks to an underclass. In Trueblood's words, "no matter how biggity a nigguh gits, the white folks can always cut him down" (p. 53). The only means of negotiating a passage beyond this underclass, Ellison's episode implies, is expressive representation.

Dr. Bledsoe, for example, endorses lying as an effective strategy in interacting with Mr. Norton and the other college trustees. And Trueblood himself adopts tale telling (which is often conflated with lying in black oral tradition) as a mode of expression that allows him a degree of dignity and freedom within the confines of a severe white hegemony. The expressive "mask," one might say, is as indispensable for college blacks as it is for those beyond the school's boundaries. Describing the initial meeting between Mr. Norton and the sharecropper, the protagonist says, "I hurried behind him [Mr. Norton], seeing him stop when he reached the man and the children. They became silent, their faces clouding over, their features becoming soft and negative, their eyes bland and deceptive. They were crouching behind their eyes waiting for him to speak—just as I recognized that I was trembling behind my own" (p. 50). The evasive silence of these blacks is as expressive of power relations in the South as the mendacious strategy advocated by Dr. Bledsoe.

When the protagonist returns from his ill-fated encounters with Trueblood and the crew at the Golden Day, the school's principal asks him if he is unaware that blacks have "lied enough decent homes and drives [from white coffers] for you to show him [Mr. Norton]" (p. 136). When the protagonist responds that he was obeying Mr. Norton's orders by showing the millionaire the "slum" regions of Trueblood rather than "decent homes and drives," Bledsoe exclaims, "He *ordered* you. Dammit, white folk are always giving orders, it's a habit with them. . . . My God, boy! You're black and living in the South—did you forget how to lie?" (p. 136).

Artful evasion and expressive illusion are equally traditional black expressive modes in interracial exchange in America. Such modes, the Trueblood episode implies, are the only resources that blacks at any level can barter for a semblance of decency and control in their lives. Making black expressiveness a commodity, therefore, is not simply a gesture in a bourgeois economics of art. It is a crucial move in a repertoire of black survival motions in the United States. To examine the status of Afro-American expressiveness as a commodity, then, is to do more than observe, within the constraints of an institutional theory of art, that the art world is a function of economics. In a very real sense, Afro-America's exchange power has always been coextensive with its stock of expressive resources. What is implicit in an analysis of black expressiveness as a commodity is not a limited history of the "clerks" but a total history of Afro-American cultural interaction in America.

In *When Harlem Was in Vogue*—a study that treats the black artistic awakening of the 1920s known as the "Harlem Renaissance"—David Levering Lewis captures the essential juxtaposition between white hegemony and black creativity as a negotiable power of exchange.[99] Writing of Charles Johnson, the energetic black editor of *Opportunity* magazine during this period, Lewis says:

> [Johnson] gauged more accurately than perhaps any other Afro-American intellectual the scope and depth of the national drive to "put the nigger in his place" after the war, to keep him out of the officer corps, out of labor unions and skilled jobs, out of the North and quaking for his very existence in the South—and out of politics everywhere. Johnson found that one area alone—probably because of its very implausibility—had not been proscribed. No exclusionary rules had been laid down regarding a place in the arts. Here was a small crack in the wall of racism, a fissure that was worth trying to widen. [P. 48]

"Exclusionary rules" were certainly implicit in the arts during the 1920s, but what Lewis suggests is that they were far less rigid and explicit than they were in other domains. Blacks thus sought to widen the "fissure," to gain what power they could to determine their own lives, through a renaissance of black expressiveness.

An ideological analysis of expressiveness as a commodity should take adequate account of the defining variables in the culture where this commercialization occurs. In Afro-American culture, exchanging words for safety and profit is scarcely an alienating act. It is, instead, a defining act in expressive culture. Further, it is an act that lies at the heart of Afro-

American politics conceived in terms of who gets what and when and how. Making a commodity of black expressiveness, as I try to make clear in my concluding section, does entail inscription of an identifying economics. But aggressively positive manifestations of this process (despite the dualism it presupposes) result from a self-reflexive acknowledgment that only the "economics of slavery" gives valuable and specifically black resonance to Afro-American works of art.

V

The critic George Kent observes a "mathematical consistency between Ellison's critical pronouncements and his creative performance."[100] Insofar as Ellison provides insightful critical interpretations of his own novel and its characters, Kent's judgment is correct. But the "critical pronouncements" in Ellison's canon that suggest a devaluing of Afro-American folklore hardly seem consistent with the implications of his Trueblood episode. And such devaluative utterances are properly regarded, I believe, as public statements by Ellison the merchant rather than as incisive, affective remarks by Ellison the creative genius.

Trueblood's duality is, finally, also that of his creator. Ellison knows that his work as an Afro-American artist derives from the "economics of slavery" that provided conditions of existence for Afro-American folklore. Black folk expression is a product of the impoverishment of blacks in America. The blues, as a case in point, are unthinkable for those happy with their lot.

Yet if folk artists are to turn a profit from their monumental creative energies (which are often counteractive, or inversive, vis-à-vis Anglo-American culture), they must take a lesson from the boss quail and move without moving. They must, in essence, sufficiently modify their folk forms (and amply advertise themselves) to merchandise such forms as commodities in the artistic market. To make their products commensurate with a capitalistic marketplace, folk artists may even have to don masks that distort their genuine selves. Ralph Ellison is a master of such strategies.

Ellison reconciles the trickster's manifestations as untrammeled creator and as god of the marketplace by providing critical advertisements for himself as a novelist that carefully bracket the impoverishing economics of Afro-America. For example, in "Change the Joke and Slip the Yoke" he writes, "I use folklore in my work not because I am a Negro, but because writers like Eliot and Joyce made me conscious of the literary value of my folk inheritance. My cultural background, like that of most Americans, is dual (my middle name, sadly enough, is Waldo)."[101] What is designated in this quotation as "literary value" is in reality market value. Joyce and Eliot taught Ellison that if he were a skillful enough strategist and spokesman he could market his own folklore. What is bracketed, of course, is the economics that required Ellison, if he wished to be an Afro-American artist, to turn to Afro-American folklore as a traditional, authenticating source for his art. Like his sharecropper, Ellison is wont to make literary value out of socioeconomic necessity. But he is also an artist who recognizes that Afro-American folk forms have value *in themselves*; they "have named human situations so well," he suggests in "The Art of Fiction," "that a whole corps of writers could not exhaust their universality" (p. 173). What Ellison achieves in the Trueblood episode is a dizzying hall of mirrors, a redundancy of structure, that enables him to extend the value of Afro-American folk forms by combining them with an array of Western narrative forms and tropes. Written novel and sung blues, polysyllabic autobiography and vernacular personal narrative, a Christian Fall and an inversive triumph of the black trickster—all are magnificently interwoven.

It is in such creative instances that one discovers Ellison's artistic genius, a genius that links him inextricably and positively to his invented share-cropper. In the Trueblood episode conceived as a chapter in a novel, one finds not only the same kind of metaexpressive commentary that marks the character's narration to Norton but also the same type of self-reflexive artist that the sharecropper's recitation implies—an artist who is fully aware of the contours and limitations, the rewards and dilemmas, of the Afro-American's uniquely expressive craft.

In the expository, critical moment, by contrast, one often finds a quite different Ralph Ellison. Instead of the *reflexive* artist, one finds the *reflective* spokesman. To return to Barbara Babcock-Abrahams, specifically to her notion of a "failed" Narcissus to illustrate the difference between the "reflective" and the "reflexive," one might say that in his criticism Ralph Ellison is not narcissistic enough.[102] His reflections in *Shadow and Act* seem to define Afro-American folk expressiveness in art as a sign of identity, a sign that marks the creator as unequivocally Afro-American and hence other. I have sought to demonstrate, however, that Ellison's folk expressiveness is, in fact, "identity within difference." While critics experience alienation, artists can detach themselves from, survive, and even laugh at their initial experiences of otherness. Like Velázquez in *Las Meninas* or the Van Eyck of *Giovanni Arnolfini and His Bride*, the creator of Trueblood is "conscious of being self-conscious of himself" as artist.[103] Instead of solacing himself with critical distinctions, he employs reflexively mirroring narratives to multiply distinctions and move playfully across categorical boundaries. Like his sharecropper, he knows indisputably that his most meaningful identity is his Afro-American self imaged in acts of expressive creativity.

Ralph Ellison's identity as a public critic, therefore, does not forestall his private artistic recognition that he "ain't nobody but himself." And it is out of this realization that a magnificent folk creation such as Trueblood emerges. Both the creator and his agrarian folk storyteller have the wisdom to know that they are resourceful "whistlers" for the tribe. They know that their primary matrix as artists is coextensive not with a capitalistic society but with material circumstances like those implied by the blues singer Howling Wolf:

> Well I'm a po' boy, long way from home.
> Well I'm a po' boy, long way from home.
> No spendin' money in my pocket, no spare meat on my bone.[104]

(One might say that in the brilliant reflexivity of the Trueblood encounter we hear the blues whistle among the high-comic thickets. We glimpse Ralph Ellison's creative genius beneath his Western critical mask. And while we stand awaiting the next high-cultural pronouncement from the critic, we are startled by a captivating sound of flattened thirds and sevenths—the private artist's blues-filled flight, the blues artist's surrender to the air in lively fulfillment of a dream of American form.)

Conclusion

I have attempted in my foregoing discussions to translate music of American junctures into practical scholarly benefits. My general aim has been to offer further delineations of the culturally specific in Afro-American life and expression. A materialistic prospect leads me to conclude that writing the culturally specific is coextensive with discovering vernacular inscriptions in American culture. What must be summoned to view are not Grecian urns, but ancestral faces. An American vernacular ancestry is as various as the multitudes who have made their way to New World shores, settled vast and difficult landscapes, discovered inhabitants who were always already settled, and given voice to their own acts and beliefs. My project is a minute beginning in the labor of writing/righting American history and literary history.

One way of considering the overall labor that needs to be performed is to see it as "reconstruction" in the manner of a recent group of Afro-American literary critics. It is essential, however, when talking of "reconstruction" to decide first whether any extant timber, or perhaps more aptly, any used crossties are worth salvaging in attempts to create a new perspective. It may ultimately prove the case that *deconstruction* is the best first step.

In an imagistic sense, a deconstructionist initial step can be conceived as a nomadic traipsing over a boundless network of American rails—that is, as a ludic and tropological stroll (interdisciplinary "bindle" in hand) that surveys America's myriad vernacular possibilities. Of course the image of the scholar as hobo, as a liminal trickster always on the move, is scarcely one that is compatible with pristine hydrias.

Nonetheless, from a blues perspective, no image is more appropriate. For if one is dedicated to discovering ancestral faces embedded in cliffs and petroglyphs, faces squinting from behind plows in midday sun, faces distorted by intense flames of steel furnaces, faces at depots or staring with vacant eyes at meager possessions—if one is dedicated to discovering such vernacular faces, one must acknowledge, at the outset of one's project, that all fixed points are problematical.

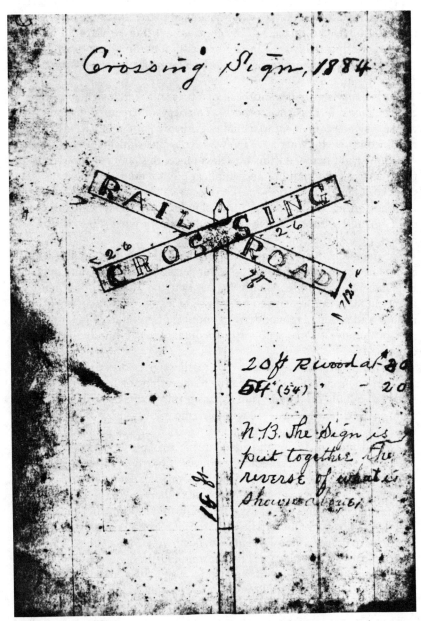

Drawing of a railroad crossbuck sign, 1884. Courtesy of the Association of American Railroads, Washington, D.C.

Fixity is a function of power. Those who maintain place, who decide what takes place and dictate what has taken place, are power brokers of the traditional. The "placeless," by contrast, are translators of the nontraditional. Rather than fixed in the order of cunning Grecian urns, their lineage is fluid, nomadic, transitional. Their appropriate mark is a crossing sign at the junction.

The crossing sign is the antithesis of a place marker. It signifies, always, change, motion, transience, process. To adept adherents of wandering, a crossing sign is equivalent to a challenge thrown out in brash, sassy tones by a locomotive blowing by: "Do what you can," it demands. "Do what you can—right here—on this placeless-place, this spotless-spot—to capture manifold intonations and implications of fluid experience!" "Do what you can," in interstices marked by crossing roads, "to play, sing, and decipher an endlessly proliferating significance of American literature, criticism, and culture." Do what you can to decode what Albert Murray so astutely refers to as the American "and also."

The fact that historical and literary-critical discourse in the United States have been powerfully arrested for generations among (and by) New England male Brahmins simply means that the "and also"—American ancestral faces that remain to be seen—are legion. The discovery of such prolific and prodigal remainders is contingent upon the willing inventiveness of the investigator who dares to situate himself productively at the crossroads.

The risk of situating oneself at the crossing sign is, of course, enormous. But the benefits are beyond price. The relinquishing of a self-certainty that strives to annul "otherness" and to masterfully fix its own place is meetly compensated. The reward, the reimbursement for translation at the crossing, is the magnificent appearance of America's blues people.

A vastly more inclusive and adequate national picture emerges with the appearance of these dark, ancestral faces. To lose a master desire, one might say, is to see a different America—singing. To locate the crossing where such a vision is possible is not difficult.

The sign is likely to appear anywhere in one's journeyings: beside defunct roadbeds in southern fields, at the intersection of thoroughfares on midwestern prairies, at town centers in northwest timber country. Like the railroad cars and locomotives that it implies, the sign is without a fixed place or an unchanging proper name. As a signal always already there, a mark signifying motion and meanings yet to be deciphered, it possesses fine blues resonance.

The task of present-day scholars is to situate themselves inventively and daringly at the crossing sign in order to materialize vernacular faces. If scholars are successful, their response to literature, criticism, and culture in the United States will be as wonderfully energetic and engrossing as the response of the bluesman Sonny Terry to the injunction of his guitar-strumming partner Brownie McGhee. Brownie intones: "Let me hear you squall, boy, like you never squalled before!" The answer is a whooping, racing, moaning harmonica stretch that takes one's breath away, invoking forms, faces, and places whose significance was unknown prior to the song's formidable inscriptions.

Notes

Introduction

1. Chicago: University of Chicago Press, 1980.

2. Though a great many sources were involved in my reoriented cultural thinking, certainly the terminology employed in my discussion at this point derives from Marshall Sahlins's wonderfully lucid *Culture and Practical Reason* (Chicago: University of Chicago Press, 1976). Sahlins delineates two modes of thinking that have characterized anthropology from its inception. These two poles are "symbolic" and "functionalist." He resolves the dichotomy suggested by these terms through the middle term "cultural proposition," a phrase that he defines as a cultural mediating ground where the material and symbolic, the useful and the ineffable, ceaselessly converge and depart.

3. The "ideology of form" as a description of Jameson's project derives from the essay "The Symbolic Inference; or, Kenneth Burke and Ideological Analysis," *Critical Inquiry* 4 (1978): 507–23. Surely, though, Jameson's most recent study, *The Political Unconscious: Narrative as a Socially Symbolic Act* (Ithaca, N.Y.: Cornell University Press, 1981), offers the fullest description of his views on ways in which cultural texts formally inscribe material/ historical conditions of their production, distribution, and consumption.

4. In *The Journey Back*, I define my project as follows: "The phrase ['the anthropology of art'] expresses for me the notion that art must be studied with an attention to the methods and findings of disciplines which enable one to address such concerns as the status of the artistic object, the relationship of art to other cultural systems, and the nature and function of artistic creation and perception in a given society" (p. xvi). The project's privileging of "symbolic anthropology" and "art" under the sign *interdisciplinary* involved exclusions that were ironical and (I now realize) somewhat disabling where a full description of expressive culture is sought.

5. The Hegelian epigraph that marks the beginning of these introductory remarks offers the best definition I know of "determinate negation." The epigraph is taken from the *Phenomenology of Spirit*.

6. I have in mind Louis Althusser and Étienne Balibar, *Reading Capital* (London: New Left Books, 1977), and Jean Baudrillard's *For a Critique of the Political Economy of the Sign* (1972; St. Louis: Telos Press, 1981) and *The Mirror of Production* (1973; St. Louis: Telos Press, 1975). By "poststructuralist" thought, I have in mind the universe of discourse constituted by *deconstruction*. Jacques Derrida's *Of Grammatology* (1967; Baltimore: Johns Hopkins University Press, 1976) is perhaps the locus classicus of the deconstructionist project. One of the more helpful accounts of deconstruction is Christopher Norris's *Decon-struction: Theory and Practice* (London: Methuen, 1982). Of course, there is a certain collapsing of poststructuralism and political economy in the sources cited previously.

7. For a full citation of Baudrillard, see note 6.

8. Ibid.

9. In *Of Grammatology*, Derrida defines a problematic in which *writing*, conceived as an iterable *differe(a)nce*, is held to be *always already* instituted (or, in motion) when a traditionally designated *Man* begins to speak. Hence, *script* is anterior to speech, and absence and *differe(a)nce* displace presence and identity (conceived as "Intention") in philosophical discourse.

10. The story appears in W. C. Handy, *Father of the Blues*, ed. Arna Bontemps (New York: Macmillan Co., 1941), p. 78. Other defining sources of blues include: Paul Oliver, *The Story of the Blues* (London: Chilton, 1969); Samuel B. Charters, *The Country Blues* (New York: Rinehart, 1959); Giles Oakley, *The Devil's Music: A History of the Country Blues* (New York: Harcourt Brace Jovanovich, 1976); Amiri Baraka, *Blues People: Negro Music in White America* (New York: William E. Morrow, 1963); Albert Murray, *Stomping the Blues* (New York: McGraw-Hill Book Co., 1976); and William Ferris, *Blues from the Delta* (New York: Anchor Books, 1979).

11. The description at this point is coextensive with the "decentering" of the subject mentioned at the outset of my introduction. What I wish to effect by noting a "subject" who is not *filled* is a displacement of the notion that knowledge, or "art," or "song," are manifestations of an ever more clearly defined individual consciousness of *Man*. In accord with Michel Foucault's explorations in his *Archaeology of Knowledge* (1969; New York: Harper & Row, 1972), I want to claim that blues is like a discourse that comprises the "already said" of Afro-America. Blues' governing statements and sites are thus vastly more interesting in the process of cultural investigation than either a history of ideas or a history of individual, subjective consciousness vis-à-vis blues. When I move to the "X" of the trace and the body as host, I am invoking Mark Taylor's formulations in a suggestive deconstructive essay toward radical christology called "The Text as Victim," in *Deconstruction and Theology* (New York: Crossroad, 1982), pp. 58–78.

12. The terms used in "The Text as Victim," ibid., are "host" and "parasite." The words of the blues are hostlike in the sense of a christological Logos-as-Host. But without the dialogical action of the parasite, of course, there could be no Host. Host is, thus, parasitic on a parasite's citation. Both, in Taylor's statement of the matter, are *para-sites*.

13. The definition of "code" is drawn from *A Theory of Semiotics* (Bloomington: Indiana University Press, 1976). All references to Eco refer to this work and are hereafter marked by page numbers in parentheses.

14. *The Phenomenology of Spirit*, trans. A. V. Miller (New York: Oxford University Press, 1977). While it is true that the material dimensions of the dialectic are of primary importance to my current study, it is also true that the locus classicus of the dialectic, in and for itself, is the *Phenomenology*. Marx may well have stood Hegel on his feet through a materialist inversion of the *Phenomenology*, but subsequent generations have always looked at that uprighted figure—Hegel himself—as an authentic host.

15. Having heard John Felstiner in a session at the 1982 Modern Language Association Convention present a masterful paper defining "translation" as a process of preserving "something of value" by keeping it in motion, I decided that the blues were apt translators of experience. Felstiner, it seemed to me, sought to demonstrate that *translation* was a process equivalent to gift-giving in Mauss's classic definition of that activity. The value of the gift of translation is never fixed because, say, the poem, is always in a transliterational motion, moving from one alphabet to another, always renewing and being *re-newed* in the process. Translation forestalls fixity. It calls attention always to the *translated*'s excess—to its complex multivalence.

16. One of the most inspiring and intriguing descriptions of the relationship between blues voice and sounds of the railroad is Albert Murray's lyrical exposition in *Stomping the Blues*.

17. Quoted in Oakley, *The Devil's Music*, p. 7.

18. I have appropriated the term "negative symbol" from Roy Wagner's *The Invention of Culture* (Chicago: University of Chicago Press, 1975), p. xvi.

19. My references to a "post-Heisenbergian universe" and to the "particle physicist" were made possible by a joyful reading of Gary Zukav's *The Dancing Wu Li Masters: An Overview of the New Physics* (New York: William E. Morrow, 1979).

20. Zukav, ibid., writes: "According to the uncertainty principle, we cannot measure accurately, at the same time, both the position *and* the momentum of a moving particle. The more precisely we determine one of these properties, the less we know about the other. If we precisely determine the position of the particle, then, strange as it sounds, there is *nothing* that we can know about its momentum. If we precisely determine the momentum of the particle, there is no way to determine its position" (p. 111). Briefly, if we bring to bear enough energy actually to "see" the imagined "particle," that energy has always already *moved* the particle from its *position* (which is one of the aspects of its existence that one attempts to *determine*) when we take our measurement. Indeterminacy thus becomes normative.

21. The "blues force" is my translational equivalent in investigative "energy" for the investigative energy delineated by Heisenberg's formulations. See note 20.

22. Eco (*A Theory of Semiotics*, p. 29) employs the metaphor of "ecological variation" in his discussions of the semiotic investigation of culture to describe observer effect in the mapping of experience.

23. New York: Random House, 1976. All citations refer to this edition and are hereafter marked by page numbers in parentheses.

24. See n. 9 above.

25. The Chehaw Station is a whistle-stop near Tuskegee, Alabama. It was a feature of the landscape of Tuskegee Institute, where Ellison studied music (and much else).

26. *American Scholar* 47 (1978): 24–48. All citations refer to this version and are hereafter marked by page numbers in parentheses.

27. *Song of Solomon* (New York: Alfred A. Knopf, 1977), p. 337.

Chapter 1

1. The story of Gideon Mantell and Iguanodon is captivatingly recorded in Edwin H. Colbert's *Men and Dinosaurs* (New York: E. P. Dutton, 1968). I want to thank Alan Mann for introducing me to both the story and the reference.

2. Michel Foucault, *The Archaeology of Knowledge*, trans. A. M. Sheridan Smith (New York: Harper & Row, 1972). All citations from the text refer to this edition and are marked by page numbers in parentheses.

3. For discussion of "descriptive integration," see Sol Tax and others, eds., *An Appraisal of Anthropology Today* (Chicago: University of Chicago Press, 1953), pp. 229 ff.

4. The classic statement of this construction of American history is, of course, Perry Miller's *Errand into the Wilderness* (Cambridge, Mass.: Harvard University Press, 1956).

5. "Of Plymouth Plantation." In *American Poetry and Prose*, ed. Norman Foerster (Boston: Houghton Mifflin, 1957), pp. 20–21.

6. Robert Spiller and others, eds., *A Literary History of the United States*, 4th rev. ed. (New York: Macmillan Co. 1974).

7. Robert E. Spiller, "The Cycle and the Roots: National Identity in American Literature," in *Toward a New American Literary History*, ed. Louis J. Budd, Edwin H. Cady, and Carol L. Anderson (Durham, N. C.: Duke University Press, 1980). All citations from the text refer to this edition and are marked by page numbers in parentheses.

8. In *Literature and the American Tradition* (New York: Doubleday, 1970), Leon Howard details the conviction held by Puritans and Pilgrims alike that their signal task was to establish New World communities that would facilitate God's plan to constitute the earthly paradise in America.

9. I am indebted to E. H. Gombrich's "In Search of Cultural History," in his *Ideals and Idols: Essays on Values in History and in Art* (Oxford: Phaidon, 1979), for its insights on Providential history and cultural history.

10. Sacvan Bercovitch, *American Jeremiad* (Madison: University of Wisconsin Press, 1978).

11. The convergence of ministers and professors, classrooms and pulpits, is a function of American higher education's beginnings and primary associations. Carved on the gates of Harvard College are the following words:

> After God had carried us safe to *New-England*, and we had builded our houses, provided necessaries for our liveli-hood, rear'd convenient places for Gods worship and settled the Civill Government; One of the next things we longed for, and looked after was to advance *Learning* and perpetuate it to Posterity; dreading to leave an illiterate Ministry to the Churches, when our present Ministers shall lie in the Dust.

Learning and religious learning, in the quoted passage, stand in a relationship of identity. The contours of Providential immigration and development that characterize the discourses Harvard was instituted to teach mark that institution's own statement of mission. Ministers at the "seminary in the wilderness" are thus capable of teaching American history and literary history because they, too, are part of the civilizing "errand." In order to fulfill their role, they are required to bring to notice and perpetuate those historical accounts and literary works of art that reveal God's divine plan for the world working itself out in his dealings with New England.

12. New York: St. Martin's Press, 1973. All citations are hereafter marked by page numbers in parentheses.

13. Roland Barthes, "Historical Discourse," in *Introduction to Structuralism*, ed. Michael Lane (New York: Basic Books, 1970). All citations from the text refer to this edition and are marked by page numbers in parentheses. I am aware of Foucault's disagreements with the structuralist project. But I am also aware that he (and his hypothetical questioner in the conclusion to *The Archaeology of Knowledge*) concede certain analytical successes to that project (*Archaeology*, p. 201). Further, I am certain that Barthes's analysis of historical discourse is far less concerned with what Foucault disparages as notions of a "constituent consciousness" (*Archaeology*, p. 203) than with the "discursive formation" of historical discourse examined in its "dispersed" totality. Looking ahead, one can say much the same of Lévi-Strauss's essay, which I refer to later in the present discussion.

14. One suspects that it was this type of "spiritual revenue" that D. H. Lawrence had in mind when he described the God of eighteenth-century America as "the supreme servant of men who want to get on, to *produce*. Providence. The provider. The heavenly store-keeper. The everlasting Wanamaker. And this is all the God the grandsons of the Pilgrim Fathers had left. Aloft on a pillar of dollars . . . He is head of nothing except a vast heavenly store that keeps every imaginable line of goods, from victrolas to cat-o-nine tails" (*Studies in Classic American Literature* [New York: Thomas Seltzer, 1923], p. 15, p. 27).

15. Robert Hayden, "Middle Passage," in *Selected Poems* (New York: October House, 1966), p. 65. All citations refer to this edition and are marked by page numbers in parentheses.

16. George Lamming, *Season of Adventure* (London: Allison & Busby, 1979). All citations refer to this edition and are marked by page numbers in parentheses.

17. Hayden, *Selected Poems*, p. 67.

18. I have chosen to employ graphics because they seemed to make the point so effectively in an earlier version of this essay presented as a lecture. The Miguel Covarrubias illustration of the inspection and sale of slaves is drawn from Malcolm Cowley, ed., *Adventures of an African Slaver: Being a True Account of the Life of Captain Theodore Canot* (Garden City,

N.Y.: Garden City Publishing Co., 1928). The picture of the "cargo" of an African slaver is from *Harper's Weekly*, 2 June 1860.

19. Claude Lévi-Strauss, "History and Dialectic," in *The Structuralists from Marx to Lévi-Strauss*, ed. Richard and Fernande DeGeorge (New York: Doubleday & Co., 1972), p. 228.

20. *Marxism and Form: Twentieth Century Dialectical Theories of Literature* (Princeton, N.J.: Princeton University Press, 1971), pp. 182–83. All citations are hereafter marked by page numbers in parentheses.

21. *New Literary History* 12 (1980): 363–80. All citations are hereafter marked by page numbers in parentheses.

22. *Critical Inquiry* 4 (1978): 507–23. All citations are hereafter marked by page numbers in parentheses.

23. *The Political Economy of Slavery* (New York: Vintage Books, 1965); *The World the Slaveholders Made* (New York: Vintage Books, 1971). I have relied heavily on the works of Genovese for my claims about slavery in the Old South.

24. *The World the Slaveholders Made*, p. 24.

25. Karl Marx, *Capital*, ed. Friedrich Engels (Chicago: Encyclopedia Britannica, 1952), p. 79. All citations refer to this edition and are hereafter marked by page numbers in parentheses.

26. In *Capitalism and Slavery* (Chapel Hill: University of North Carolina Press, 1944), Eric Williams develops this point of view in some detail.

27. *The World the Slaveholders Made*, p. 122.

28. *The Souls of Black Folk*, in *Three Negro Classics*, ed. John Hope Franklin (New York: Avon Books, 1965), p. 304. All subsequent citations refer to this edition and are marked by page numbers in parentheses.

29. In *Tropics of Discourse: Essays in Cultural Criticism* (Baltimore: Johns Hopkins University Press, 1978), p. 5. Subsequent citations are marked by page numbers in parentheses.

30. New York: Oxford, 1972, p. 159.

31. Quoted from Paul Oliver, *The Story of the Blues* (London: Chilton, 1969), p. 79.

32. "Sleepy John Estes," *Saturday Review* (10 November 1962), p. 57.

33. In *Great Slave Narratives*, ed. Arna Bontemps (Boston: Beacon Press, 1969), pp. 4–192. Subsequent citations refer to this edition and are marked by page numbers in parentheses.

34. "The Symbolic Inference," p. 504.

35. *Narrative* (New York: New American Library, 1968). All citations refer to this edition and are hereafter marked by page numbers in parentheses.

36. *Incidents in the Life of a Slave Girl* (New York: AMS Press, 1973). Subsequent citations refer to this edition and are marked by page numbers in parentheses.

37. *Communities of Women: An Idea in Fiction* (Cambridge, Mass.: Harvard University Press, 1978). Subsequent references to this work are marked by page numbers in parentheses.

38. Bloomington: Indiana University Press, 1981.

39. Urbana: University of Illinois Press, 1978. All citations from *Their Eyes Were Watching God* in my discussion refer to this edition and are hereafter marked by page numbers in parentheses.

40. Ralph Ellison, *Invisible Man* (New York: Vintage Books, 1972). All citations from the text refer to this edition and are marked by page numbers in parentheses.

41. Examples of the works of Chicano, Native American, and Asian American scholars (to list but three prominent "minorities") are represented in the Modern Language Association of America's volume, *Three American Literatures: Essays in Chicano, Native American, and Asian American Literatures for Teachers of American Literature* (New York: MLA, 1982). I had the pleasure of editing this volume.

Chapter 2

1. Lewis S. Feuer, *Ideology and Ideologists* (Oxford: Basil Blackwell, 1975), p. 70.

2. Thomas S. Kuhn, *The Structure of Scientific Revolutions* (Chicago: University of Chicago Press, 1970).

3. Richard Wright, "The Literature of the Negro in the United States," in *White Man, Listen!* (Garden City, N.Y.: Anchor Books, 1964), pp. 69–105. All citations from Wright's essay refer to this edition and are hereafter marked by page numbers in parentheses.

4. Brown, Davis, and Lee, eds., *The Negro Caravan* (New York: Dryden Press, 1941; reprinted, New York: Arno Press, 1969), p. 7. All citations from the work refer to this edition and are hereafter marked by page numbers in parentheses.

5. In *The American Negro Writer and His Roots, Selected Papers from the First Conference of Negro Writers, March, 1959* (New York: American Society of African Culture, 1960), pp. 39–40.

6. For historical details on the events of this period, the reader may wish to consult John Hope Franklin, "A Brief History," in *The Black American Reference Book*, ed. Mabel M. Smythe (Englewood Cliffs, N.J.: Prentice-Hall, Inc., 1976), pp. 1–89.

7. The phrase was originally uttered as part of a call-and-response chant between Carmichael and his audience during the course of a several-day protest march in Mississippi.

8. From Stokely Carmichael and Charles V. Hamilton, *Black Power, The Politics of Liberation in America* (New York: Vintage Books, 1967), pp. 43–44.

9. In *Home, Social Essays* (New York: William Morrow, 1966), p. 110. All citations of the essay refer to this edition and are hereafter marked by page numbers in parentheses.

10. For an account of this enterprise, the reader can consult Theodore R. Hudson, *From LeRoi Jones to Amiri Baraka: The Literary Works* (Durham, N.C.: Duke University Press, 1973), pp. 20–25.

11. In Addison Gayle, Jr., ed., *The Black Aesthetic* (New York: Doubleday & Co., 1971), p. 272.

12. Stephen Henderson, "Introduction: *The Forms of Things Unknown*," in *Understanding the New Black Poetry, Black Speech and Black Music as Poetic References* (New York: William Morrow & Co., 1973), pp. 1–69. All citations refer to this edition and are hereafter marked by page numbers in parentheses.

13. Parenthetical page numbers in my text in the following discussion all refer to Kuhn's book.

14. Two collections of essays provide excellent overviews of responses to Kuhn's work and of Kuhn's own responses to his critics. These two collections are the sources I have in mind as I briefly rehearse in the next paragraph and a half the kinds of claims that have been made about *The Structure of Scientific Revolutions*. The two volumes are Imre Lakatos and Alan Musgrave, eds., *Criticism and the Growth of Knowledge* (Cambridge: Cambridge University Press, 1970); and Gary Gutting, ed., *Paradigms and Revolutions: Applications and Appraisals of Thomas Kuhn's Philosophy of Science* (Notre Dame, Ind.: University of Notre Dame Press, 1980).

15. In "The Artworld," which appears in Joseph Margolis, ed., *Philosophy Looks at the Arts* (Philadelphia: Temple University Press, 1978), pp. 132–45, Arthur Danto writes: "terrain is constituted artistic in virtue of artistic theories, so that one use of theories, in addition to helping us discriminate art from the rest, consists in making art possible." The *theoretical* constraints of the integrationist paradigm excluded "Negro" expressive works from the American literary artworld.

16. Albert Hofstadter, "On the Grounds of Aesthetic Judgment," in *Contemporary Aesthetics*, ed. Matthew Lipman (Boston: Allyn & Bacon, 1973), pp. 473–74. In both the concept "artworld" and "reference public," I have interpreted the Black Aesthetic as an institutional theory of art. For a recent critique of such theories, the reader may consult Marx W. Wartofsky, "Art, Artworlds, and Ideology," *Journal of Aesthetics and Art Criticism* 38

(1980): 239–47. In contrast to the "institutional" dimensions of the Black Aesthetic are its idealistic assumptions, whch I will discuss shortly.

17. For reflections on field theory and on the work of Trier, see John Lyons, *Semantics* (Cambridge: Cambridge University Press, 1977), 1: 250–61.

18. I have discussed the romantic idealism of the Black Aesthetic in "The Black Spokesman as Critic: Reflections on the Black Aesthetic," the fifth chapter of my book, *The Journey Back: Issues in Black Literature and Criticism* (Chicago: University of Chicago Press, 1980), pp. 132–43.

19. Stephen Henderson, "Saturation: Progress Report on a Theory of Black Poetry," *Black World* 24 (1975): 14.

20. The words on the creation of system are, of course, those of William Blake's Los, drawn from *Jerusalem.* Los, like the Black Aestheticians, also refused at points to "reason" or "compare," feeling that the imperative "business" was "to create."

21. Henderson, "Saturation," p. 9.

22. Stephen Henderson, "The Question of Form and Judgement in Contemporary Black American Poetry, 1962–1977," in *A Dark and Sudden Beauty: Two Essays in Black American Poetry by George Kent and Stephen Henderson*, ed. Houston A. Baker, Jr. (Philadelphia: Afro-American Studies Program of the University of Pennsylvania, 1977), p. 24.

23. Ibid., p. 32.

24. I have in mind Robert E. Hemenway, author of *Zora Neale Hurston, a Literary Biography* (Urbana: University of Illinois Press, 1977), and Lawrence W. Levine, author of *Black Culture and Black Consciousness, Afro-American Folk Thought from Slavery to Freedom* (New York: Oxford University Press, 1977).

25. Ron Karenga, "Black Cultural Nationalism," in Gayle, ed. (see n. 11 above), p. 33.

26. Larry Neal, "The Black Contribution to American Letters: Part II, The Writer as Activist—1960 and After," in Smythe, ed., pp. 781–82. All citations refer to this edition and are hereafter marked by page numbers in parentheses.

27. I have in mind the conferences of black writers sponsored by the Howard University Institute for the Arts and the Humanities. Also important, I think, were the symposia held at the University of Pennsylvania in 1975 and 1977. Proceedings of these national gatherings can be found in *The Image of Black Folk in American Literature* (Washington, D.C.: Howard University Institute for the Arts and the Humanities, 1976), and in *Reading Black: Essays in the Criticism of African, Caribbean, and Afro-American Literature*, Monograph Series No. 4 (Ithaca, N.Y.: Cornell University Africana Studies and Research Center, 1976).

28. The symposium was entitled "The Function of Black American Poetry, 1760–1977," and it was sponsored by the Afro-American Studies Program at the University of Pennsylvania, March 24–26, 1977. Selected proceedings of this symposium appeared in the edited volume *A Dark and Sudden Beauty.*

29. Feuer, *Ideology and Ideologists*, p. 57.

30. I have discussed this phenomenon at length in *The Journey Back*, pp. 126–31.

31. It is difficult to date the first contemporary usage of this term. Ben J. Wattenberg and Richard Scammon's article, "Black Progress and Liberal Rhetoric" (*Commentary* [April 1973], pp. 35–44), which proclaimed that 52% of Black Americans could be called "middle class," certainly gave life to ongoing attempts to define what E. Franklin Frazier designated the "Black Bourgeoisie" in his seminal study *Black Bourgeoisie* (1957). The special issue of *Ebony* magazine entitled "The Black Middle Class" (August 1973) seems to have been prompted as much by the necessity to answer Wattenberg and Scammon as by a desire to "update" Frazier at a time when (between 1960 and 1970) the number of blacks employed in professional and technical operations had increased by 131% and the number of blacks in the clerical force had grown by 121%. Some of the major investigative issues that are signaled by the employment of the term "new black middle class" are addressed by William Julius Wilson

in his study *The Declining Significance of Race: Blacks and Changing American Institutions* (Chicago: University of Chicago Press, 1978). In 1979 and 1980, the Afro-American Studies Program of the University of Pennsylvania took up the issues raised by Wilson and by the concept of a "new black middle class" in its annual spring symposia. The proceedings of those symposia can be found in Joseph R. Washington, Jr., ed., *The Declining Significance of Race? A Dialogue among Black and White Social Scientists* (Philadelphia: Afro-American Studies Program of the University of Pennsylvania, 1979), and in "Dilemmas of the New Black Middle Class," ed. Joseph R. Washington, Jr. (manuscript). Essentially, the term "new black middle class" seems to denote a stratum of Afro-American professionals whose education, occupations, and incomes place them on a level near that of their similarly employed white counterparts.

32. Quoted from William Julius Wilson, "The Declining Significance of Race: Myth or Reality," in Washington, ed., p. 15.

33. Dexter Fisher and Robert B. Stepto, eds., *Afro-American Literature: The Reconstruction of Instruction* (New York: Modern Language Association of America, 1979). All citations refer to this edition and are hereafter marked by page numbers in parentheses.

34. Sir David Ross, *Aristotle* (London: Methuen, 1923), pp. 73–74. "Prime" matter is unlike "secondary matter" since the latter cannot only "exist apart" (e.g., "tissues" may or may not be combined into organs) but can also be severed in reality (i.e., organs may be broken up into their component tissues). It is the inseparability of "form" and "matter" where Stepto is concerned (his "myth" is both structured and structuring) that gives his pregeneric myth the character of "prime" or "informed" matter. (See Ross, p. 71.)

35. *Metaphysics*, in *Aristotle's Metaphysics*, ed. John Warrington (London: J. M. Dent, 1956), p. 346. When Aristotle discusses "The Prime Mover" in one of the books of the *Metaphysics*, he sets forth what according to Sir David Ross is his only "systemic essay in theology" (Warrington, p. 331). Stepto, in adducing the agentless operation of his pregeneric myth, is on similar theological ground, attempting to find something that is "eternal, substance, and actuality" (Warrington, p. 345) to move the great sphere of Afro-American literary lights.

36. Quoted from *Afro-American Literature*, pp. 20–21.

37. T. S. Eliot, "Tradition and the Individual Talent," *Selected Essays* (New York: Harcourt, Brace, 1950), pp. 3–11. According to Eliot, the poet cannot know what valuable poetic "work" is to be done "unless he lives in what is not merely the present, but the present moment of the past, unless he is conscious, not of what is dead, but of what is already living" (p. 11).

38. Matthew Arnold, "The Study of Poetry," in *The Works of Matthew Arnold* (New York: AMS Press, 1970), 4:2. All citations refer to this edition and are hereafter marked by page numbers in parentheses. Arnold, of course, is following in the tradition of German philosophy and earlier English and German "aesthetic" theory when he makes art theological in character. Such "aesthetics" and theory trace their origins to early eighteenth-century Germany.

39. These "factors" are treated in detail by Samuel R. Levin in *The Semantics of Metaphor* (Baltimore: Johns Hopkins University Press, 1977) and by Robert Rogers in *Metaphor, a Psychoanalytic View* (Berkeley and Los Angeles: University of California Press, 1978). Additional theoretical discussion of metaphor can be found in the stimulating issue of *Critical Inquiry* vol. 5 (Autumn 1978), devoted to the subject.

40. I refer, of course, to Neal's "The Black Contribution to American Letters," which I discussed in an earlier section of this essay.

41. Genette defines the text as "subject" in *Figures* (Paris: Editions du Seuil, 1966). Georges Poulet and Paul Ricoeur have also reflected on the process whereby "critical thought *becomes* the thought criticized." The quotation here is from Maria Corti's *An Introduction to Literary Semiotics* (Bloomington: Indiana University Press, 1978), p. 43.

42. I have discussed the concept of "the destruction of the text" in *The Journey Back*, pp. 127–28. In his essay "And Shine Swam On," which serves as the "Afterword" for the anthology *Black Fire*, ed. Larry Neal and LeRoi Jones (New York: William Morrow, 1968), Neal says that true Afro-American poetry lies in verbal and musical performance, not in *written* texts: "The text could be destroyed and no one would be hurt in the least by it" (p. 653).

43. By "Whorfianism" I mean the scholarly position assumed by Benjamin Lee Whorf. In his studies of the Hopi Indians, Whorf emphasized the interpenetration of language and reality; the world view of the Hopi, according to Whorf, is encoded in their language. Hence, language and world view are coextensive (mild Whorfianism) or coterminous (strong Whorfianism), and this makes for a kind of linguistic determinism in human affairs. For a more detailed view of Whorf's thought, a reader can consult John B. Carroll, ed., *Language, Thought and Reality*, a collection of Whorf's essays published by the M.I.T. Press in 1956.

44. Instead of language determining world view, the individual world view (under the aspect of "privacy") determines, or fashions, its own peculiar language.

45. Umberto Eco, *A Theory of Semiotics* (Bloomington: Indiana University Press, 1976), pp. 6–7.

46. This is not, however, an injunction to regard Henderson as an expert on Black English Vernacular as a subject of study *in itself*. For such expert testimony one must turn to the work of Geneva Smitherman, William Labov, and others. A good beginning, of course, is Lorenzo Turner's pioneering study *Africanisms in the Gullah Dialect*.

47. Karl Mannheim, *Ideology and Utopia, An Introduction to the Sociology of Knowledge* (New York: Harcourt, Brace, 1936), pp. 82–83. My reading in "ideology" and the "sociology of knowledge" prompted this essay on generational shifts. It seemed appropriate to situate the discussion within its proper ambit as a means of concluding.

48. In *The Journey Back* I discuss the assumptions and methodology of this approach to literary study.

49. Jean Baudrillard, *The Mirror of Production* (St. Louis: Telos Press, 1975). All citations refer to this edition and are hereafter marked by page numbers in parentheses.

50. Robert Stepto, when last I conversed with him, indicated that his scholarly work on Afro-American storytelling and written fiction was proceeding well. Henry Louis Gates has found the vernacular form of the "toast"—especially the toast known as "The Signifying Monkey"—wonderfully suggestive and useful for his own scholarly endeavors. When he and I last talked, he indicated that he believed the vernacular was, indeed, the privileged domain of Afro-American expression.

51. Two books by Murray, *Stompin the Blues* (New York: McGraw-Hill Book Co., 1976) and *The Hero and the Blues* (Columbia: University of Missouri Press, 1973), contain fine descriptions of what it means to be improvisationally nimble in the blues break.

Chapter 3

1. *International Encyclopedia of the Social Sciences* (New York: Macmillan Co. and Free Press, 1968), 10:576–82. Page numbers are hereafter found in parentheses.

2. For example, Margaretta Matilda Odell's *Memoir and Poems of Phillis Wheatley* (Boston: Light & Horton, 1835) or Benjamin Brawley's *Paul Laurence Dunbar, Poet of His People* (Chapel Hill: University of North Carolina Press, 1936).

3. One of the more notable recent examples of the tendentious cliché is Amiri Baraka's condemnation of Wheatley in his essay, "The Myth of a Negro Literature," *Home: Social Essays* (New York: William Morrow & Co., 1966), p. 106. Baraka (at the time he wrote the essay, he had not yet changed his name from LeRoi Jones) writes: "Phyllis Wheatley and her pleasant imitations of 18th century English poetry are far and, finally, ludicrous departures from the huge black voices that splintered southern nights with their *hollers, chants, ar-*

whoolies, and *ballits.*" Since Wheatley was hundreds of miles removed—geographically—from the scene of such forms as Baraka champions, it seems understandable that she would not have imitated them. The condemnation is, thus, gratuitous and tendentious; it merely serves in the office of a particular, ideological, historical interpretation. Wheatley criticism abounds in such critical acts. A reading of M. A. Richmond's *Bid the Vassal Soar* (Washington, D.C.: Howard University Press, 1974), makes this clear.

4. Robert Bone, *The Negro Novel in America* (New Haven: Yale University Press, 1965), p. 42.

5. Kenny Jackson Williams, "The Making of the Novelist," in *A Singer in the Dawn, Reinterpretations of Paul Laurence Dunbar*, ed. Jay Martin (New York: Dodd, Mead & Co., 1975), p. 195.

6. One of the most notable essays in this debate is James Baldwin's "Everybody's Protest Novel," which appears in the collection *Notes of a Native Son* (Boston: Beacon Press, 1955), pp. 13–23. For an update of the issues involved in the debate, one might turn to Hoyt Fuller's essay, "The New Black Literature: Protest or Affirmation," which appears in *The Black Aesthetic*, ed. Addison Gayle, Jr. (New York: Doubleday & Co., 1971), pp. 346–69.

7. Addison Gayle, Jr., "Literature as Catharsis: The Novels of Paul Laurence Dunbar," in ibid., p. 149. Gayle brings forth essentially the same argument in his study of the Afro-American novel, *The Way of the New World* (Garden City, N.Y.: Anchor Press, 1975).

8. *L. Wittgenstein: Lectures and Conversations on Aesthetics, Psychology and Religious Belief*, ed. Cyril Barrett (Berkeley and Los Angeles: University of California Press, 1967), p. 24.

9. Roland Barthes, "Historical Discourse," in *Introduction to Structuralism*, ed. Michael Lane (New York: Basic Books, 1970), pp.145–55.

10. *Structuralist Poetics* (Ithaca, N.Y.: Cornell University Press, 1975), p. 116.

11. In *How to Do Things with Words* (Cambridge, Mass.: Harvard University Press, 1975), the volume containing the William James Lectures delivered at Harvard by J. L. Austin, and edited by J. O. Urmson and Marina Sbisa, one finds the following definition of a "performative": "One of our examples was, for instance, the utterance 'I do' (take this woman to be my lawful wedded wife), as uttered in the course of a marriage ceremony. Here we should say that in saying these words we are *doing* something—namely, marrying, rather than *reporting* something, namely *that* we are marrying. And the act of marrying, like, say, the act of betting, is at least *preferably* (though still not *accurately*) to be described as saying *certain words*, rather than as performing a different, inward and spiritual, action of which these words are merely the outward and audible sign." The characterization appears on pp. 12–13. For a discussion of speech acts in ordinary language, one can also turn to John R. Searle's *Speech Acts: An Essay in the Philosophy of Language* (Cambridge: Cambridge University Press, 1969).

12. I am indebted for this insight to Barbara Herrnstein Smith's "Poetry as Fiction," which appears in *New Directions in Literary History*, ed. Ralph Cohen, (Baltimore: Johns Hopkins University Press, 1974), pp. 165–87.

13. John Ellis, *The Theory of Literary Criticism* (Berkeley and Los Angeles: University of California Press, 1974).

14. Jacques Derrida, "Limited Inc.," *Glyph* 2 (1977): 162–254.

15. Paul Laurence Dunbar, *The Sport of the Gods* (1901; reprinted, New York: Arno Press, 1969), p. 255. All citations from the novel in my text come from this edition and are, subsequently, marked by page numbers in parentheses.

16. The notion captured by this phrase is that human beings are motivated in their present actions by their expectations of the future. For a further discussion of the notion in the history of psychology, one can consult C. S. Hall and Gardner Lindzey's *Theories of Personality* (New York: John Wiley & Sons, 1978), pp. 160–61.

17. For a useful discussion of the Plantation Tradition in American letters, one can

consult Jean Fagan Yellin's *The Intricate Knot: Black Figures in American Literature, 1776–1863* (New York: New York University Press, 1972). For a brief and provocative analysis of this tradition, one can turn to Addison Gayle's essay, "Cultural Hegemony: The Southern White Writer and American Letters," which appears in *Amistad I* (New York: Random House, 1970), pp. 1–24.

18. Langston Hughes and Milton Meltzer, *Black Magic: A Pictorial History of Black Entertainers in America* (New York: Bonanza Books, 1967), pp. 47–48.

19. Ibid., p. 48.

20. Albert Murray, *The Hero and the Blues* (Columbia: University of Missouri Press, 1973), p. 101.

21. A discussion of Bloch's essay occurs in Fredric Jameson, *Marxism and Form* (Princeton: Princeton University Press, 1971), pp. 131–32.

22. Turner, p. 577.

23. I have in mind Baldwin's "Everybody's Protest Novel" and "Many Thousands Gone," which appeared in *Notes of a Native Son*, a collection of essays first published in 1955.

24. Ellison's essay appears in his stunning collection entitled *Shadow and Act* (New York: Random House, 1964). All citations from "The World and the Jug" refer to this edition and are hereafter marked by page numbers in parentheses.

25. The essay appears, as my earlier note indicates, in *Notes of a Native Son* (New York: Bantam Books, 1979). All citations refer to this edition and are marked by page numbers in parentheses. Quotations from "Many Thousands Gone" are also drawn from this edition and similarly marked.

26. Louis Althusser and Étienne Balibar, *Reading Capital* (New York: Schocken Books, 1970), p. 29.

27. In *Marxism and Literature* (Oxford: Oxford University Press, 1977) Raymond Williams provides a concise account of such aesthetics. In my following discussion, I not only shall offer my own conceptions but also shall introduce the observations of Williams himself. All citations from *Marxism and Literature* refer to the noted edition and are hereafter marked by page numbers in parentheses.

28. Ibid.

29. Of course, the designation of Ellison's essay as a "condemnation," and that alone, can only be heuristically proposed. The larger context of Ellison's essay is Irving Howe's "socially engaged" *charge* against the author of *Invisible Man*—a charge leveled by Howe in valorization of Richard Wright. It is, perhaps, "natural" that Ellison answered Howe in his own absolutely best bourgeois "aesthetic" voice. Henry Louis Gates, Jr., has fascinating things to say about the critical-discursive relationship between Ellison and Wright in his book *The Signifying Monkey* (forthcoming from Oxford University Press).

30. Hayden White, *Tropics of Discourse* (Baltimore: Johns Hopkins University Press, 1978).

31. Ibid., p. 91.

32. Gary Zukav, *The Dancing Wu Li Masters: An Overview of the New Physics* (New York: Bantam Books, 1979), p. 184. *The Dancing Wu Li Masters* serves as the source for most of my observations on black holes. It is an engaging introduction to the worlds of General Relativity and Quantum Mechanics. After completing the initial draft of the present essay, I discovered that both *Discover* and *Omni* magazines for the month of December (1982) contained accounts of the "state of the art" in black hole research.

33. Stephen Henderson, *Understanding the New Black Poetry: Speech and Black Music as Poetic References* (New York: William Morrow, 1973).

34. Richard Wright, *Black Boy* (New York: Harper Bros., 1966). All citations refer to this edition and are hereafter marked by page numbers in parentheses.

35. For me the "blues life" is the economically determined, ground-level existence that

emerges from the codifications of Afro-American folklore—in particular and most expressly from the Afro-American blues. Two blues stanzas provide an idea of the type of life I am suggesting with the phrase. The first stanza says: "Well I'm a po' boy, long way from home./ Well I'm a po' boy, long way from home./ No spendin' money in my pocket, no spare meat on my bone." The second asserts: "I'm setting here a thousand miles from nowhere, in this one-room country shack./ Well, Lawd, I'm setting here a thousand miles from nowhere in this one-room country shack./ All the crickets keep me company, you know the wind howling round my feet." "Blues life" is energized by blues song. One might say that the "triumph" of a culture over a bleak situation is announced in the *singing* itself.

36. Roland Barthes, *A Lover's Discourse*, trans. Richard Howard (New York: Hill & Wang, 1980). Citations are hereafter marked by page numbers in parentheses.

37. Under the prospect of "Self-Consciousness" and "The Truth of Self-Certainty," Hegel sets forth a characterization of *desire* in the *Phenomenology of Spirit*. I am indebted to Mark Taylor, a colleague at the National Humanities Center during 1982–83, for calling my attention to the Hegelian project and guiding me through it. I also wish to acknowledge my indebtedness to Howard Zeiderman and Richard Bjornson for suggesting critical sources on the subject of "desire."

38. Roland Barthes, *Writing Degree Zero*, trans. Annette Lavers and Colin Smith (New York: Hill & Wang, 1967). The discussions of Barthes's project in Fredric Jameson's *The Prison-House of Language* (Princeton: Princeton University Press, 1972) and in Julia Kristeva's *Desire in Language* (New York: Columbia University Press, 1980) have been useful for my essay.

39. Julia Kristeva's *Desire in Language* contains an illuminating discussion of Bakhtin and the "carnivalesque" in the essay entitled "Word, Dialogue, and Novel."

40. In her discussion of Bakhtin in *Desire in Language*, Kristeva defines the "ambivalent word" as follows: "the writer can use another's word, giving it a new meaning while retaining the meaning it already had. The result is a word with two significations: it becomes *ambivalent*. This ambivalent word is therefore the result of a joining of two sign systems" (p. 73).

41. Ibid., p. 102. Future citations are marked by page numbers in parentheses.

42. Jameson, in *The Prison-House of Language*, defines this term from Russian Formalism's repertoire as "the deliberate attracting of the reader's attention [by a narrative] to the basic technique of narration itself" (p. 61).

43. Arnold Van Gennep, *The Rites of Passage*, trans. Monika B. Vizedom and Gabrielle L. Caffee (Chicago: University of Chicago Press, 1960).

44. Edmund Leach, *Culture and Communication* (Cambridge: Cambridge University Press, 1976). The diagram in question occurs on p. 78.

45. "The Black Writer and His Role," in *The Black Aesthetic*, ed. Addison Gayle, Jr. (New York: Doubleday, 1971), pp. 370–78.

46. Zora Neale Hurston, *Their Eyes Were Watching God* (Urbana: University of Illinois Press, 1978). Hurston's novel was first published in 1937. All citations refer to the Illinois edition and are marked by page numbers in parentheses.

47. Ralph Ellison, *Invisible Man* (New York: Vintage Books, 1972), pp. 554–55.

48. René Girard, *Deceit, Desire, and the Novel* (Baltimore: Johns Hopkins University Press, 1966), p. 294. Girard typifies "desire" as triangular—the subject, object, and *mediator* occupying three points of an isosceles triangle. For Girard, *desire* is never *unmediated*, though human subjects always fancy that it is so. The theological paradigm of mediation is Christian *desire* for salvation, mediated by Christ, and expressed in the subject's imitation of His life.

49. The graphics that follow were created by Jean Williams of the National Humanities Center. Her skill, patience, and suggestions were extemely helpful in arriving at the final result.

50. The title of Williams's outstanding critical book is *Give Birth to Brightness*.

51. "Big Boy Leaves Home," in Richard Wright's *Uncle Tom's Children* (New York: Harper Bros., 1969), p. 39. All citations refer to this edition and are hereafter marked by page numbers in parentheses. *Uncle Tom's Children* first appeared in 1938.

52. "The Man Who Lived Underground," in Richard Wright's *Eight Men* (New York: Pyramid Books, 1969), pp. 22–74. All citations refer to this edition and are hereafter marked by page numbers in parentheses.

53. John M. Reilly has presented a very suggestive statement on this authorial strategy in "The Reconstruction of Genre as Entry into Conscious History," *Black American Literature Forum* 13 (1979): 3–6. Reilly discusses Wright's novel *The Outsider*. Michel Fabre locates the motivation for Wright's composition of "The Man Who Lived Underground" in the author's reading of a 1941 story in *True Detective* magazine. For an elaboration of Fabre's point of view, see: "Richard Wright: The Man Who Lived Underground," *Studies in the Novel* 3 (1971): 165–79. In *The Unfinished Quest of Richard Wright* (New York: William Morrow & Co., 1973), Fabre discusses Wright's abiding interest in detective fiction. And the reader familiar with *Black Boy* will be aware of the young Wright's attraction to pulp thrillers and stories of murder and mayhem.

54. Robert Bone, *The Negro Novel in America* (New Haven: Yale University Press, 1968), pp. 201–2.

55. "Notes from Underground," in *Man Alone*, ed. Eric and Mary Josephson (New York: Dell Books 1963), p. 360, 364.

56. For a perspective on this proposition and others in the present essay concerning philosophies of existence, a reader can consult Jean Wahl, *Philosophies of Existence: An Introduction to the Basic Thought of Kierkegaard, Jaspers, Marcel, Sartre* (New York: Schocken Books, 1969). For a briefer view, the reader can turn to Jean Wahl, *A Short History of Existentialism* (New York: Philosophical library, 1949). Wright's connection with French existentialist thinkers is discussed by Fabre in *The Unfinished Quest*.

57. Wahl, *Philosophies of Existence*, p. 38.

58. The notion, as elaborated by Freud, is more complicated than I have represented it here. For Freud's hypotheses on guilt and anxiety are intended to explain the origin and prevalence of these mental states in the developmental history of mankind. Eros and aggression, instinct and ego, are postulated by Freud to stand in a relationship that is determinatively conditioned by the killing of the "primal father." Ontogeny recapitulates phylogeny as each infant leaves the womb and commences interacting with fatherly "authority." The struggle between love and hate, and its attendant anxieties ("trauma"), Freud feels, are indigenous to human history and hence repeat themselves in each individual life history. Anthropologically, Freud's suggestive rendition of the Oedipus myth is without support. But his clinical reports on anxiety and his provocative theses connecting modern psychosocial malaise with certain tribal practices are enduringly fascinating. For further details, the reader can turn to James Strachey, trans., *Totem and Taboo* (New York: W. W. Norton & Co., 1950), and to Strachey, trans., *Civilization and Its Discontents* (New York: W. W. Norton & Co., 1962).

59. Discussing the thought of Heidegger in *Philosophies of Existence*, Wahl writes:

> We are in this world limited in our very being. The only way to take our destiny upon ourself—for this finally is the meaning of the Heideggerian decision—is to want ourselves to be limited by death. It is therefore by way of dread and the thought of death that we arrive at repetition. We must take what we are upon ourselves. That is what Heidegger calls the anticipatory resolute decision by which we live our own death in advance. We overcome our failure by becoming conscious of that failure. [P. 74]

60. Wahl, *Philosophies*, p. 60.

61. Mary Douglas, *Purity and Danger: An Analysis of Concepts of Pollution and Taboo* (New York: Frederick A. Praeger, 1966).

62. Edmund Leach, "Anthropological Aspects of Language: Animal Categories and Verbal Abuse," in *Reader in Comparative Religion*, ed. William A. Lessa and Evon Z. Vogt (New York: Harper & Row, 1972) p. 210.

63. Mary Douglas, "Pollution," in *Reader in Comparative Religion*, ibid., p. 200.

64. In R. L. Gregory and E. H. Gombrich, eds., *Illusion in Nature and Art* (New York: Charles Scribner's Sons, 1973), Gombrich writes:

> There is a theory of the mind which links its capacity to produce illusions—artistic or otherwise—with the quest for satisfactions which real life too often denies us. According to Freud our whole psychic life might be described in terms of a conflict between what he calls the pleasure principle and the reality principle. The first rules the "lower reaches of the soul," the latter the higher ones. The pleasures of illusion are generally bought at the expense of reality testing. [Pp. 216–17]

65. The discussion of the development of consciousness that follows relies on Giuseppina Chaira Moneta's *On Identity: A Study in Genetic Phenomenology* (The Hague: Martinus Nijhoff, 1976).

66. Ibid., pp. 37–70.

67. Socrates, speaking to the ever-dense (but amiable) Glaucon says of the prisoners of the cave: "prisoners so confined would have seen nothing of themselves or of one another, except the shadows thrown by the fire-light on the wall of the Cave facing them." Quoted from trans. Francis MacDonald Cornford, *The Republic of Plato*, (Oxford: University Press, 1960), p. 228.

68. Wahl, *Philosophies*, p. 74.

69. Ralph Ellison, *Shadow and Act* (New York: Signet Books 1966), pp. 89–104. Ellison's essays in *Shadow and Act* comprise the bulk of his critical canon, and all my references in the present discussion are confined to these essays. All references to "Richard Wright's Blues" that follow will be marked by page numbers in parentheses.

70. *Shadow and Act*, p. 148–68. All references to "Hidden Name and Complex Fate" that follow are marked by page numbers in parentheses.

71. *Shadow and Act*, pp. 61–73. All references to "Change the Joke and Slip the Yoke" that follow are marked by page numbers in parentheses.

72. "The Art of Fiction: An Interview," in *Shadow and Act*, p. 172. Quoted phrases in the following sentence derive from this same interview.

73. Clifford Geertz, "Deep Play: Notes on the Balinese Cockfight," *The Interpretation of Cultures* (New York: Basic Books, 1973), p. 443. All citations refer to this edition and are hereafter marked by page numbers in parentheses.

74. *Modern Language Notes* 89 (1974): 911–37. All citations refer to this source and are hereafter marked by page numbers in parentheses.

75. *Shadow and Act*, pp. 115–47. All references to "The World and the Jug" that follow are marked by page numbers in parentheses.

76. Ralph Ellison, *Invisible Man* (New York: Vintage Books 1972), p. 52. All citations from *Invisible Man* refer to this edition and are hereafter marked by page numbers in parentheses.

77. Sigmund Freud, *Totem and Taboo*, trans. James Strachey (New York: W. W. Norton, 1950). The general statement of hypothesis to which I refer in this present discussion occupies pp. 141–46. One of the general questions provoking Freud's inquiry into totemism is, "What is the ultimate source of the horror of incest which must be recognized as the root of exogamy?" (p. 122).

78. Victor Turner, *The Forest of Symbols: Aspects of Ndembu Ritual* (Ithaca, N.Y.: Cornell University Press, 1967). All references are to this edition and are marked by page numbers in parentheses.

79. Paul Radin, *The Trickster* (London: Routledge & Kegan Paul, 1955).

80. For a stimulating discussion of "The Trickster" in his various literary and nonliterary guises, see Barbara Babcock-Abrahams's essay, " 'A Tolerated Margin of Mess': The Trickster and His Tales Reconsidered," *Journal of the Folklore Institute* 2 (1975): 147–86. She writes: "In contrast to the scapegoat or tragic victim, trickster belongs to the comic modality or marginality where violation is generally the precondition for laughter and communitas, and there tends to be an incorporation of the outsider, a levelling of hierarchy, a reversal of statuses" (p. 153).

81. "Myth and Symbol," in *International Encyclopedia of the Social Sciences* (New York: Macmillan Co. and Free Press, 1968), 10:580.

82. "Betwixt and Between: The Liminal Period in *Rites de Passage*," in *The Forest of Symbols*, pp. 93–112.

83. "Myth and Symbol," p. 577.

84. Ibid., p. 580.

85. "Betwixt and Between," p. 98.

86. I am grateful for some enlightening conversations with Kimberly Benston on the Trueblood episode's parodic representation of the Fall. Benston explores these representations at some length in a critical work in progress.

87. *how i got ovah: New and Selected Poems* (New York: Doubleday & Co., 1975), pp. 11–12. All citations refer to this edition.

88. The sharecropper's incestuous progeny may be said to carry the same weight of significance as that possessed by the broken link of leg chain Brother Tarp presents to the invisible man during his early days in the Brotherhood. "I don't think of it in terms of but two words," says Tarp, "*yes* and *no*; but it signifies a heap more" (*Invisible Man*, p. 379).

89. Samuel Charters, *The Legacy of the Blues* (New York: Da Capo, 1977), p. 22.

90. Quoted in Giles Oakley, *The Devil's Music: A History of the Blues* (New York: Harvest, 1976), p. 6.

91. Charters, *Legacy*, p. 183.

92. Fredric Jameson, "The Symbolic Inference; or, Kenneth Burke and Ideological Analysis," *Critical Inquiry* 4 (1978): 510–11.

93. Hayden White, "Literature and Social Action: Reflections on the Reflection Theory of Literary Art," *New Literary History* 12 (1980): 363–80. Further citations of White's work are marked by page numbers in parentheses.

94. The term is, of course, drawn from George Lamming, *Season of Adventure* (London: Allison & Busby, 1979), p. 93.

95. "Change the Joke and Slip the Yoke," p. 63.

96. Ibid., p. 64.

97. Charters, *Legacy*, p. 168.

98. "*Blues People*," *Shadow and Act*, p. 249. Ellison introduces his own claim in contradiction to the assertions on blues of LeRoi Jones, whose book *Blues People* he is reviewing in his essay.

99. David Levering Lewis, *When Harlem Was in Vogue* (New York: Alfred A. Knopf, 1981). All citations refer to this edition and are marked by page numbers in parentheses.

100. George Kent, *Blackness and the Adventure of Western Culture* (Chicago: Third World, 1972), p. 161.

101. "Change the Joke and Slip the Yoke," p. 72. The implicit "trickiness" of Ellison's claim—his use of words to "signify" quite other than what they seem to intend on the surface—is an aspect of the Afro-American "critic as trickster." Henry Louis Gates, Jr.,

analyzes the trickster's "semiotic" manifestation in *The Signifying Monkey* (New York: Oxford University Press, forthcoming). In Gates's terms, the Afro-American folk figure of the "signifying monkey" becomes an archetype of the Afro-American critic. In the essays "Change the Joke and Slip the Yoke" and "The World and the Jug," one can certainly think of Ellison demonstrating an elegant mastery of what might be termed the "exacerbating strategies" of the monkey.

102. Barbara Babcock-Abrahams, "Reflexivity: Definitions and Discriminations," *Semiotica* 30 (1980): 4.

103. Ibid. One of the most intriguing recent discussions of the Velazquez painting is that of Michel Foucault in *The Order of Things*. The Van Eyck is briefly discussed in the introduction to Jay Ruby's edited volume *A Crack in the Mirror: Reflexive Perspectives in Anthropology*.

104. Quoted from A. S. Nicholas, ed., *Woke up This Mornin': Poetry of the Blues* (New York: Bantam Books 1973), p. 85.

Index

221

ARAPAHOE COMMUNITY COLLEGE

PS 153 .N5 B23 1984
Baker, Houston A.
Blues, ideology, and Afro-
   American literature

DUE

LIBRARY
ARAPAHOE COMMUNITY COLLEGE
5900 SOUTH SANTA FE
LITTLETON, COLORADO 80120